Peter Davison
GEORGE ORWELL

Linda Wagner-Martin
SYLVIA PLATH

Felicity Rosslyn
ALEXANDER POPE

Ira B. Nadel
EZRA POUND

Richard Dutton
WILLIAM SHAKESPEARE

John Williams
MARY SHELLEY

Michael O'Neill
PERCY BYSSHE SHELLEY

Gary Waller
EDMUND SPENSER

Tony Sharpe
WALLACE STEVENS

Joseph McMinn
JONATHAN SWIFT

Leonée Ormond
ALFRED TENNYSON

Peter Shillingsburg
WILLIAM MAKEPEACE THACKERAY

John Mepham
VIRGINIA WOOLF

David Wykes
EVELYN WAUGH

John Willams
WILLIAM WORDSWORTH

Alasdair D.F. Macrae
W.B. YEATS

Literary Lives
Series Standing Order ISBN 0–333–71486–5 hardcover
Series Standing Order ISBN 0–333–80334–5 paperback
(*outside North America only*)

You can receive future titles in this series as they are published by placing a standing order. Please contact your bookseller or, in case of difficulty, write to us at the address below with your name and address, the title of the series and one of the ISBNs quoted above.

Customer Services Department, Macmillan Distribution Ltd, Houndmills, Basingstoke, Hampshire RG21 6XS, England

Ezra Pound

A Literary Life

Ira B. Nadel

First published 2004 by
PALGRAVE MACMILLAN
Houndmills, Basingstoke, Hampshire RG21 6XS and
175 Fifth Avenue, New York, N.Y. 10010
Companies and representatives throughout the world

PALGRAVE MACMILLAN is the global academic imprint of the Palgrave
Macmillan division of St. Martin's Press, LLC and of Palgrave Macmillan Ltd.
Macmillan® is a registered trademark in the United States, United Kingdom
and other countries. Palgrave is a registered trademark in the European
Union and other countries.

ISBN 0–333–58256–X (HB)
ISBN 0–333–58257–8 (PB)

This book is printed on paper suitable for recycling and made from fully
managed and sustained forest sources.

A catalogue record for this book is available from the British Library.

Library of Congress Cataloging-in-Publication Data
Nadel, Ira Bruce.
  Ezra Pound : a literary life / Ira B. Nadel.
    p.   cm. — (Literary lives)
  Includes bibliographical references (p.) and index.
  ISBN 0–333–58256–X (hardback) — ISBN 0–333–58257–8 (pbk.)
  1. Pound, Ezra, 1885–1972.   2. Poets, American—20th century—
  Biography.   3. Critics—United States—Biography.   I. Title.
  II. Literary lives (Palgrave Macmillan (Firm))

  PS3531.O82Z758 2004
  811'.52—dc22
  [B]
                                                    2004041502

10   9   8   7   6   5   4   3   2   1
13 12 11 10 09 08 07 06 05 04

Printed and bound in Great Britain by
Antony Rowe Ltd, Chippenham and Eastbourne

For Dara & Ryan
With memories of the castle &
Mary, if she wants it

If a man writes six good lines he is immortal – isn't that worth trying for?
                                                    Ezra Pound, 1912

Yeats used to say I was trying to provide a portable substitute for the British Museum.
                                                    Ezra Pound, 1934

I can't say my remarks were heeded. I thought I had got 'em simple enough. . . . I have, however, never asked for sympathy when misunderstood. I go on trying to make my meanin' clear and then clearer.
                                                    Ezra Pound, 1941

Contents

Acknowledgements

Many have assisted with this project, not all of them Poundians. In Vancouver, John X. Cooper proved a willing ear for many fanciful notions, while Keith Alldritt offered stimulating conversations and controversial views of Pound's life and work, as well as details about visits to the 'Hidden Nest.' Ramona Montagnes challenged, corrected and consistently argued for the need to be concise. Pound's 'Make it New' found cogent restatement in 'Make it Short.' My children, Dara and Ryan, aided in numerous ways, not the least in being willing travelers to Brunnenburg and courageous in confronting the crow. Anne MacKenzie provided new direction, and encouragement at a time when it was most welcomed. In New York, Glenn Horowitz and Sarah Funke generously allowed me to examine several new Pound items and provided wonderful hospitality.

Poundians who have journeyed with me include George Bornstein, Massimo Bacigalupo, Ronald Bush, Reed Way Dasenbrock, Bernard Dew, Burton Hatlen, Alec Marsh, Zhaoming Qian, Tim Redman, Richard Sieburth, Robert Spoo and Hugh Witemeyer. They have all substantially contributed to my understanding of the life and work of Pound. Patricia Cockram has been especially helpful with suggestions, sources and assistance, while Peter Brooker's work on Pound and bohemian London identified many new doors to open. The late James Laughlin and the late Donald Gallup both offered important inspiration for a neophyte 'Poundian,' while Pat Fox and Declan Spring at New Directions have consistently afforded useful guidance. Mary de Rachewiltz has remained gracious not only in sharing her knowledge but in offering suggestions, while ensuring that the story of Pound be thoroughly told. Walter de Rachewiltz has also been supportive. Finally, the Ezra Pound Association of Hailey, Idaho: their restoration of the Ezra Pound birthplace and co-sponsorship of the 20th International Ezra Pound Conference in July 2003 provided a wonderful gathering point for ideas and news that stimulated the completion of this book.

Extracts from the writing of Ezra Pound are reprinted by permission of New Directions Publishing Corporation and Faber and Faber Ltd, and extracts from James Laughlin's poem 'Collage' are reprinted by permission of James Laughlin, copyright © 1983.

List of Abbreviations

AA	Pound, Ezra, ed. *Active Anthology*. London: Faber and Faber, 1933.
ABCR	Pound, Ezra. *ABC of Reading*. NY: New Directions, 1960.
ALSp	Pound, Ezra *A Lume Spento and Other Early Poems*. NY: New Directions, 1965.
AMF	Hemingway, Ernest. *A Moveable Feast*. NY: Scribner's, 1964.
Am EP	Flory, Wendy Stallard. *The American Ezra Pound*. New Haven: Yale University Press, 1989.
Am Rt	Wilhelm, J.J. *The American Roots of Ezra Pound*. NY: Garland Publishing, 1985.
Auto	Pound, Ezra, 'An Autobiographical Outline (written for Louis Untermeyer),' *Paris Review* 28 (1962): 18–21.
AV	Yeats, William Butler. *A Vision*. London: Macmillan, 1938; 1956.
C&R	Pound, Ezra. *Canzoni and Ripostes*. London: Elkin Mathews, 1913.
CtoC.	Pound, Ezra and Marcella Spann, eds. *Confucius to Cummings: An Anthology of Poetry*. NY: New Directions, 1964.
Case	*A Casebook on Ezra Pound*, eds. William van O'Connor and Edward Stone. NY: Thomas Crowell, 1959.
CEP	Pound, Ezra. *The Collected Early Poems of Ezra Pound*. ed. Michael John King. intro. Louis L. Martz. NY: New Directions, 1976.
CPost	Pound, Ezra. *Canti Postumi*, a cura di Massimo Bacigalupo. Milan: Mondadori, 2002.
CrH	*Ezra Pound: The Critical Heritage*, ed. Eric Homberger. London: Routledge and Kegan Paul, 1972.
CST	*The Cantos of Ezra Pound: Some Testimonies*. NY: Farrar & Rinehart, 1933.
DE	*Dear Editor: A History of Poetry in Letters, The First Fifty Years, 1912–1916*. eds. Joseph Parisi and Stephen Young. NY: Norton, 2002.
Death	Aldington, Richard. *Death of a Hero*. London: Hogarth Press, 1984.

Des Imagistes	*Des Imagistes: An Anthology.* NY: Albert and Charles Boni, 1914.
Dis	de Rachewiltz, Mary. *Ezra Pound, Father and Teacher: Discretions.* NY: New Directions, 1975.
End	H.D. [Doolittle, Hilda.] *End to Torment: A Memoir of Ezra Pound with poems from 'Hilda's Book' by Ezra Pound.* eds. Norman Holmes Pearson and Michael King. NY: New Directions, 1979.
EP/ACH	*The Letters of Ezra Pound to Alice Corbin Henderson.* ed. Ira B. Nadel. Austin: University of Texas Press, 1993.
EP/JJ	*Pound/Joyce: The Letters of Ezra Pound to James Joyce,* ed. Forrest Read. NY: New Directions Publishing, 1971.
EPCA	*Ezra Pound: A Critical Anthology,* ed. J.P. Sullivan. London: Penguin, 1970.
EPCP	Pound, Ezra. *Ezra Pound's Poetry and Prose: Contributions to Periodicals.* 11 vols. eds. Lea Baechler, A. Walton Litz and James Logenbach. NY: Garland, 1991.
EPDS	Pound, Ezra. *Ezra Pound and Dorothy Shakespear: Their Letters 1909–1914.* eds. Omar Pound and A. Walton Litz. NY: New Directions, 1984.
EP/JL	Pound, Ezra. *Ezra Pound and James Laughlin, Selected Letters.* ed. David M. Gordon. NY: W.W. Norton, 1994.
EP/JQ	Pound, Ezra. *The Selected Letters of Ezra Pound to John Quinn, 1915–1924.* ed. Timothy Materer. Durham, NC: Duke University Press, 1991.
EPLR	Pound, Ezra. *Pound/The Little Review,* eds. Thomas L. Scott *et al.* NY: New Directions, 1988.
EP/LZ	Pound, Ezra. *Pound/Zukofsky, Selected Letters of Ezra Pound and Louis Zukofsky.* ed. Barry Ahearn. NY: New Directions, 1987.
EP/MC	*Ezra Pound and Margaret Cravens: A Tragic Friendship, 1910–1912.* eds. Omar Pound and Robert Spoo. Durham, NC: Duke University Press, 1988.
EPS	Pound, Ezra. *'Ezra Pound Speaking,' Radio Speeches of World War II,* ed. Leonard W. Doob. Westport, CN: Greenwood Press, 1978.
EPVA	Pound, Ezra. *Ezra Pound and the Visual Arts.* ed. Harriet Zinnes. NY: New Directions, 1980.

EPWB	Pound, Ezra. *The Correspondence of Ezra Pound and Senator William Borah*, ed. Sarah C. Holmes. Urbana: University of Illinois Press, 2001.
GB	Pound, Ezra. *Gaudier-Brzeska: A Memoir*. [1916]; NY: New Directions, 1970.
GK	Pound, Ezra. *Guide to Kulchur*, 1938; NY: New Directions, 1970.
HER	Doolittle, Hilda [H.D.] *HERmione*. NY: New Directions, 1981.
HR	Pound, Ezra. *How to Read*. London: Harmsworth, 1931.
Ind	Pound, Ezra. 'Indiscretions,' *Pavannes and Divagations*. Norfolk, CT: New Directions, 1958.
JM	Pound, Ezra. *Jefferson and Mussolini*. London: Stanley Nott, 1935.
LC	Pound, Ezra and Dorothy Pound, *Letters in Captivity 1945–1946*. eds. Omar Pound and Robert Spoo. NY: Oxford University Press, 1999.
LE	Pound, Ezra. *Literary Essays*, ed. T.S. Eliot, 1954; NY: New Directions, 1976.
Metric	[Eliot, T.S.] *Ezra Pound: His Metric and Poetry*. NY: Knopf, 1917.
MN	Pound, Ezra. *Make It New*. London: Faber and Faber, 1934.
NA	*New Age*.
O/E	Conover, Anne. *Olga Rudge and Ezra Pound*. New Haven: Yale University Press, 2001.
PAesth	Pound, Ezra. 'Pragmatic Aesthetics,' *Machine Art and Other Writings*, ed. Maria Luisa Ardizzone. Durham, NC: Duke University Press, 1996, 155–9.
PC	Pound, Ezra. *The Pisan Cantos*, ed. Richard Sieburth. NY: New Directions, 2003.
PD	Pound, Ezra. *Pavannes and Divagations*. NY: New Directions, 1958.
Per	Pound, Ezra. *Personae: The Shorter Poems of Ezra Pound*. rev. edn. ed. Lea Baechler and A. Walton Litz. NY: New Directions, 1990.
P/F	Pound, Ezra. *Pound/Ford, The Story of a Literary Friendship*, ed. Brita Lindberg-Seyersted. NY: New Directions 1982.
RP	Hall, Donald. *Remembering Poets*. NY: Harper & Row, 1978. Includes 'E.P. An Interview,' originally in *Paris Review* 28 (1962): 22–51.

SB	Pound, Homer. *Small Boy: The Wisconsin Childhood of Homer L. Pound.* ed. Alec Marsh. Hailey, ID: Ezra Pound Association, 2003.
SCh	Carpenter, Humphrey. *A Serious Character: The Life of Ezra Pound.* London: Faber and Faber, 1988.
SL	*Selected Letters of Ezra Pound, 1907–1941*, ed. D.D. Paige. NY: New Directions Publishing, 1971.
SLMM	Moore, Marianne. *Selected Letters of Marianne Moore.* ed. Bonnie Costello. London: Penguin, 1998.
SP	Pound, Ezra. *Selected Prose, 1909–1965*, ed. William Cookson. London: Faber and Faber, 1973.
SPP	Pound, *Selected Poems.* ed. T.S. Eliot. London: Faber and Gwyer Ezra 1928.
SR	Pound, Ezra. *The Spirit of Romance* 1910; NY: New Directions, 1968. Rev. edn.
VL	*The Venice Library of Ezra Pound and Olga Rudge.* NY: Glenn Horowitz Bookseller, 1999.
WCW/JL	Williams, William Carlos and James Laughlin, *Selected Letters.* ed. Hugh Witemeyer. NY: W.W. Norton, 1989.

Introduction

Ezra! Ezra! . . . you are (odd) strange – elusive – of other habits of
thought than I (shall ever be able to) can understand.

Dorothy Shakespear's early reaction to Ezra Pound was not unusual.[1]
Throughout his life, Pound provoked, disturbed and challenged the *status
quo*, whether in literature, politics or morals. In many ways, of course,
this was justified as he threatened, if not overturned, outdated poetic
practice, political attitudes, social behaviour and literary reputations,
while marshalling the arrival of modernism and the departure of Victor-
ianism. Universities fired him, governments indicted him, poets reviled
him and America jailed him. Yet through his instruction of Yeats, promotion of Joyce and editing of Eliot – plus his constant encouragement
of writers through essays, editorials, anthologies and letters – Pound
had a profound effect on the establishment of modernist writing,
although not without controversy.

Biblically, Ezra was a minor prophet but even minor prophets can
shock. Ezra Pound did this from his youthful entrance in an oriental
robe at a Halloween party witnessed by H.D. in 1901 to his arrival in
Naples after his release from St Elizabeths hospital in 1958 when he
raised his arm in the fascist salute. Pound was defiant and throughout
his life he startled, upset and challenged philistine ideas, conventional
poetics, and trite ideas. Provoked by politicians and bureaucrats, he
tried to correct many wrongs. Yet his motive was always moral, echoing
Confucius: 'if the world were in possession of right principles, I should
not seek to change it' (in Emerson 8: 410). Pound's unorthodox life
is one of iconoclastic efforts to re-establish 'right principles', which
sometimes meant the overthrow of poetic, social, political and even
historical ideals. The 'radiant world' was no longer a place 'where one

1

thought cuts through another with clean edge' (*MN* 351). He sought to restore it.

Pound's vigorous attack on complacency and convention was initially literary. He challenged English poetry, especially Victorian, and the entrapment of poets by iambic pentameter; he found textbooks an anathema, teaching a curse. Traditional works like Whitman's *Leaves of Grass* were stultifying and narrow, at one point telling his father 'it is impossible to read it without swearing at the author almost continuously' (*SL* 21). Yet Pound also had a generosity of understanding; if energy was present, it was valued: 'one doesn't need to like a book or a poem or a picture in order to recognize its artistic vigor' he announced (*LE* 384). His stringent criticism and sharp tone, expressed in journals like *The Little Review*, *Poetry* and even his own short-lived periodical, *The Exile*, reveal a mind stimulated by literature on three continents: America, Europe, and Asia. Inter-continental readings which cut through history summarize Pound's approach expressed in directives, commands and a hortatory style that frequently reduced itself to statements of concision to get readers reading: 'Premier principe – RIEN that interferes with the words, or with the utmost possible clarity of impact of words on audience....' (*SL* 169). Or, in more colourful language, 'if you weren't stupider than a mud-duck you would know that every kick to bad writing is by that much a help for the good' (*SL* 158). The recipient of this advice was William Carlos Williams.

Imagism became not only a literary style but a metaphor of Pound's determination to slice, pare and concentrate ideas, language and expression in his criticism and writing. 'Cut direct' is his admonition (*GB* 19). The aggressiveness of his writing, the immediacy of his words, is part of the energy of his ideas and eagerness to 'make it new' which shaped his life as well as his literature. 'I have never known anyone worth a damn who wasn't irascible' he wrote to Margaret Anderson and he met this *dicta* completely (*SL* 111). His agenda was clear, his plan precise: 'When did I ever, in enmity, advise you to use vague words, to shun the welding of word and thing, to avoid hard statement, word close to the thing it means?', he rhetorically asks Williams (*SL* 158). 'Against the metric pattern' he tells the poet Mary Barnard, 'struggle toward natural speech. You haven't *yet* got sense of quantity' (*SL* 261). The best '*mechanism* for breaking up the stiffness and literary idiom *is* a different metre, the god damn iambic magnetizes certain verbal sequences' (*SL* 260). 'To break the pentameter, that was the first heave' he writes in *The Cantos* (LXXXI/538). Pound's own plan was exact and even his eccentric spellings and erratic letters had purpose: to emphasize, stress, underscore, intensify and condense his ideas, even if he had to revert, for effect, to an earlier, Biblical style:

> Oh HELL, how shall I put it. My son, elucidate thine own bloody damn point of view by its contrast to others, not by trying to make the others conform.
>
> (*SL* 235)

Pound wanted precision, explaining to Harriet Monroe in 1915 that 'Poetry must be *as well written as prose*':

> Its language must be a fine language, departing in no way from speech save by a heightened intensity (i.e. simplicity). There must be no book words, no periphrases, no inversions. It must be as simple as De Maupassant's best prose, and as hard as Stendhal's.... there must be no cliches, set phrases stereotyped journalese. The only escape from such is by precision, a result of concentrated attention to what is writing... objectivity and again objectivity... when one really feels and thinks, one stammers with simple speech.
>
> (*SL* 48–9)

This is Pound's programme, summarized in a sentence from 1912: 'Technique is the means of conveying an exact impression of exactly what one means in such a way to exhilarate.' 'Language,' he added, 'is made out of concrete things' (*SP* 33; *SL* 49).

Yet literature for the poet was always moral despite its most radical forms and midway in his career he will shift his energy from aesthetic to social concerns. But language is always the catalyst: 'with the falsification of the word everything else is betrayed' (*SP* 277). But Pound's concentration resulted in a certain irritation with ideas, culture and history: 'a sound poetic training is nothing more than the science of being discontented' he believed (*EPCP* II: 11). Only through the active work of art and the artist can society be redeemed: 'to set the arts in their rightful place as the acknowledged guide and lamp of civilization [is the goal]. Artists first, then, if necessary, professors and parsons' (*SL* 48). Words, Pound re-iterated, must be 'Objective – no slither; direct – no excessive use of adjectives, no metaphors that won't permit examination. It's straight talk, straight as the Greek!' (*SL* 11).

One site of energy for Pound is the page: on it, the visible form of his writing leaps about in irregular lines and voices, from the stanzas of *Mauberley* to the irregular arabesques of *The Cantos*. Pound, in his poetry as well as prose, is always alive; before Vorticism or Futurism, two movements that stressed action on the page, Pound had chosen textual combat as his preferred mode of existence. One of his appropriately titled projects was his 1933 collection, *Active Anthology*. Sixteen years earlier, he admonished William Carlos Williams for not displaying enough poetic action, turning his aggressive encouragement into a threat: 'I demand of you more robustezza. Bigod sir, you show more robustezza, or I will come over to Rutherford [N.J.] and have at you, *coram*, in person' (*SL* 124). Pound's militant defence of literature, of what was first rate, further expressed his explosive energy, ego and self-confidence. Throughout his career, he vigorously attacked the mediocre, outrageous and moribund.

Pound's literary, social, political and moral restlessness was also physical: Williams registered this when he and Pound dined in London in 1910. Enjoying *risotto* and a cheap wine, Pound could not sit still: he was in constant motion, looking 'boldly about him, wriggling in his chair, turning to examine the faces about him in his bold way, while I sat indifferent across the table eating' (Williams 116). But this could have hardly surprised Williams who recounts how the lunging Pound startled him during an informal fencing match with canes. Instead of a parry came a wild plunge 'without restraint and hit me with the point of the cane above my right eye to fairly lay me out' (Williams 65). Those who played tennis with Pound confirmed his unorthodox moves: his short dives and erratic movements about the court made the game almost unrecognizable. Watching Pound play tennis with Ford Madox Ford, Brigit Patmore wrote that the two looked 'readier to spring at each other's throats than the ball' (Patmore 55). Confusingly, Pound would also habitually sit down on his side of the court and then leap up in time to meet his opponent's volley. Playing tennis against Pound, Ford once remarked, was like 'playing against an inebriated kangaroo' (*P/F* 87). Another observer later commented that Pound's tennis was 'eccentric, surprising and scattershot, filled with bounding rushes, wheezes, shouts and many cries of "Egad!"' (*SCh* 446). His prowess at boxing (his instructor was Hemingway) was no better, his teacher commenting that Pound 'leads with his chin and has the general grace of the crayfish or crawfish' (*SCh* 425).

Pound was equally erratic, energetic and forceful on the dance floor. Once, at the Boule Blanche club in Paris, Pound – accompanied by Caresse Crosby, wife of the publisher Harry Crosby – leapt from his chair, declared that the band from Martinique had no idea of rhythm, and began a kind of tattoo. He then seized the cigarette girl and 'began a sort of voodoo prance, his tiny partner held glued against his piston-pumping knees'. The other dancers stopped and 'formed a ring to watch until the music crashed to an end: Ezra opened his eyes, flicked the cigarette girl aside like an extinguished match and collapsed into the chair beside me. The room exhaled a long orgasmic sigh – I too' writes Crosby (255).[2] Even Pound's walk suggested energy. In 1939, during a short trip to Washington, DC to visit Senator William Borah, among other Congressman, Pound made a lasting impression on the Senator's aide, not because of his ribboned, broad-brimmed hat and open-necked shirt, but because of his walk: 'he appeared to bounce along at about four feet to a stride, announcing himself halfway through the door, "Hello, hello, hello!"' (*EP/WB* 81). As Charles Olson would remark much later when visiting Pound at St Elizabeths hospital in Washington, 'he's got the jump – his wit, the speed of his language, the grab of it' has returned despite his arrest, his trial and his imprisonment: 'E.P.', he concluded, 'is a tennis ball' (Olson 99). Pound's energy on the dance floor, in the ring and in the halls of Congress equaled his efforts in promoting writers, cajoling editors, and corralling projects. He welcomed the title Wyndham Lewis bestowed on him: 'demon pantechnicon driver, busy with removal of old world into new quarters' (*CrH* 116).

Of course, accompanying his energy and frantic actions was his impatience. Pound wanted things done and done quickly. A June 1942 radio broadcast begins, with this sentence: 'People are allus tellin' me to be PATIENT.' This, he knows, is impossible, partly because he feels an urgency to write, to lecture, to harangue and to declaim: 'Well, I have said before, said it in poetry and said it in prose. I was twenty years late in startin'' and he needed to catch up (*EPS* 179). Any pause upsets him: 'I am held up, enraged, by the delay needed to change a typing ribbon' he declares in a 1942 radio broadcast (*EPS* 192). 'If I am not patient, thank God I am persistent' he later exclaimed (*EPS* 206). The problem with America is that it's 'lazy, and muddled, and jitterbug' (*EPS* 179). A lively search for the facts becomes his method: 'Dig in. Look up the ECONOMIC background of Cromwell' he orders (*EPS* 180). Speed and passion are essential.

An active, energetic Pound is the figure that emerges in this portrait, for Pound is energy charged with meaning seeking transmission. 'Electrified arguments' define his many exchanges as he became a bundle of 'moving energies' whose very kisses, according to H.D., were 'electric' (*GB* 46; *MN* 351; *End* 4). Pound wrote of Gaudier-Brzeska that 'his stillness seemed an action' but it applies more directly to himself (*GB* 39). With unknown prescience, he summarized his ethos *and* the nature of this narrative when he wrote that 'we might come to believe that the thing that matters in art is a sort of energy, something more or less like electricity or radioactivity, a force transfusing, welding, and unifying' (*LE* 49). He wrote this in 1913.

1
'Mastership at One Leap': 1885–1908

> I could write a whole American history by implication stickin' to unknown folks, in four or five families.
>
> (Pound, May 1942)

Hailey, Idaho – even in 1885 – seems at first an unlikely place for the birth of one of America's, and later Europe's, most controversial if not provocative writers. But in that lawless town that had one hotel and fifty bars on its unpaved streets, Ezra Loomis Pound was born on 30 October to Homer and Isabel Pound. What brought the Pounds to the west was work: the son of Congressman Thaddeus C. Pound of Wisconsin (former member of the Wisconsin State Assembly and Lieutenant Governor of the state in 1869), Homer Pound needed a job and through his father's influence received an appointment at the newly opened Federal Land Office in Hailey.

Money was made and lost quickly in this western frontier. One day a man would be out of work but the next he might have $10,000 in the bank. A maid that Isabel Pound had employed left one day to become the wife of an overnight millionaire. Not only did Homer register claims and try to keep order in the lawless region but he also assayed the silver or lead being mined to test its purity. Years later he would become an assayer for the US Mint in Philadelphia. He also got the land bug and acquired various lots around town as investments. Like his father Thaddeus, who owned two silver mines in the area and wanted his son to keep an eye on them, Homer saw the potential of Hailey. Isabel Pound at first seemed out of place. A Wadsworth on one side of her family with connections to Henry Wadsworth Longfellow, on the other she was a Weston, a family with connections throughout the east, especially in New York where Isabel grew up in a boardinghouse with her mother.

But life in Hailey was trying for a woman concerned with appearances and cultivating formality. She was unable to locate reliable help and found the rough and ready ways unappealing, although she brought glamour to the frontier town. Soon, the Pounds found a busy social life, participating in church events, amateur theatricals and civic activities.

Homer had little formal education, attending a military academy for several years before heading to West Point for college at his father's direction. On the train to the school, however, Homer decided it wouldn't do and got off at a stop half way and returned. Being born in northern Wisconsin taught him some degree of independence, and he soon learned the details of running a business working for his father and his uncle's company, the Union Lumbering Company. During the early 1870s, the lumber business did not flourish and Thaddeus saw that transportation was partly the problem. He thought a railroad would be the answer and began to build one in the region. Canto XXVIII of *The Cantos* records this feat. Cantos XII and XCVII cite other accomplishments of his grandfather – cited as T.C.P. in the poem; the independence and entrepreneurmanship of Thaddeus clearly appealed to his grandson who further celebrated him in his essay, 'A Visiting Card' (*Impact* 64–5).

In a memoir written in 1929, Homer Pound admiringly writes about his father's cunning and imagination. A State Assemblyman (1864–69), he was also elected Lieutenant Governor of Wisconsin in 1869 and despite a divorce in 1871 and business reversals, he was elected to the US Congress in 1876, serving three terms until 1882. In the memoir *Small Boy*, Homer details the bravery of his father in securing railroad right of ways, marshaling the lumber company into an economic force and even venturing into bottling Chippewa Falls water. That Thaddeus at one point issued his own money when no other source would lend him any had a lasting impression on Pound (see Canto XCVII). Defeated in the Congressional race of 1882, Thaddeus went back to Wisconsin, although his bills in support of conservation and improving the state of the native Americans met with reasonable success in Congress (*Am Rt* 21).

As a public man, Thaddeus found that his private life could not be sustained by his withdrawn and conservative wife and they soon separated. When he went to serve in the Wisconsin Assembly, Thaddeus took up with a new woman who accompanied him to Washington after his election to Congress despite a possible scandal. This union, which Pound describes in his autobiography *Indiscretions*, anticipates the poet's own later behaviour as he maintained a long love affair with Olga Rudge, while continuing his own marriage with Dorothy Shakespear. Later, during a fiercely contested presidential campaignof 1884, Thaddeus published a broadside at his own expense against the Republican candidate. His rhetoric fiercely upheld public morality without attention to private behavior. Wisconsin duly turned against the candidate. Pound would later offer similar declarations upholding the public good as the first step toward a civilized society.

Thaddeus's marrying a second time, while maintaining his liaison, led to further complications, although Pound does not mention this in his idealized portrait of his grandfather in *Indiscretions*. Yet Thaddeus's action, energy, enterprise and enthusiasm for new ideas imprinted itself on Pound. When he died in 1914, penniless in a Chicago hospital, Thaddeus was eulogized at the Wisconsin State Capital as man of vigor and independence who took a stand against the banks and monopolies like the Weyerhauser Lumber company. He was called 'a Republican of the radical type' which his grandson took to mean someone in the tradition of Jefferson who challenged the interfering politicians and robber barons of the nineteenth century (*Am Rt* 26). The freedom to assert one's individual rights became essential to Pound, as his eminent grandfather demonstrated.

Homer's memoir of his Wisconsin childhood surprisingly exhibits various habits seen in his son's writing: an eagerness for adventure, a determination to meet the powerful in Washington (there is a humorous account of his encounter with the Secretary of Agriculture) and a love of movies, especially westerns (*SB* 43, 48, 114). There is also a similarity of style: 'Let me get out of my system an item about horses' an impatient Homer writes at one point; at another, he imitates the frantic, almost stream-of-consciousness style of Pound himself. Chapter 5 opens with:

Indicative mood present tense look alive cut and over the fence. High low jack and the game is to X as H.D., A.E., WB, S.T.E.E. [are to] Jesse James, Bill Nye, J.W.R., Cam.B. James Joyce, H.J.W.J.W.C.W. F.B.M.F.B.F.E.W.A.R.O.H.M.M.A and others were unknown to fame. Quality not quantatee.

(*SB* 35)

Homer also clarifies an incident cited in Canto XXVII involving TCP (*SB* 96–7). Although simple in presentation, Homer's memoir evokes past concerns, while anticipating future habits of his son including a love of books (*SB* 105).

When his father was elected to Congress in 1876, Homer first stayed behind in Wisconsin to work for the family business. But he soon found the mystique of Washington irresistible and moved there, enjoying an active social life. At one event, he met a woman from New York, Frances Weston, later to be better known as Aunt Frank. She lived with her husband Ezra Weston at 24 East 47th Street in New York, a boardinghouse he owned, and she invited the young Homer Pound to visit. During his stay he met and fell in love with Isabel Weston who was residing there with her mother, Mary, whose marriage to Harding Weston had dissolved largely because of his unsuccessful business schemes and spendthrift behaviour that prevented them from establishing a proper family life. The mother did not approve of the undereducated Homer but finally allowed her daughter to marry him because she hoped that his father's connections – he was a lumberman, railroad builder *and* politician – might provide opportunities for the young couple who were married on 26 November 1884. Following a long honeymoon which included Niagara Falls, Milwaukee, and Chippewa Falls, where Homer was born, they arrived in Hailey, preceded by Isabel's maid.

Pound, born at home, was among the first – if not *the* first – child christened at the newly built Emmanuel Church of Hailey, only a few blocks from their house at the corner of 2nd and Pine.[1] The severity of the winter that December, meant, however, that Isabel and her infant son would move to a better heated hotel. As Homer prospered, playing an increasingly important social and governmental role in the town, his father sought to increase his holdings. But politics (Homer was a Federal appointee) made his tenure in Hailey unstable, especially after the assassination of President James Garfield (a supporter of Thaddeus Pound) and the election in 1884 of Grover Cleveland, a Democrat, as President. His father soon fell out of favor. Coupled with his wife's discomfort, the Pounds sought more security in the east (*Ind* 41).

In the winter of 1887, New York, not Hailey, was the Pound's destination. His family headed east to stay with Uncle Ezra Weston, his mother's brother, at his five storied brownstone boardinghouse on 47th Street between Madison and Fifth Avenue. Soon acquiring leases for adjacent buildings, the Weston's had a series of linked brownstones and operated an establishment called The Weston until 1906 when the entrepreneur who owned the properties tore them down to build the Ritz-Carlton Hotel. In *Indiscretions*, Pound paints a portrait of Uncle Ezra Weston as a man accustomed to comfort who tried to transmit that to his boardinghouse tenants by displaying a hospitality more southern than northern. His business dealings in the South and relatives in

Virginia authenticated this attitude which an entourage of black servants at the establishment confirmed. The young Pound, living with his aunt and uncle, soon developed a fascination with the Weston past and some of its mythology, including a Thomas Weston from London who supposedly helped to transport Puritan refugees to America; the family also believed that Weston, Massachusetts was named after this figure, mentioned in Canto LXII.

Like Pound's exposure to life in Idaho, retold to him by his father but recalled with less romance by his mother, life at a New York boardinghouse never left him. Many of the characters that came and went reappeared to him when incarcerated at Pisa in 1945. In Canto LXXIV of *The Pisan Cantos*, he recalls:

> the remains of the old South
> tidewashed to Manhattan and brown-stone
> or (later) the outer front stair
> leading to Mouquin's
>
> (LXXIV/467)

The reference to a favoured restaurant on Herald Square underscores the lasting image of New York for Pound. Additionally, frequent political debates and social upheavals in New York surrounded the impressionable young Pound which he would not forget.

Uncle Ezra Weston became a marvellous, if not towering, figure of good humour and comfort for the youthful Pound who later adopted the same voice of 'Uncle Ez' in numerous letters and writings. Pound clearly remembered his death in 1892 as *Indiscretions* recounts. In that work, he restates his affection for Uncle Ezra, as well as the report that Pound threw his baby rocking chair across the room at the age of six when he heard that Grover Cleveland won the Presidency in 1892. He did it in protest and for economic reasons, believing that a change in government would mean that his father would likely lose his job (*Ind* 28). Politics, economics and action found early expression for the poet to be – just as the example of his grandfather Thaddeus showed him a man who could get things done.

The youthful Pound also spent time at Grandmother Weston's, Isabel's mother, who had a home at 52nd and Lexington. Emphasizing the Wadsworth connection, 'Ma' Weston would constantly read to him from Longfellow and conveyed to him her love of romantic literature. In particular, she shared with him the novels of Scott and retelling romantic colonial history until her death when Pound was twelve.

He also traveled; at two-and-a-half, his grandmother and parents took him to Newport; at three, he went to Wisconsin to the house of his grandfather Thaddeus Pound and his Great-Grandfather, Elijah. A blurred photo from that period records the visit and shows four generations of Pounds, the infant Pound perched on the knee of Thaddeus, while an erect Homer bisects the formal arrangement with great-grandfather Elijah seated on the right.

By 1889, however, Homer could not in good conscience continue to live off his brother-in-law and began to apply for work at the US Mint because of his experience with minerals. No jobs existed in Washington but he learned of an opportunity at the Philadelphia branch where he had briefly worked as an assistant assayer in the early 1880s. He got the job in 1889 and in weeks the family of three left for Philadelphia, although Pound's affection for New York never departed, frequently returning to 47th street over the next two decades. The act of making money, evident at the Mint and in the activities of Charles and William Wadsworth, both involved with the New York Stock Exchange, provided the matrix from which Pound himself would examine, criticize and later reject the capitalist monetary system.

Ezra Pound arrived at 166 Fernbrook Avenue in Wyncote, Pennsylvania, a suburb of Philadelphia, at the age of four; this would remain his legal address until he left for Europe in the spring of 1908 when he was twenty-three. It would remain the home of his parents until their move to Rapallo to be with their son in 1928. The wooden, three-storied house stood two blocks from the train station on top of a hill and had a front porch and, most importantly for the adolescent Pound, a tower-room which functioned as his 'den.'[2] One part of the community, however, was not just upper middle class but wealthy and that was where John Wanamaker of department store fame, among others, lived. Lyndenhurst, the Wanamaker mansion was built above a private lake. When it burned to the ground in 1907, Homer and Pound tried to rescue some of its art, an event recalled in *The Cantos*. Other notable residents in the area included Cyrus Curtius whose company published *The Saturday Evening Post* and his assistant, George Horace Lorimer, who use to cut through the Pound's back yard – an event Pound recalled in Canto LXXXI. But socially aware Wyncote was not the first residence of the Pounds in Philadelphia.

When they first arrived, they went to a home on South 43rd Street at the western edge of the city. After a short while, they headed north of the city to a home at 417 Walnut Street in Jenkintown, across the tracks from Wyncote, moving in on 22 March 1890. Two years later, they moved again, staying in Jenkintown but moving to Hillside Avenue but that house was unsuitable so in less than a year, the Pounds moved to Fernbrook Avenue in Wyncote. Such dislocation, following the shift from Hailey to New York may have implanted the constant sense of activity and action that would define the young poet's life who, until he settled in Italy in 1924, was a restless resident of Venice, London, and Paris.

Promotion to Assistant Assayer in 1891 increased Homer's income to $2000 a year, but the costs involved in purchasing and running the home in Wyncote required more capital; 'Ma' Weston, Isabel's mother, helped. Mary Weston provided the funds necessary for purchase, although occasionally the Pounds took in paying guests to defray expenses. In this way, however, Mary Weston exerted a certain control over the family which her daughter also exerted over her son which he soon understood as interference but others understood as strong matriarchal control. Pound later admitted his adoration of his father but also his objection to his mother's domineering manner, referring to her once as 'the Presbyterian Peacock' (*Am Rt* 71; Flory *Am EP* 16). Somewhat affected in manner, although attractive, Isabel Pound was also fond of offering witticisms or epigrams that only she seemed to understand, a habit her son would soon imitate according to H.D. (*End* 22).

Meanwhile, Homer solidified his job at the Mint, housed in a Greco-Roman style building near the ornate City Hall. Pound visited his father often, describing those trips to the temple of money in *Indiscretions*. H.D. recalled visiting Homer Pound at the Mint with friends and his hearty, informal and jovial manner as he showed everyone the minute weights and measures and explained the analysis of gold – before he opened the vault stacked with gold bars and neatly piled coins. Commenting on its architecture, the son noted that the Mint had a 'moderate number of sensible columns ... befitting the deity of coinage rather than the harpies of fluctuation' (*Ind* 47). Concern over the making and distribution of money remained with Pound throughout his life, recalling the act of shoveling in silver coins to be melted in Canto XCVII. In a 1962 interview, Pound drew an analogy between the making of money and the weighing and testing of every word in the making of literature (*RP* 235). On a 1902 trip to Europe with his father, Pound and his father purposely visited the British Mint which they found formal and the staff overbearing.

But the church, not the Mint, became Homer's interest at this time. Reared as a Quaker, Homer converted to Presbyterianism in Wyncote and became active in the Calvary Presbyterian Church which he and

Isabel helped to found. It was eventually located one block from their home. He also became president of a young people's society to promote enlightened forms of Christian action. Both Homer and Isabel were also active in missionary work, assisting the Italian community of central Philadelphia, actually living there in the summers, helping to establish what would become the First Italian Presbyterian Church. Indeed, in 1902, Homer lived part of the year in the city to be closer to his work at the Mint. In 1910–11, the parents moved for a year to the city center to be closer to their Christian Endeavor work and Homer's job. Pound would describe this work in an article published in the *New Age* entitled 'Through Alien Eyes' in January/February 1913.

One striking feature of the Wyncote years was that while anti-Semitism appeared in slights and comments in the locale press, it was not an attitude or view expressed by his parents who acted in the opposite manner attempting to find ways to include minority groups, namely Italians, into the fabric of Philadelphia life. In 1902/03, the Pounds, in fact, rented their home to the President of the Jewish Hospital Association (*Am Rt* 75; Flory 288). The wealthy neighbors of the Pounds may certainly have been anti-Semitic but it was not expressed openly in the suburban life of Wyncote. But later, in London, when Pound examined international banking and the role of the Rothschilds, and came under the influence of the views of A.R. Orage, Wyndham Lewis and Major C.H. Douglas, his prejudice towards Jews and finance became stronger.

Religion for Pound was unexceptional. He professed his faith at the Calvary Presbyterian Church in 1897 and maintained it in word, at least, until his death some seventy-five years later when he was buried with Protestant rites on the island of San Michele in Venice in the section reserved for non-Catholics. But he also found deep attraction to mysticism, Confucianism and Neoplatonism. Reverend Carlos Tracy Chester, pastor of the Wyncote Church, had a great influence on Pound, not the least because he was well-read and encouraged the young Pound's early literary efforts. Chester not only published short stories and articles, but helped to edit the *Booklover's Magazine* and *Book News Monthly*. Pound dedicated *Exultations* to him in 1909. Reverend Chester would later suggest Hamilton College (his *alma mater*) to the Pounds as an alternative for their son, when Pound encountered difficulties at the University of Pennsylvania.

Small private schools provided Pound's earliest formal education, necessary because public schools were limited in Wyncote at this time. But when the Public School opened in 1895, Pound enrolled. Before that, he attended Miss Elliott's school and Chelten Hills School run by the Heacock family whose founder was an ardent suffragette. The feminism at the school may have influenced Pound's later valuation of independent and self-reliant women. He also spent time at a temporary Wyncotte school where one teacher, Florence Ridpath, made a great impression on him. As late as 1958, two months before his release from St Elizabeths, he wrote to her to praise her opposition to bureaucracy.

The absence of a high school in Wyncote meant that Pound had to transfer to the Cheltenham Military Academy in 1897. This was noted in the *Jenkintown Times-Chronicle* where a 'Ray Pound' (Ray, or sometimes Ra, was an early nickname) is cited. Between the ages of 12 and 16, Pound attended the military academy in nearby Ogontz where he walked everyday from his home. Uniforms and daily drill were the order of the day, supplemented by Latin, history and math. Frederick James Doolittle (unrelated to the poet Hilda Doolittle) taught him Latin and taught him well, Pound later reporting in an interview that 'I got into college on my Latin; it was the only reason they *did* take me in' (*RP* 229). A photo of Pound at this time in uniform shows him staring at the camera surrounded by other 'cadets' and wearing glasses. Suffering from acute astigmatism through childhood, he cured the ailment with the help of a Dr. George Gould of Philadelphia to whom he later referred James Joyce. At Cheltenham, he competed in fencing and tennis: crossed foils hung on the wall of his tower-room at Fernbrook Avenue. But disliking the military tenor of the academy, Pound was eager to graduate and he completed his studies at fifteen in 1901, the year Queen Victoria died.

Growing up, Pound could count on the esteem of his parents. He could change his bedroom whenever he wanted and was read to a great deal by his mother before he began school (and teased by his classmates for his polysyllabic vocabulary). Pound's father was, throughout his life, one of his greatest admirers. And it was he who, at his son's request, asked that the University of Pennsylvania award a PhD to Pound for *The Spirit of Romance*. He also frequently kept the local press informed of his son's European triumphs. In 1930, Homer proudly leaned across to Max Beerbohm in Rapallo to say 'You know, Mr. Beerbohm, there isn't a darn thing that boy of mine don't know' (*SCh* 9). Pound admired his father whom he called 'the naïvest man who ever possessed sound sense,' while gently satirizing his mother's pretensions to gentility (*Ind* 8). Similar to his own father, the gregarious Pound became a kind of father-figure to the modernists, dispensing advice, direction, manuscripts and, when possible, money.

Pound began his international education before his graduation from Cheltenham Military Academy when he took his first trip to Europe in 1898 with his Aunt Frank and his mother (although his account in *Indiscretions* fails to mention his mother's presence). From June to September, the three traveled to Genoa, Lake Como, Venice, Rome, Naples, Granada, Seville and Tangiers where Aunt Frank bought him a green robe which he proudly wore to numerous social events. Canto LXXIV/467, the first of *The Pisan Cantos*, recalls some of the adventures which introduced him to southern France and northern Italy which he would frequently revisit (also see *Am Rt* 91–4). In 1902 at the age of sixteen, Pound made a second trip to Europe, traveling again with Aunt Frank and his parents. London and Venice were included, as well as a stop at the British Mint where his father's authority allowed entry but not a tour of its workings (*Ind* 45). Between the ages of thirteen and twenty six, Pound made five trips to Europe, each of them providing what he called 'the old kick to the senses' (*Ind* 3). For some, however, these trips created a questionable rather than cultured reputation because he had been exposed to exotic locales and ideas at an impressionable age. Nevertheless, Pound's early European travels laid the groundwork for the method (first-hand research) and content (European culture) of his finest poetry, from *A Lume Spento* (1908) to *Drafts & Fragments* (1969). Supporting this was his desire to incorporate the past into the present. He summarized the reason for his constant travels in 1912: 'my pawing over the ancients and semi-ancients has been one struggle to find out what has been done, once for all, better than it can ever be done again, and to find out what remains for us to do...' (*LE* 11).

In September 1901, when Pound began the University of Pennsylvania at age 15 (he would turn sixteen the following month), there was a lengthy hazing period for freshmen and in Pound's year, all incoming freshman were forbidden to wear flashy socks. The day after this announcement, Pound arrived wearing 'lurid, loud socks' and was promptly thrown in the lily pond by the second year students, earning him the nickname, 'Lily Pound' (H.D. *End* 14; *Jenkintown Times-Chronicle* 19 April 1902). The seemingly shy boy from Cheltenham military school had protested against the Establishment, asserting his rights and setting a pattern he would follow in his literary practice as well as political and private life: independence. He proudly referred to the freshman incident many years later, as he proudly referred to his reddish golden beard in his adolescence: 'I make five friends for my hair, for one for myself' (EP in *End* 3). Ungraceful but dramatic, 'one would dance with him for what he might say' not how he would move wrote H.D., his youthful admirer

(*End* 3). Pound always made himself conspicuous even at the Philadelphia Academy of Art where he would dash at a picture and then stand 'in his then Whistler manner in the (then novel) horn-rimmed spectacles before various . . . atrocities and commenting in a loud voice' (H.D., *CST* 18). Pound's outspokenness included the classroom where he once challenged the Shakespearean expert Professor Felix Schelling during his MA studies at Penn with the declaration that 'Shaw is greater than Shakespeare' (H.D., *CST* 17; *Am Rt* 103). This was heresy. He also read loudly, shouting more than reading a poem of William Morris's to H.D. in a field, raising his voice even more at the end of each verse. He brought *brie* to a picnic making everyone aware of their lack of sophistication and 'general lack of polish and [lack of] European culture because we did not appreciate the cheese' (H.D., *CST* 18). The green robe was also a form of outspokeness and it so impressed Hilda Doolittle that, when she saw it at a Halloween party Pound's freshman year, she was startled. The sixteen-year-old Pound told the fifteen-year-old H.D. that it was not Chinese but that he had gotten it on a trip to Europe some years before in Tunis (not so; he only went as far as Tangiers). But Ezra 'had Gozzoli bronze-gold hair and the coat caught up with his hair and odd eyes' (H.D. *CST* 17). Others were less sure of his hair color, referring to it as gold, red, brown, sandy and even blonde (*SCh* 59). The coat, however, became infamous because Pound gave it to the sister of a friend of H.D.'s who was suffering from anxiety. The girl visited H.D. while Pound was present and he suddenly insisted that she take the coat to cheer her up (H.D., *CST* 17). Generosity and self-dramatization began to define him.

Pound chose the University of Pennsylvania partly for economic reasons. His father could not afford to send him away, but the son could commute which he did the first year at the expense of establishing new friendships that might emerge from dormitory living. He was also two years younger than most freshman but compensated by being overly self-assured. In an 'Autobiographical Outline' written for the critic Louis Untermeyer, Pound wrote that he entered university 'with the intention of studying comparative vales in literature (poetry) and began doing so unbeknown to the faculty. 1902 enrolled as special student to avoid irrelevant subjects' (*Auto* 18). He officially registered for a Bachelor of Science degree (exempting him from Greek) in September 1901 and did well in Solid Geometry but failed Algebra and Trigonometry. In English Composition, as well as in Latin, Public Speaking and German, he had no more than a Pass. He improved in second term continuing with Algebra, German, English Grammar and more Latin (*Am Rt* 98).

Pound made only a few close friends in his first year at Penn, one of them the young artist William Brooke Smith who had a studio near the downtown area. However, the sickly Smith would die in 1908, a loss Pound would mark by dedicating his first book, *A Lume Spento*, to the painter. The title is partially borrowed from Canto III of Dante's *Purgatorio* where the remains of the son of the Holy Roman Emperor, Frederick II, are carried from his place of death 'with tapers quenched.' Hence the title, *A Lume Spento* referring to the premature death of Smith. There is also the suggestion that the painter, like the poet Pound, is an outcast. But more importantly was Smith's education of Pound's visual sense, something that he would cultivate throughout his life, as well as his friendship with later artists, notably Gaudier-Brzeska (to die tragically in World War I), Wyndham Lewis, Picabia, Brancusi and Oscar Kokoschka. The 'seen form,' what Guido Cavalcanti called the *veduta forma*, influenced Pound's emphasis on the visual in his poetry (Canto XXXVI/177).

Hilda Doolittle was another other important figure from Pound's first year, a tall blond with a 'long jaw but gay blue eyes,' later known as H.D. (Williams 67). The youngest daughter (by his second marriage) of the Professor of Astronomy and Director of the Flower Astronomical Observatory, Charles Doolittle, H.D. possessed what William Carlos Williams described as 'a breathless impatience' and, like Pound, had a 'provocative indifference to rule and order.' Pound was 'wonderfully in love with her' in part, perhaps, because of her romantic nature and romantic attitude toward writing (Williams, *Auto* 67–8). After Williams told her how *he* preferred a neat desk before he could begin to write poetry, she explained that it was a greater help for her to start by putting some ink on her pen and then 'splash it on her clothes to give her a feeling of freedom and indifference toward the mere means of the writing' (Williams, *Auto* 69).

H.D. and Pound shared a love of classical literature, a curiosity about mythical traditions and an appreciation of the arts. He fondly addressed her as the 'Dryad.' In her one year at Bryn Mawr – her career interrupted by her stormy engagement to Pound which saw her at home studying and writing for the next five years – H.D. spent one third of her fifteen credit hours studying Latin; another third was spent on English literature, the remainder on science. Greek, unofficially studied by both, also became a kind of secret language for them. H.D. was Pound's first serious romance and for a time they were 'unofficially' engaged. They met at the Halloween party where the sixteen-year-old Pound entered in his striking green robe. Their walks in the lyrical woods in

Upper Darby, where the Observatory was located, were occasions for poetic exchanges and an identity with nature which Pound expressed in one of his poems about her: 'She hath some tree-born spirit of the wood/ About her, and the wind is in her hair,' anticipated by the lines 'My Lady is tall and fair to see/ She swayeth as a poplar tree' (*End* 84, 73).

Pound took her to a performance of Richard Mansfield's *Peer Gynt* in Philadelphia and 'he read me William Morris ["The Gilliflower of Gold" and "The Defence of Genevere"] in an orchard under blossoming – yes, they must have been blossoming – apple trees' (*End* 22). Pound also began his habit of instructing others what to read, bringing the young H.D. Ibsen, Shaw, Swendenborg, Rossetti, Whistler's *Ten O'Clock* lecture, and a reprint of the romance of Tristram and Iseult. He also wrote, or tried to write, a sonnet a day for her, which were later bound in vellum and called *Hilda's Book*. He also brought her a historical novel, *The Gadfly* (1897), set in mid-19th century Italy about the illegitimate son of an Italian prelate involved in revolution who also publishes political verse lampoons under the pseudonym of 'The Gadfly.' His signature is the sketch of a gadfly with spread wings, which the youthful Pound adopted as the motif for his own signature for a time. The hero is eventually captured, court-marshaled and executed, partially foreshadowing Pound's own later experiences (and fears) which prompted H.D. in her memoir *End to Torment* to conclude that Cocteau's phrase – the artist is 'a kind of prison from which the works of art escape' – applied literally and meta-phorically to Pound whose incarceration at Pisa and then St Elizabeths was the catalyst to a kind of compulsive creation. The result was *The Pisan Cantos* (*End* 56).

Early classical interests, beginning with his study of Latin at Cheltenham, carried over to Pound's youthful identity as an 'aesthetic pagan' and celebration of Ovid which influenced H.D. His study of Early Latin suggested a new pagan renaissance was necessary to break free from the stultifying Victorian period. 'Why write what I can translate out of Renaissance Latin or crib from the sainted dead?' he asked William Carlos Williams (*SL* 4). To H.D. he would bring translations of Theocritus by Andrew Lang and Dante's *Vita Nuova*. The use and application of classical tropes and figures carried through to all of his work, competing with his renditions of Troubadour poetry and Provençal for importance. From early works in imitation of Catullus (see Δώρια [Doria] from *Ripostes* [*CEP* 193]) to his use of Homer to begin *The Cantos* and his late translation of the *Women of Trachis*, the classical tradition is the bedrock of Pound's writing. His borrowing, appropriating and even stealing lines and phrases from Greek and Latin poets reflect his absorption with romance languages and romance. And his inspiration was his 'Dryad,' H.D. *Hilda's Book* consists of twenty-five poems written for H.D. in the manner of Morris, Rossetti and Swinburne, handbound by Pound, first published as an epilogue to *End to Torment* (1979).[3] Composed between 1905–7, when he still believed that the two might marry, the volume, presented to H.D. in 1907, is Pound's first book, although not his first publication. Part of the poetry is about his making the book and writing:

> I strove a little book to make for her,
> Quaint bound, as 'twere in parchment very old,
> That all my dearest words of her should hold,
> Wherein I speak of mystic wings that whirr
> Above me when within my soul do stir
> Strange holy longings[...]
>
> (*End* 69)

Syntax and diction evoke the Pre-Raphaelites which his later poetry would reject and replace with more concrete language and original meter, although the use of Latin, Italian and some experimentation anticipate what he will do on a larger scale years later. The lyrical mixes with the Romantic through an imitative classical trope as in 'Per Saecula:'

> Where have I met thee? Oh Love tell me where
> In the aisles of the past were thy lips known
> To me, as where your breath as roses blown
> Across my cheeks?
>
> (*End* 75)

The engagement between H.D. and Pound ended over objections from her father, a tall gaunt man who, in the words of William Carlos Williams, 'seldom even at table focused upon anything nearer, literally, than the moon' (Williams 67). Her mother also found Pound unacceptable.

H.D.'s novel *HERmione*, written in 1927 but not published until 1981, recounts her love affair with Pound which was intense, emotional and defined by mutual trust. They became engaged in 1905 which the novel vividly describes. Her poem 'Winter Love' records their fiery kisses which were 'Electric, magnetic, they do not so much warm, they magnetize, vitalize' she wrote in *End to Torment* (4). But her parents adamantly disapproved of Pound because of his upbringing, behavior and lack of respectability – but this did not prevent intense arguments with her mother over her future which Hermione narrates. Told that she must have something to live on, Hermione responds with:

> I can live on sunlight falling across little bridges. I can live on the Botticelli-blue cornflower pattern on the out-billowing garments of the attendant to Aphrodite and the pattern of strawberry blossoms and little daisies in the robe of Primavera.
>
> (*HER* 98)

Could Pound have provided for H.D. as an unemployed poet? Professor Doolittle and his wife were convinced he could not. And while H.D. could not willfully renounce her family, Pound could not accept her domestic tendencies and matriarchal nature. He wanted her to be more 'ornate, more worldly...more of a companion' rather than a homemaker (Robinson 18). In *End to Torment*, H.D. blamed Pound for severing her '(psychically) from friends and family' (48). In the novel, Hermione becomes ambivalent as the family's opposition grows: she 'wanted George to make one of his drastic statements that would dynamite her world away for her' but he does not (*HER* 63). Her ambivalence then becomes oppressive; despite her love for Pound, at a certain level H.D. was trying to break away from him and the powerful emotional net entangling them which Pound found increasingly confining. H.D. understood: Pound, she writes, 'broke it by subconscious or even conscious intention, the little "scandal"' (*End* 47).

The reference is to Pound's dismissal from Wabash College in 1907 and rumors that he was involved with other women in the area – Mary Moore, Bessie Elliot, Louise Skidmore. This gossip caused H.D., the Doolittles and even 'Philadelphia' to reject him (*HER* 44). Only 'daily duties and necessities' and the claim of 'a forceful effort toward artistic achievement' that disallowed domesticity camouflaged the 'two-edged humiliation, from the friends and family, from Ezra' of the broken engagement (*End* 48). Pound feared that H.D. might limit his freedom as a poet, as a note composed in 1908 confirms: 'art and marriage are not incompatible but marriage means art death often because there are so few sufficiently great to avoid the semi-stupor of satisfied passion – whence no art is' (*CEP* 322). He planned his departure to Europe shortly after the breakup and H.D. turned to her confidant and soon to be her lover, Francis Gregg, for support. Gregg, a friend of both H.D. and Pound – he called her 'the Egg' – also wrote and accompanied H.D. to

Europe in 1911; in 1912, Gregg married Louis Wilkinson and settled in
Europe, beginning to contribute poems and brief prose pieces to *Poetry*,
The New Freewoman, The Egoist, Dial, Smart Set and the *Adelphi*. Nevertheless, despite a possible engagement to Mary Moore of Trenton at this
time, Pound asked H.D. to elope with him when he finally decided to
leave for Europe early in 1908. Her hesitation brought an end to their
'official' engagement (Robinson 22; *End* 15). But she felt desolate, which
her poem 'Callypso Speaks' recorded:

> He has gone
> he has forgotten;
> he took my lute and my shell of crystal –
> he never looked back –
>
> (*Sel Poems* 61)

This would not be true, however, for they renewed their relationship
when H.D. came to Europe partly in pursuit of her poet and, according
to her biographer, faced another marriage proposal from Pound, while he
was engaged to Dorothy Shakespear, soon to become his wife (Robinson
23–5).

   In his second year at Penn, Pound encountered a young medical
student who also had writerly ambitions. William Carlos Williams, the
son of an Englishman who grew up in the West Indies and a mother
from that region of Spanish, French and Jewish ancestry, had graduated
from the Horace Mann High School in New York and spent a year in
Europe with his parents before beginning medical school. He also had
artistic aspirations and continued with medicine only because he realized
early that he needed an income. Introduced to Pound through a mutual
friend who responded to Williams' violin-playing by telling him there
was an interesting young man around who was curious about writing
poetry, the two established a lifelong friendship. Pound, allowed by his
parents to stay in the dorms for his second year, developed a number of
new friendships. But Williams' lasted and they met in London in 1910,
Paris in the early twenties and the US in 1939 when Pound made
a quick visit. It was also at Williams' home where Pound spent his last
night in America before returning to Italy in June 1958. During Pound's
later confinement to St Elizabeths mental hospital, Williams wrote letters
in support, although he disagreed with a number of Pound's ideas.

   The presentational poetry of Williams, emphasizing objects rather
than ideas, appealed to Pound. 'No ideas but in things' from *Paterson*

found echo in *The Cantos*. Their differences, however, would also emerge, beginning in 1919 when Williams, defending those poets who remained in America and who were less seduced by European traditions, wrote that Pound did little to forward US verse. Pound vigorously objected (see *SL* 156–161). During the war years, Williams would also object to Pound's racist radio broadcasts, although he defended him as a remarkable poet and helped to win his release from US custody.

In his second year at Penn, Pound began to concentrate on Latin, including a study of the outspoken, epigrammatic poet Catullus, as well as Propertius, and Virgil. He continued an interest in chess and fencing which began in high school, taking lessons from Signor Terrone, the Penn coach. They weren't entirely successful but Pound maintained his love for the sport and even sent Terrone a copy of his fist book of poems (*SCh* 40). Pound did not make the team, turning, instead, to lacrosse. That career was even shorter according to Williams (56).

Pound also never learned to play the piano, although his mother tried to teach him, but in typical style Pound 'played' nonetheless, or thought he did. He 'attacked' the keyboard and 'everything... resulted except music' Williams recounted (56). But as with much that he did, Pound 'took mastership at one leap,' playing coherently in his own mind. 'It was part of his confidence in himself' (56–7). This included his role as a captive maiden in the chorus of Euripides' *Iphegenia in Aulis*, performed in Greek by Penn undergraduates in April 1903. Williams, witnessing the production, noted how Pound 'waved his arms about and heaved his massive breasts in ecstasies of extreme emotion' (Williams 57). Enjoying the performance in the audience was Aunt Frank and her companion, a Dr James Louis Beyea. Nevertheless, Pound was 'the liveliest, most intelligent and unexplainable thing I'd ever seen and the most fun' Williams summarized (58). What Williams disliked about him, however, was his posturing as a poet.

Mediocre grades – he did not receive a single Distinction (equal to an A), failed one history course and received an incomplete in another – and inability to find instruction in areas he sought at the end of his second year at Penn meant a transfer to another, perhaps less distracting, university for Pound. Reverend Chester, the former pastor of the Pounds, suggested Hamilton College in Clinton, New York. Following an interview there in June 1903, Pound wrote to his parents to say how he and the President of the college hit it off; in turn, Dr Stryker, the President, was willing to gamble on the youngman who had a grasp of Latin and a solid grounding in chess. He was accepted as a transfer student and given credit for all Penn courses except the failures and incompletes.

Grades alone did not force Pound's departure from Penn: he couldn't take the courses he wanted, the rules forbidding study in Junior year of any language not studied in the first two. At Hamilton, he could add Italian and Spanish to his knowledge of Latin and German. Pound, who at 15 thought he wanted to be a poet, understood that he had to know the best that had been written in a variety of languages.[4] Restrictive course requirements brought about by low grades forced Pound to look elsewhere; Hamilton College was the answer. At Hamilton he took forty units of languages in two years: French, Italian, Spanish and Provençal, in addition to Anglo-Saxon and Hebrew, plus English literature. Two professors, William Shepard and Revd. Joseph Darling Ibbotson (who taught Anglo-Saxon, English and Hebrew), became his mentors. When he returned to Penn for graduate work in 1905, he took every Romanics course offered by Hugo Rennert except Portugeuse (McDonald 12).

Pound arrived at Hamilton with his mother in the fall of 1903 and settled in a largish suite on the ground floor of a dorm. Hamilton had approximately two hundred students and no women. The absence of girls did not curb his pursuit, however. He soon made the acquaintance of Viola Baxter through a church group in nearby Utica, NY. He dated her in his senior year but that year (1904), he also met and fell in love with an older woman, the Jewish pianist Katherine (Kitty) Ruth Heyman. Their platonic affair – she was eight years older than Pound – lasted until Pound settled in London in 1908. A distinguished interpreter of Scriabin, Heyman likely met Pound in Philadelphia (she's mentioned as an older threat in H.D.'s *HERmione* under the name Stamberg), perhaps through one of his parents' musical evenings. Kitty found the younger Pound fascinating, at one point giving him a diamond ring that was her mother's. When Pound was involved with Mary Moore, but unable to purchase a ring, he gave her Kitty's ring, telling Mary how he obtained it.

Kitty's tour of Europe in the spring of 1908 and her presence in Venice when Pound arrived may have been more than coincidental. His poem 'Scriptor Ignotus' in *A Lume Spento* is dedicated to K.R.H. Parallels between Pound and Kitty, and Dante and Beatrice, are suggested by the narrator who dreams of completing a world-epic on a beloved organist, analogous to Kitty (*ALS* 38–40). Pound omitted the poem from *Personae* of 1926, likely because it revealed his as of yet unfulfilled wish to write an epic and because it recorded his love-for-Kitty.

Hamilton introduced Pound to oratory, 'Prex,' – President Stryker – a fine if vitriolic speaker, who during chapel, would rail against higher education and President Teddy Roosevelt at the same time he argued for the necessity of practical action in life. Canto XCVIII echoes the emphasis on practical education; in his anthology *Confucius to Cummings*, Pound included Stryker's translation of a poem by Martin Luther. But Pound did not easily fit in with the Hamilton community; only his roommate, Claudius A. Hand, understood the poetic obsessions of the young Pound, who would frequently wake Hand in the middle of the night to have him listen to his poetry (*Am Rt* 127).

At this early stage in his writing career, Pound began to talk of leaving the country and living abroad and he began to think of a great epic. But with the support of his teachers – Herman Brandt of the German Department, Arthur Saunders of Chemistry (who also staged musical events at the school) and William Shepard, Professor of Romance Languages and Literatures – Pound flourished. Shepard, in particular, was important, introducing Pound to Dante in Italian. Pound's copy of the three volume Temple Classics bilingual edition of *The Divine Comedy* contains numerous glosses in Pound's hand.[5] When Pound later told Donald Hall that his idea of writing *The Cantos* evolved during his Hamilton days, he added that 'it was a question of dealing with material that wasn't in the *Divina Commedia*.' The problem was to find a form – 'something elastic enough to take the necessary material. It had to be a form that wouldn't exclude something merely because it didn't fit' (*RP* 222). He was also becoming an expert in Provençal, the language of the Troubadours of Southern France which greatly influenced his earliest poetry.

Joseph Ibbotson, a specialist in Hebrew, Anglo-Saxon and Middle English, was Pound's closest friend and faculty mentor at Hamilton. Known as 'Bib,' Ibbotson was a presence on the campus, and Pound took full advantage of their friendship, often showing up at Ibbotson's house at odd hours to talk about poetry and the Anglo-Saxon tradition (*Am Rt* 132). With the encouragement of such instructors, Pound did much better academically than at Penn and even found time to do extra courses in Provençal and the Troubadours of Dante with Shepard. While at Hamilton, Pound also published a translation of a bilingual poem which he entitled 'Belangal Alba,' most of the work written in Latin with several Provençal refrains. It appeared in the *Hamilton Literary Magazine* for 1905, the year Pound graduated.

Pound returned to Wyncote after two successful years at Hamilton and entered the MA program at Penn, although he initially thought it would be part-time, while he taught at a locale prep school. When no opportunities emerged, he began a full-time program in Romance languages, while H.D. was preparing to enter Bryn Mawr, William Brooke Smith was establishing his studio near Franklin Square and William

Carlos Williams was working on his medical degree. Pound renewed his acquaintance with Professors Felix Schelling (English drama) and Child (medieval). He only studied with a Latinist, Professor Walton Brooks McDaniel, and with Professor Hugo Rennert, a specialist in Romance languages. Rennert had published on Lope de Vega and in a note to *The Spirit of Romance*, Pound provides a clever portrait of Rennert commenting on his efforts to translate the irregular rhythm of *El Cid* (*SR* 67). Rennert also appears in Canto XXVIII in a description of a classroom scene. Earlier, in Canto XX, he is shown telling Pound that if he is serious about mastering Provençal and the work of Arnaut Daniel, he should go to Freiburg to visit the renowned scholar, Emil Lévy. Pound would.

Because Pound did well in Rennert's classes, he won a $500 Harrison Foundation Fellowship in 1906, selecting Spain as the place for his summer research. The trip was his third to Europe, but his first alone, departing on 28 April from New York and arriving in Gibralter in early May. He recalled his earlier experiences of the place in Canto LXXIV. In Canto XXII, Pound narrates his adventure with his Jewish guide, Yusuf Benamore. Traveling under the pseudonym of Mr Freer, Pound became friendly with Yusuf who took him to an Arab holy man, as well as a synagogue, where Pound noted the social cohesiveness and his acceptance marked by sharing their snuff (XXII/105). As he later wrote in Canto LXXVI:

> in the synagogue in Gibraltar
> the sense of humour seemed to prevail
> during the preliminary parts of the whatever
> but they respected at least the scrolls of the law
> from it, by it, redemption...
>
> (LXXVI/474)

Pound began his studies at the Royal Library in Madrid where he read the works of Lope de Vega. He was to analyze the role of the *gracioso* in the plays of the Spanish playwright. There, he met a young priest whom he would later re-encounter in London after World War I and who was helpful in getting a Cavalcanti manuscript for Pound. This Father Elizondo had both an artistic sense and an appreciation of classical literature. Pound spent other moments at the Prado where the paintings of Valesquez fascinated him. He left Madrid for Burgos, home of El Cid, the Spanish hero and on his return to Philadelphia, he would publish 'Burgos: A Dream City of Old Castile' with photographs in *Book News Monthly* (Oct. 1906). Canto III narrates some of Cid's adventures in

Burgos. Pound then went north through the mountains of southern France and visited Bordeaux, Orleans, Paris, London and, finally, New York, stopping to see Aunt Frank. While abroad, he continued to write poetry, completing 'Capilupus... to Grotus' in 1906 in Paris and 'Scriptor Ignotus' to Kitty Heyman in London. Spanish epics, Provençal songs and classical odes to women registered his personal encounter with the European past.

Pound returned to Philadelphia in the fall of 1906 ready to continue his studies, boosted by his renewed love for H.D., although he also saw other women, including Viola Baxter and, soon, Mary Moore. He continued, as well, to take every course Rennert offered except Portuguese, focusing on Old Provençal, Spanish Drama and the Chanson de Roland. Courses with other professors were less successful, however; in fact, he flunked Professor Penniman's Literary Criticism course (Penniman was also Dean of the College faculty and would soon become Provost) and abandoned Schelling's course in Spanish Drama. Other classes were also left incomplete. This meant Pound lacked by seven the necessary twenty-four course hours needed to graduate.

Pound could not countenance academic bureaucrats and in his 1929 essay, 'How to Read,' castigated the kind of professor who treated their subjects as no more than drill manuals and yet rose to 'positions of executive responsibility' (LE 15). In the same essay, he critiqued his favored Rennert when he defended the study of inferior literature. Pound wanted to study Comparative Literature, a field not yet organized at the university level, which favored literature divided along national lines. Pound soon fell out of favor: in the spring of 1907, he was told that his fellowship would not be renewed and that he would be asked to stay on only as an instructor. He was upset at this change and remained angry at Penn for years, ending a 1929 letter to the Alumni Secretary, for example, with this postscript: 'All the U. of P. or your god damn college or any other god damn American college does or will do for a man of letters is to ask him to go away without breaking the silence' (SL 225).

At this time, the twenty-one year old graduate student published the first of his anti-philological essays, 'Raphaelite Latin,' in Book News Monthly (Sept. 1906) edited by Reverend Chester. In it, he stresses the beauty of the Latin language rather than the life or context of the poet, anticipating the formalist criticism he would later favor and which would be applied by those who defended his work in the face of his objectional racial and political views. Too much emphasis occurs on 'endless pondering over some utterly unanswerable question of textual criticism' and not on the inspired elements of language he argues (*EPCP* I:5). A teacher, for Pound, must do more than provide facts. Provincialism is the enemy he would declare in 1917 in a four- part essay of the same name which appeared in the *New Age* (July–August 1917).

Pound's earliest publication may have actually appeared in 1902, the early protest poem, 'Ezra on the Strike,' a doggerel work of four, eight-line stanzas about current events published in the *Jenkintown Times Chronicle*, 8 Nov. 1902, although this is disputed. Pound, himself, told Dr Kavka at St Elizabeths that his first poem was a limerick published in the same paper on 7 Nov. 1896 on the defeat of William Jennings Bryan – a protest against his loss. Humphrey Carpenter claims this as Pound's first published poem, although in his authoritative bibliography of Pound, Donald Gallup lists 'Ezra on the Strike' as Pound's first publication and has no reference to an 1896 work (*Am Rt* 83; *SCh* 36, Gallup C 0). Pound was seventeen when 'Ezra on the Strike' appeared.

Pound continued to write poetry while at Penn. Most of the manuscript of *A Lume Spento*, his first book, had in fact been completed before he would leave the US two years later, the early poems reflecting his unperfected talent as William Carlos Williams noted. Williams would often visit Pound's rooms at Penn to hear his works read, including 'some of those in *A Lume Spento*. It was a painful experience' (Williams 56). But interestingly, according to Williams, Pound 'never explained or joked about his writing as I might have done, but was always cryptic, unwavering and serious in his attitude toward it. He joked, crudely, about anything but that' (Williams 57–8).

At the same time he was suffering academic reversals, Pound's Aunt Frank was experiencing business upheavals. A hotel she invested in and managed, The New Weston at 49th and Madison which opened in 1906, did poorly and went into receivership by 1909. Aunt Frank and her third husband, Dr Beyea, could not make the mortgage payments and they soon found themselves without any equity or savings. The New Weston was 'the drain wot swallered all the fambly forchune & left me bareassed on the pavement' Pound wrote to the poet Louis Zukofsky in 1931 (*EP/LZ* 98). Yet Pound forgave her and remembered her with affection in Canto LXXXIV:

> at least she saw damn all Europe
> and rode on that mule in Tangiers
> and in general had a run for her money
> (LXXXIV/559)

At this academic and financial low-point, Pound met Mary Moore. Unlike the ethereal H.D., more of a Greek nymph than Professor's daughter, Mary Moore was the girl next door. A vivacious young woman, who wore bright, loose-fitting dresses, Moore was carefree and not moody or introspective like H.D. Pound met her in Scudder Falls, New Jersey, where he was tutoring a young man trying to get into Williams College. The young man went off to fetch Moore, likely his girlfriend, and they returned to meet Pound who thrived on the brashness of the young woman. Throughout the summer of 1907, Pound enjoyed himself with Moore, picnicking, boating and exploring the Delaware river. During this idyllic time, Pound was sure he wanted to marry Moore. Two years later in London, Pound would dedicate *Personae* to her, repeating the dedication in the expanded edition of the book in 1926. But as the summer of 1907 drew to a close, Pound needed a job.

Through the Penn Graduate School, Pound heard of a position at Wabash College in Crawfordsville, Indiana, a small liberal arts school. It was advertised as Chair of the Department of Romance Languages consisting of a department of one, the new hire. Pound interviewed for the job in Philadelphia and the new president of the college hired him on the spot. Pound was at first elated and saw a bright future ahead. But could the *poète* become eminent in the town whose most illustrious citizen was the author of *Ben Hur*, Lew Wallace? Even before he left, Pound expressed anxiety over leaving the cultured East and the good company of Mary Moore. But in the midst of a series of flirtatious letters they would soon exchange, she dropped a shocker: she was in love with another man, which made Pound's isolation in Indiana even more difficult.

Pound went to Crawfordsville in September 1907, staying, first, at a hotel and celebrating the southern character of the town to his parents. But soon, conflict, if not friction, emerged beginning with smoking which Pound enjoyed but the college and state forbid. The president, whose office was near Pound's, caught him smoking at least once. But the *peccadillo* was overlooked: Pound was an effective teacher and needed, offering elementary Spanish, and two beginning French classes. Pound had, meanwhile, moved from the hotel to a residence where he soon became infatuated with the sister of his landlady, a widow from the South. Unfortunately, the president of the college was also smitten with the young girl and Pound had to forego his flirtation.

Pound took to entertaining his students in his rooms but the owners frowned on the situation. They soon asked Pound to leave; by 20 October, he had found new rooms and it is here where Pound met a stranded vaudeville girl who was living across the hall from him and to whom he gave food and coffee. A letter to his friend Lewis B. Hessler from November 1907 details the arrangement (*Am Rt* 171). Pressures of various sorts caused Pound to move again, now to a house owned by the spinster Hall sisters, social figures in the small town and well- known to the Wabash administration. During this time, Pound made friends on the faculty and sought out acquaintances in town while writing poetry. Many of the poems would appear in *A Lume Spento*, which also included homages to François Villon, what he called Villonauds, while other works imitated a pagan Keats or overwrought Rossetti. 'Cino,' a troubadour monologue about the unsuccessful rejection of love, was likely written at this time, while other poems marked his desire to live free of conformity and pursue a kind of creative wandering in the tradition of the Troubadours. But faculty friendships and a few local acquaintances, such as the painter Fred Vance, could not substitute for the 'decadence' of the East and what he called 'kissable girls.' That lack led to the incident that caused his sudden departure and the lasting 'scandal' of Crawfordsville.

The episode, recounted by many but best told, although perhaps not entirely believed, by Pound deals with the so-called 'orphan-in-the-storm' situation. During one bitterly cold winter night, likely in February 1908, Pound walked outside in a blizzard to mail a letter. On the street, he met a penniless girl from a stranded burlesque show. He took her to his rooms where she spent the night in his bed and he on the floor of his study. In the morning, he went off to class but when the Misses Hall came up to make the bed they found the girl.[6] They immediately phoned the president of the college and a trustee. Pound was contacted and his act of charity was deemed an act of licentiousness. Characteristically, Pound did not easily give in; he held his ground, maintaining his innocence and then had to be paid off to leave. An agreement was quickly reached: Pound would be paid to the end of the month but depart immediately. On 12 February, he was issued payment and on Valentine's Day he left. Ironically, throughout his stay at Wabash, Pound's name appeared in print both in college publications and the newspaper as 'Pounds.'

Chagrined, the twenty-two year old returned to Wyncote, thinking the entire time of how to explain the incident to his parents, while anxiously considering his future. His attitude towards America also began to shift. Until then a patriot, he began to question the country's commitment to culture and its values in the face of such narrow mindedness.

But more pressing was his relationship with Mary Moore and H.D. To them, he told the truth, at least the truth of the orphan-in-the-storm story. His parents were shocked, although the loyal Isabel Pound was unwilling to acknowledge any wrongdoing on her son's part, while Homer good naturedly forgave his son. The rest of Wyncote and all of Philadelphia it seemed – with the exception of Mary Moore, H.D. and William Brooke Smith – were scandalized by Pound's actions. H.D.'s novel *HERmione* records the shock when the news hit Philadelphia and offers a dialogue between Hermione and her mother where she dismisses the incident in her desire to marry the poet-hero:

'But I thought that was all forgotten and anyhow everyone knew George [Pound] took the poor creature to his room to feed her.'

'People don't take people to their rooms to feed them. You're out of your mind, Hermione'

replies her mother (*HER* 94). The daughter continues to defend George, telling her mother that society cuts him because he's had books published and that, besides, they are *all* provincials. But she also acknowledges her dilemma: 'I can't go away with George, I can't stay here without George' (*HER* 95–6). But despite H.D.'s support, Philadelphia society and academia turned its back on Pound.

Mary Moore rejected his proposal of marriage. Pound then turned to H.D. but despite his renewed affection, her father adamantly maintained his objections. Nevertheless, H.D. wrote to William Carlos Williams on 12 February 1908 that she and Pound were engaged and she wore a sapphire ring given to her by Isabel Pound on her son's behalf. But when Pound got the courage up to ask her father for her hand, Professor Doolittle was speechless and cried "*What!* Why... you're... nothing but a *nomad*" (Norman 5)! A depressed H.D. returned Pound's ring, finding his plan that they both go to Europe to marry unrealistic. But for Pound, Europe was the only solution, although money an immediate problem.

The payment from Wabash was a start but not enough to live on, nor to publish his first book, which he planned to do soon after arriving overseas, thinking, perhaps, that a European rather than American colophon would be more authoritative and exotic. But he had to ask his father for funds. Homer agreed if the son could provide some testimony that his poetry had merit. Pound thought of the poet Witter Bynner (also an editor of *Mclure's Magazine*) as one who might understand his early work. Pound wrote to Bynner and received an invitation to send the poems and meet the editor in New York. A colorful Pound appeared extravagantly dressed in a riot of colors according to Bynner (Norman 26). Pound read his poetry outloud with enthusiasm and energy and Bynner compared his work to Vachel Lindsay. The editor/poet was more than happy to write a supportive letter for Homer. Aunt Frank was next to contribute, although she was herself in a perilous financial situation. With this support, Homer confidently gave his son the money for a cheap ticket to Europe. Pound bought passage to Gibraltar from a travel agent named Smith who then wrote a letter of introduction to another Mr Smith in London who would tell Pound about an opening as a lecturer at the London Polytechnic Institute where Pound would deliver a series of lectures in 1910 on the Troubadours and Dante. But that is getting ahead of the story. An invitation to Mary Moore to see him off at the dock in New York and a quick visit to Williams in Rutherford, New Jersey preceded his departure on the R.M.S. *Slavonia* on 17 March 1908, St Patrick's Day, with Mary waving, H.D. alone and Pound turned towards Europe with almost forty unpublished poems in his bag.

2
'My Music is Your Disharmony': 1908–14

Venice struck me as an agreeable place.... I announced an intention to return.

(Pound, *Indiscretions*)

Preceded by Proust and followed by Thomas Mann, Ezra Pound arrived in Venice in April 1908. That same year, Hugo von Hofmannsthal published an essay about a late summer stop in the dreamlike and alluring city, while Claude Monet settled for two-and-a-half months to paint. That same summer, Rilke sat in Paris and wrote three poems about the world Ruskin called 'the amphibious city.'[1] Pound arrived in Venice after stops in Gibraltar, Tangiers, Cadiz and Seville. The trip across had been stormy but his characteristic restlessness took on a lyrical tone: 'here today & on the wind tomorrow' he wrote his mother from Gibraltar (*Am Rt* 192). He at first thought his trip to Europe would be brief, an exit not an exile from America, but he would not return for two years.

Landing in Gibraltar, Pound unexpectedly re-connected with Yusuf Benamore met on his trip with Aunt Frank ten years earlier, and may have gotten involved with some minor money exchange as an autobiographical statement noted: '1908 landed in Gibraltar with 80 dollars and lived on the interest for some time' (*Auto* 19). He briefly acted as a tour guide around Spain for an American family but after ten days returned to Gibraltar and took a boat to Genoa, continuing by train to Venice, arriving at the end of the month. Venice, however, was expensive, Pound recalling in Canto III sitting on the Dogana (Custom House) steps because the 'gondolas cost too much, that year' to tour (III 11). In Venice, he moved about from the San Vio Quarter, where he lived over a bakery near the Academy Bridge, to 942 calle dei Frati, described in Canto LXXVI (482) where remembering also becomes a text. 'Dove sta

33

memoria' ('where memory liveth'), alluding to *Donna mi prega* by Cavalcanti, forms the refrain in a Canto that with Canto XVII are perhaps the best guides to Pound's early Venetian life (LXXVI/477). From calle dei Frati he had a view of the Grand Canal and the Giudecca Quarter; next to him was the garden of the San Trovaso Church. Near a gondola repair shop cited in Canto XVII, the out-of-the-way location, far from the tourists, was 'a fit abode for a poet. Stage setting at least correct' as he wrote to Mary Moore (*SCh* 93).

In this cultural *milieu*, Pound renewed his poetic imagination and sense of artistic purpose, overcoming his distress from the Crawfordsville incident. With understatement, he wrote in *Indiscretions* that Venice was 'an excellent place to come to from Crawfordsville, Indiana' (*Ind* 5). Freed from midwestern provincialism and Philadelphia gossip, Pound discovered that Venice encouraged new artistic confidence which his early poems, 'Alma Sol Veneziae' and 'San Vio,' record. Venice, his new *locus vivendi*, would remain his center throughout his life.

But Pound was eager to draw attention to his work. At his own expense, he made arrangements with a printer, A. Antonini, to prepare his first collection, *A Lume Spento*. One hundred and fifty copies of the paperbound book appeared in July 1908. Checking proof, however, created doubts and he momentarily considered throwing the pages into the canal (LXXVI/480). He had earlier tried to publish the volume with Thomas Bird Mosher of Maine, but was unsuccessful; now, the 72-page work (including misprints) would display his early efforts and be available for readers not only in Europe but the US. As the book was being printed, Pound told his parents with characteristic bravado that an 'American reprint has got to be worked by kicking up such a hell of a row with genuine and faked reviews that Scribner or somebody can be brought to see the sense of making a reprint. I shall write a few myself and get someone to sign em' (Gallup 4). This didn't work and no American edition appeared until 1965. While he waited for the book, Pound wrote two short stories that he thought he could sell to *Smart Set*. Entitled 'La Dogesa's Necklace,' and 'Genoa,' and written as first person monologues, they do not survive. He did admit to his parents, however, that he had no talent for fiction and found the form too mechanical.

Kitty Heyman arrived in Venice in June on a recital tour of Europe and Pound was quick to join her, announcing that he would act as her manager; he held a press conference for her and assisted her with details concerning her Venetian performance. He even considered joining her for her Paris and London concerts, but settled, instead, for a poem – 'Nel Biancheggiar' – about the effect of her Venice performance which was quoted in a Venice newspaper (*ALSp* 109). Before her arrival, he had looked for work, from teaching Italian to taking, very briefly, lessons as a gondolier. When not with Kitty and her entourage, Pound worked on a set of new poems to follow his first collection, copying them in an exercise book labeled 'San Trovaso,' the name of an area of Venice where he lived. The city was his principal subject, an absorption deflected only by the appearance of *A Lume Spento* in the third week of July. However, the first twenty copies or so of the book were spoiled by poor trimming by the printer who cut off too much margin making 'the thing look like a Sunday School hymn book' (*SCh* 94). Pound made sure that the rest of the run was trimmed properly and fifteen copies went by mail to his father – as well as copies to Williams, Mary Moore, H.D. and, perhaps most boldly, to Yeats who replied that he found the verses 'charming,' a remark Pound interpreted to mean approval: 'I have been praised by the greatest living poet' he wrote to Williams whose own criticism of the book led to a lengthy defense by Pound (*SL* 7–8, 3–5).[2]

The poems in *A Lume Spento* embody the two traditions that had the greatest influence on Pound before 1912: medieval literature of southern France and British literature from roughly 1840 to 1900, especially Browning and the Pre-Raphaelites, plus the early Yeats. Combining these two traditions, that of Provençal and the late nineteenth century including the 1890s, characterized Pound's work at this time. Self-consciously, he described the effect of this union on readers in 'Anima Sola' when he wrote 'my music is your disharmony' (*ALSp* 32). Swinburne, who died in 1909, was an early hero, as was Browning, both supplementing his reading of the aesthetes of the 90s: Lionel Johnson, Ernest Dowson, Fiona MacLeod and Arthur Symons whose 'Wanderer's Song' likely inspired Pound's 'Cino.' Yeats' Celtic poems also found a reworking in *A Lume Spento*, one example, 'The Tree,' modeled on Yeats' 'He Thinks of His Past Greatness When a Part of the Constellations of Heaven' from *Wind Among the Reeds* (1899). Also influential was the Decadent Movement which Symons defined as a 'dutiful waiting upon every symbol by which the soul of things can be made visible;' poetry then becomes the 'evocation of a passing ecstasy, arrested in mid-flight' (Symons 8–9, 120).

'Spiritual romanticism' characterizes Pound's writing in *A Lume Spento*, which the first poem, 'Grace Before Song' initiates, mixing a classical prayer for inspiration with a statement of poetic principles:

As bright white drops upon a leaden sea
Grant so my songs to this grey folk may be:

> As drops that dream and gleam and falling catch the sun,
> Evan'scent mirrors every opal one
> Of such his splendor as their compass is,
> So, bold My Songs, seek ye such death as this.
>
> *(ALSp 13)*

Throughout the volume, Pound seeks a poetry of essences through a set of recurrent image patterns using what he would later call the *phantastikon* or image-making faculty (*SR* 92). Later, in the first version of Canto I, he expands this idea: 'Oh, we have worlds enough, and brave *décors*.' Extending the concept, he writes, 'And from these like we guess a soul for man/ And build him full of aery populations' (*Per* 234). Disembodied spirits and dreams are only two of the features in the poetic universe created by poems in his first book. Headnotes explain the more arcane Troubadour tales, while a line from Browning often sets up an imitative monologue, with verses in Latin, Italian or French acting as prefaces for other poems. The opening of 'Comraderie' is typical:

> '*E tuttoque io fosse a la compagnia di molti, quanto alla vista.*'
>
> Sometimes I feel thy cheek against my face
>   Close-pressing, soft as is the South's first breath
>   That all the subtle earth-things summoneth
> To spring in wood-land and in meadow space.
>
> *(ALSp 47)*

Few of the works in the book exhibit the energetic pose and line that will soon characterize his writing; 'To the Dawn: Defiance' is an exception:

> Ye blood-red spears-men of the dawn's array
> That drive my dusk-clad knights of dream away,
> Hold! For I will not yield.
>
> My moated soul shall dream in your despite
> A refuge for the vanquished hosts of night
> That *can* not yield
>
> *(ALSp 67)*

The tension that emerges in *A Lume Spento* between the self-conscious literary language of the Decadents and the straight talk originally encountered through the direct narratives voiced in Browning suggests a path Pound's later work will follow. A line from 'Canto I' of 1917 summarizes the shift: to Wordsworth, the narrator declares 'avoid speech figurative/ And set out your matter/ As I do, in straight simple phrases' (*Per* 232). Through the opinionated assurance of the morally wrong characters of Browning (and the gradual importation of Anglo-Saxon language), Pound understood the value of direct speech. *A Lume Spento*, despite its arabesques of language and artifice, hints at new directions for Pound and which the rules of his new poetry, to be called Imagism, would soon confirm, rejecting the associative symbols and indefinite allusions of his pseudo-Decadent verse. The wind, the dream, the dawn and the fire, all recurrent images in Pound's first book, would vanish in his new aesthetic.

Venice, however, was becoming financially difficult (he had no work as either a teacher or gondolier) and to his father, who sent on additional funds, he explained that he would like a month in England to 'meet Bill Yeats & one or two other humans if convenient' (*SCh* 93). The appeal of Yeats, he would later explain, was that the poet knew more about poetry than anyone else and that he had 'ripped away the rhetoric of English verse' (*P/J* 219). Pound had read Yeats at the University of Pennsylvania but missed a visit to the campus by the poet in 1903 because he was at Hamilton. Nevertheless, he was convinced that Yeats was *the* poet of the moment and had to meet him, for it was Yeats who 'has once and for all stripped English poetic of its perdamnable rhetoric. He has boiled away all that is not poetry – and a good deal that is.' Yeats, he announced, 'has made our poetic idiom a thing pliable, a speech without inversions' (*LE* 11–12). A month after the printing of *A Lume Spento*, Pound left Venice for England, with copies to distribute and to track down Yeats. It did not take the self-confident poet long.

London to Pound was 'the *centre* of at least anglo-Saxon letters, and presumably of intellectual action.' He approached the city with typical energy and a sense of active expectation: 'I go to London on divers chances. . . . Here goes . . . ' and arrived on 14 August 1908 (*SCh* 97 96). A musical connection through Kitty Heyman led to her refereeing his re-application for a Readers Ticket at the British Museum, followed by his unabashed entrance to the shop of Elkin Mathews on Vigo street just off Piccadilly. Pound knew that poets and critics frequented Mathews' book shop and that Mathews, with John Lane, had published *The Yellow Book*. Sympathetic to the young American, Mathews agreed to display Pound's first volume. Lecturing did not materialize, however, and Mathews hesitated to take on Pound's new collection from the 'San Trovaso' notebook. Ebullient despite his unemployment, Pound still sought to have his work published, sending the manuscript of poems to J.M. Dent, although they returned it. Money was also becoming a problem, resolved only with the late September arrival of fresh funds from his

father. But despite nothing concrete, the whirling Pound extended his
activities: 'put out some new lines and am trying to keep in motion' he
told his father on 11 October (*SCh* 100).
Most days were spent in the British Museum writing. Impatient, Pound
selected fifteen poems from his Venice notebook and went to a printer
in Mortimer Street and paid to have them printed in a booklet called *A
Quinzaine for this Yule*, 'quinzaine' sounding more exotic than fifteen.
One hundred copies were printed with a dedication to Kitty Heyman.
To sustain the image that he did not publish the book himself, the title
page gave the impression that the printers, Pollock & Co., published the
work. An epigraph he made up on beauty prefaced the work. But in this
thin collection, hastily written in Venice, only 'Night Litany' stood out.
By November that year, Pound was still undiscovered, although he
could write that 'there is no town like London to make one feel the vanity
of all art except the highest' (*SL* 8) – a sentiment he felt more strongly
after Mathews ordered an additional one hundred copies of a selection
from *A Quinzaine*, with several additions by Pound, to sell in his shop
with a new colophon: 'Printed for Elkin Mathews, Vigo Street, London
W.' The title of the new work was *Personae*, a title Pound would later use
for a much expanded edition which appeared in 1926. The 1909 edition,
published in April, less than a week after the death of Swinburne, contained the dedication, 'This book is for Mary Moore of Trenton, if she
wants it.' Sent a copy, Moore didn't notice the dedication until some
months after when a friend pointed it out to her. Notices of the book
varied from indifference to praise, Edward Thomas in the *English Review*
celebrating the intensity of the feeling and understanding the battle
between the soiled world of an independent but isolated soul set
against the need for language that was beautiful, rare and antique. The
melancholy, resignation and superficiality of contemporary verse were
absent. Personality and power dominated the text creating a reaction
that unsettled 'The Square' (a literary club founded by G.K. Chesterton
which included Masefield and Walter de la Mare), since Thomas had
discovered a new talent none of them had read (Hutchins 62).
Just before *Personae* was released, but too late to be included, Pound
wrote perhaps his most successful early work, 'Sestina: Altaforte,' a
Browningesque dramatic monologue spoken by Bertran de Born, a trou-
badour-knight. Dante placed him in hell because he stirred up strife,
but Pound capitalized on Bertan's irascibility and love of battle. Pound
wrote the first strophe in his rooms on Langham Street and then went
around to the British Museum to 'make sure of the right order of
permutations' and did 'the rest of the poem at a sitting. Technically it is

one of my best ... ' (*EPCP* I: 147). A rendering of one of Bertran's war
songs, the work startles as it shatters the languor that had recently
characterized Pound's writing: 'Damn it all! all this our South stinks
peace. / You whoreson dog, Papiols, come! Let's to music!/ I have no life
save when the swords clash' the poem opens (*Per* 26).
The aggressive tone anticipated how Pound liked to think of himself
in his contrarian manner, as he identified with the pose he constructed.
Eliot singled the work out as a complete success in his draft notes for
the introduction to the *Selected Poems of Ezra Pound* (1928). Importantly,
Pound showed how he could re-invent a traditional form, the sestina,
and make it new, removing the air of artificiality that often haunted the
genre. At the same time, Elkin Mathews was instrumental in enlarging
Pound's circle. He sent Pound to meet Ernest Rhys, for example, who
edited the *Everyman* series and he, in turn, introduced Pound to the
novelist May Sinclair. She did her part: believing that 'Sestina: Altaforte'
should appear in a new magazine, the *English Review*, she took Pound to
Holland Park Road in West London to the meet the editor, Ford Madox
Hueffer (later to change his name to Ford to de-emphasize his German
roots). He quickly accepted the poem.[3]
Different in manner and style from Pound who promoted the image
of a poet, Ford looked more like a 'caterer' according to Wyndham
Lewis or 'a flabby lemon and pink giant, who hung his mouth open as
though he were an animal at the Zoo inviting buns' (Lewis, *Rude* 122).
Ford had published twenty five books including two collaborations
with Joseph Conrad. Yet, he tended to boast, if not inflate, his literary
adventures which Richard Aldington in his autobiography details, calling
him a 'literary Falstaff,' although he also admitted that 'Ford had the
rare merit of believing in the republic of letters' and that writers and artists,
whatever their differences, should support each other publically. But no
other figure, with the exception of Pound, did so much to help other
writers, Aldington writes (Aldington, *Life* 158).
Ford was an astute, quick-minded critic whose conversation was
jewel-like if opinionated: 'Fordie/ never dented an idea for a phrase's
sake' Pound satirized in Canto LXXXII/545. But Pound actually preferred
Ford's conversation to Yeats' 'consisting in *res* non *verba*,/ despite
William's anecdotes' (*ibid.*). However, Ford postured as much as Pound,
so the two got on well. In his memoir, Ford affectionately recounts the
active, sometimes dangerously active, and energetic Pound:

> he was astonishingly meager and agile. He threw himself alarmingly
> into frail chairs, devoured enormous quantities of your pastry, fixed

his pince-nez firmly on his nose, drew out a manuscript from his pocket, threw his head back, closed his eyes ... and looking down his nose would chuckle like Mephistopheles and read you a translation from Arnaut Daniel.

(Ford, *Return* 373)

(Years later in Paris, Gertrude Stein would shudder as Pound threw himself into one of her chairs which immediately collapsed.) Nevertheless, Ford encouraged Pound, enjoyed his banter and published his 'Sestina: Altaforte,' giving Pound a tremendous boost: 'I suppose the sestina is about the most blood curdling thing the good city has seen since dear Kit Marlowe's day but it seems to have affected an entrance' he wrote (*SCh* 112).

Several years later, in 1911, Ford memorably criticized Pound's newest effort, reacting with Poundian vigor to the language of *Canzoni*. Ford, said Pound, who visited the writer in Giessen in August 1911, rolled on the floor at my 'jejune provincial effort to learn *mehercule*, the stilted language that then passed for "good English" in the arthritic mileu that held control of the respected British critical circles.' This *milieu* he glossed as 'Newbolt, the backwash of Lionel Johnson, Fred Manning, the Quarterlies, and the rest of 'em.' His third volume, Pound admits, 'displayed me trapped, fly-papered, gummed and strapped down' (*SP* 432). 'That roll,' Pound famously wrote, 'saved me at least two years, perhaps more. It sent me back to my own proper effort, namely, toward using the living tongue' (*P/F* 172). Ford, he pronounced, 'believes in an exact rendering of things' (*EPCP* I: 112). Years later, in his introduction to the 1964 reprint of *A Lume Spento*, Pound characterized his problem as writing in the imitative manner of an antique style and its archaic grammar. But Pound's double entry into Edwardian London, as troubadour scholar and brash, self-advertising American, was no longer in conflict. The first may have been medieval and old-fashioned and the second might wreck the furniture but his exuberance always caught people's attention.

Ford, who led a bohemian life, was having an affair with Violet Hunt at South Lodge, a villa at 80 Campden Hill, where her mother, widow of the Pre-Raphaelite painter Alfred William Hunt, lived. This was up the hill from 10 Church Walk, Kensington, where Pound had moved in August 1909. At first, Douglas Goldring, Ford's editorial assistant at the *English Review*, thought Pound was a charlatan, confirmed by the 'showy blue glass buttons on his coat;' indeed, his entire outfit seemed 'operatic:'

Ezra with his mane of fair hair, his blond beard, his rimless pince nez, his Philadelphian accent and his startling costume, part of which was a single turquoise ear-ring, contrived to look 'every inch a poet.'

(Goldring 48, 40)

But gradually, this 'cosmopolitian Yankee Muse' made a genuine impact and became master of social ceremonies at South Lodge (Goldring 48). The tennis courts across from South Lodge became a gathering point, not only for attempts at the game but as a social occasion, followed by a return to the 'villa' to discuss *vers libre*, 'the prosody of Arnaut Daniel and, as Ford records, "the villainy of contributors to the front page of the Times Literary Supplement"' (Goldring 47). Intensifying the afternoons was Violet Hunt's parrot which screamed 'Ezra ! Ezra!' when everyone returned from tennis. Indoors, Pound never sat still, always jumping and twisting with a 'backward jerk of the head, as he emphasized each point,' endangering every chair he sat on, on one occasion memorably breaking a delicate cane and gilt construction (Bottome 71; *SCh* 132).

At South Lodge, Pound enjoyed the role of poet, mistaken on one occasion for Browning by Violet Hunt's elderly mother. ' "Tell him to go away, tell him to go home, he always makes too much noise, that young Mr. Browning" shouted Violet Hunt's bedridden mother when Pound came to visit' writes H.D. (*End* 49). Pound also delighted in the story of the elderly Mrs Hunt saying 'Mr Browning is waiting in the drawing-room – ah, I mean Mr Ezra Pound' (HD *CST* 18).

In London, Pound enjoyed numerous flirtations with the so-called fast set of young women he met at South Lodge: Brigit Patmore, unhappily married to Coventry Patmore's grandson; Phyllis Bottome, who had published a novel at 21; Ione de Forest, stage name of a young French dancer, Jeanne Heyse, aka Joan Hayes and a member of the *New Freewoman* circle and likely the subject of his 1912 poem 'Dance Figure.'[4] In his short story, 'Nobody's Baby' (1932), Aldington satirized Pound's supposed conquests; earlier, he parodied Pound in his novel, *Death of a Hero* (1929) of whom it is said of Mr Upjohn, the Pound figure, that while discreet about his conquests, he was 'always prepared to talk about love, and to give subtle erotic advice.' Any experienced man, however, would suspect that Upjohn was 'at best a fumbler and probably still a virgin' (*Death* 116).

Through the South Lodge circle, Pound met Ford's new protege, D.H. Lawrence. Ford, publishing Lawrence's poems, wanted Pound to meet the young writer and the two surprisingly got on, Lawrence finding the

American poet 'a good bit of a genius, & with not the least self-consciousness.' Pound, at first, treated Lawrence condescendingly, and although he did not like Lawrence's ornate style, referring to it as 'fruity with a certain sort of emotion,' Pound did admire his poetry (*EPCP* II: 20). But at times overshadowed by new figures, Pound often reacted by behaving outlandishly – as when to capture the attention of Yeats, who was offering yet another monologue to Lawrence, Ford, F.S. Flint, and Ernest Rhys, Pound decided to devour one of the red tulips floating in glasses on a dinner table. Yeats did not notice the act and 'the rest of us were too well bred to take any notice. Ezra, having found the tulip – some say it was a rose – to his taste, did the same with a second flower' writes Rhys. After the second had been consumed, Mrs Rhys turned to Pound, inquiring '"Would you like another rose, Mr Pound?"' (Rhys 251ff).

James Gryffyth Fairfax, another young poet, introduced Pound to a Knightsbridge hostess, Mrs Alfred Fowler. Mrs Fowler held a salon which sometimes included Max Beerbohem and Robert Bridges. Pound became a regular. Although he never met Beerbohem or Bridges there, he did meet Mrs Olivia Shakespear who invited him to tea at her own home at 12 Brunswick Gardens where he went with Frederick Manning, an Australian poet.

Pound and others considered Mrs Shakespear one of the most attractive women in London, her secret affair with Yeats, ten years after her marriage to her solicitor husband, Henry Hope Shakespear, one source of her glamour. Yeats described her cultured poise in his posthumous *Memoirs* as a woman who seemed content with leisure and good conversation. The love affair began in 1895 and lasted a year. When Pound met her in January 1909, she had renewed her friendship but not intimacy with Yeats. The year before she met Yeats, she began a series of novels which dealt with women trapped in loveless marriages and saddled with late Victorian conventions. Pound at this time had lost interest in Kitty Heyman whom he saw in London. She was at least eight years older than Pound (there is some question about her birth date); his new interest, Olivia Shakespear, was twenty-one years older, although this did not deter him. A romantic friendship suited him perfectly, although another member of the family began to record his frequent visits: Dorothy Shakespear, Olivia's daughter and a year younger than Pound.

Reserved and beautiful, Dorothy largely accompanied her striking mother on her various social rounds. At twenty-two she had no romantic interests, although excitedly she wrote in her notebook about the young American visitor: 'Listen to it – Ezra! Ezra! – And a third time – Ezra! He has a wonderful, beautiful face, a high forehead . . . a strange mouth, never still & quite elusive' (*EPDS* 3). But Olivia, not Dorothy, enthralled him and he took her to a recital by Kitty Heyman, Dorothy tagging along. These social adventures, however, did not provide any income and he reluctantly planned to return to America, booking passage to depart on 10 March 1909. At the last minute, he changed his mind. A lecture series plus new friendships contributed to the decision. His six talks at the Polytechnic Institute of London, which began on 21 January 1909, soon brought him attention. The topic was the development of the literature of Southern Europe and he advised his father to trumpet him in any future publicity as 'Lecturer on Romance Literature for the London Polytechnique' (*SCh* 102). Thirty-five formed the audience for the first lecture on the 'Essential Qualities of Literature;' fewer appeared for his next lecture on the writing of the troubadours, although Olivia and Dorothy Shakespear attended all of the talks. While writing the lectures, he also began an essay on Whitman with whom he grappled, acknowledging his fundamentally American style but not necessarily admiring it. When he was soon compared to Whitman, Pound explained that their likeness was only generic: 'the feel of the air, the geomorphic rhythm force' (*SCh* 102).

Pound took his Thursday, 5pm lectures seriously, often wearing a dinner jacket in an effort to give the event some tone. On other occasions, he affected a more Bohemian, rakish look: a green shirt with the collar half open and tie knotted loosely as if it were a cravat. Spats covered his shoes and a black velvet jacket off-set by vermilion socks, trousers of green billiard cloth and perhaps a grey overcoat whose buttons were replaced by squares of lapis lazuli topped off the look. Pince-nez replaced glasses; soon, a thin moustache and a small goatee appeared (*P/F* 84; *SCh* 129). At twenty-four, Pound became a popular vision of the artist, or what he believed an artist in Europe might look like. Not only did he identify with this persona but he behaved as an artist, although the clothes, especially the hats, varied: on one occasion it would be a sombrero, the next a Panama, the entire look dressed-up with an ebony cane to guide the blowing and billowing of his clothes. At the Square Club, Pound would often enter with a mass of bright hair, occasionally a beard and frequently wearing a velvet coat with one turquoise ear-ring according to Edgar Jepson, a member. The model was Whistler and Kensington, where Pound lived from late September 1909 until 1920, his natural habitat.

The title and content of the Polytechnic lectures almost equaled the dress of the speaker and on their completion Pound was ready to publish *The Spirit of Romance*, 'an attempt to define somewhat the

charm of the Pre-Renaissance Literature of Latin Europe' – or more
exactly, an attempt to define the canon of his own poetic tradition (EP
in Hutchins 76). Taken by Dent on the recommendation of Rhys, the
original volume lacked notes (added in 1929 and 1932) and the present
Chapter 5, 'Psychology and Troubadours.' The aim of the book was to place
the roots of medieval romance with the Romans and connect the various
literatures of medieval Europe. Romance was not an invention of
12th century France but something broader Pound argues. Much of the
book consists of examples, through translation, to support Pound's
thesis – a technique his later critical practice will also follow – although
the text goes very little in the direction of defining its title. Classical
precision rather than lyrical romanticism appears to be its focus,
although in his lectures Pound celebrates the 12th century troubadour
poets. Among this group, Arnaut Daniel is closest to Dante in his
attempt to express a 'vivid and accurate description of...emotion' (*SR* 28).
'Proença,' Chapter 3, is a quick tour of the troubadour poetic tradition,
while Chapter 4 focuses on *The Cid*. Subsequent chapters deal with the
Italian lyric, Dante and François Villon.

Importantly, *The Spirit of Romance* contains Pound's later ideas in
embryo. In the first lecture, he outlines the link between poetry and
science and its need for precision later expanded through his concept of
Imagism and then summarized in the *ABC of Reading*. But it is in *The
Spirit of Romance* where he writes that 'poetry is a sort of inspired math-
ematics' which 'gives us equations, not for abstract figures, triangles,
spheres, and the like, but equations for the human emotions' (*SR* 14).
Anticipating his own involvement with music and the visual arts,
Pound establishes the unity of poetry with these forms: 'true poetry is
in much closer relation to the best of music, of painting, and of sculpture,
than to any part of literature which is not true poetry.' 'The spirit of the
arts,' he emphasizes, 'is dynamic,' embodying his own aesthetic of
action, movement and energy (*SR* 222).

Pound often gave Yeats as his reason for heading for London,
although he did not at first find contact with the poet that easy. But
a determined Pound formed an assault on 18 Woburn Buildings, the
Celtic stronghold of Yeats whose Monday night gatherings were
infamous. Pound likely first met Yeats in early May 1909 when Olivia
Shakespear took him to the Woburn Buildings in Camden. Although
they intersected briefly during the interim, it was not until October
that they began to talk seriously because Yeats was in Ireland throughout the summer. But October was a *mensis mirabilis* for Pound:
his new poem 'The Ballad of the Goodly Fere' appeared in the *English*

Review, his new book, *Exultations* dedicated to Reverend Carlos Tracey Chester was published and he re-met Yeats, telling his father that 'Yeats has at last arrived and I had about five hours of him yesterday' (Wilhelm I 40). The timing of their meeting was equally important for Yeats. In the fall of 1909, Yeats was seeking new poetic forms as he was stalled between his so-called 'Celtic twilight' period and the need to express Irish cultural nationalism. Spiritualism and archetypes, originating in Byzantium and/or Japan, also began to interest him. At first suspicious, Yeats, nevertheless, did admire Pound's knowledge of the troubadours, believing that his poetry 'is more definitely music with strongly marked time and yet it is effective speech' (Yeats, *Lett.* 543). But Yeats also recognized Pound's dilemma: 'a rugged headstrong nature, he is always hurting people's feelings but he has, I think, some genius and great good-will' he told William Rothenstein (in Hutchins 85). Nonetheless, a long and sustained friendship developed

At the time he met Pound, Yeats was considering a change of style, turning to more colloquial language, which stripped away redundancies and ornament to find a new precision and uncompromised effect as he had seen in Synge who had recently died. Yeats realized that 'the literary imagination has become dramatic in our time, while the stage has refused its opportunity to learn' (in Foster 439). Drama held less attraction for him, although the placement of dramatic effects in his poetry became his new goal, while seeking rhetorical simplification: 'I always try for the most natural order possible' to make thought plain (in Foster 439). This coincided with Pound's emerging view that poetry must be 'objective,' renouncing the excessive use of adjectives or dysfunctional metaphors: it must be 'straight talk' (*SL* 11). Pound's energy and unorthodoxy also challenged the good manners of the stuffy literary world of Gosse and others Yeats now saw as inhibiting. Their collaboration was still several years off, but after Pound returned from a trip to America in 1910, he and Yeats began to meet daily, starting when they found themselves in Paris in May 1911.

Beginning as an acolyte, Pound gradually made Yeats a disciple. When Goldring accompanied Pound to one of Yeats's evenings, he was startled by the way Pound distributed Yeats's cigarettes and Chianti. Pound controlled the conversation which focused on prosody and reduced Sturge Moore to silence; Yeats, himself, met the request of a young Indian woman in a sari to sing 'Innisfree,' despite being almost tone deaf. A 'dirgelike incantation' resulted to the chagrin of most (Goldring 49). Pound himself recalls a soirée at Yeats' in Canto LXXXII/544–5.

When William Carlos Williams visited Pound in 1910, he was taken to an evening with Yeats, more like a seance than a meeting. Tiptoing into a room illuminated by a single candle, Yeats was reading Ernest Dowson's 'Cynara' to a small group from the Abbey Theatre. He paid no attention to the entrance of Pound and Williams who quietly seated themselves. After a while, the two rose to leave but as they were at the door, Yeats called out: '"Was that Ezra Pound who was here?" Yes, someone answered and Yeats issued his command: "Tell him to wait a moment, I'd like to speak to him"' (Williams 114). Pound went in alone to talk to the master; Williams was impressed.

A visit to Yeats by the Italian Furturist Marinetti was less successful. Pound, Aldington and Sturge Moore acted as interpreters for Yeats who read a few of his poems 'which Marinetti would have thought disgustingly *passéistes* if he had understood them' and then Yeats, through Moore, asked Marinetti to recite something of his. Marinetti sprang up and "in a stentorian Milanese voice began bawling:

> '*Automobile,*
> *Ivre d'espace,*
> *Qui piétine d'angoisse," etc.,*

until Yeats asked him to stop because neighbors were knocking 'in protest' on the floor, ceiling and party walls (Aldington *Life* 108).

At one of Yeats's Monday nights Pound met Bride Scratton, the bored wife of a businessman. Three years older than Pound, she was outspoken and clearsighted. He fell for her at once and likely kept an image of her in his rooms, which Williams found mysterious since Pound never identified her to him. She reciprocated Pound's love for the next decade, although economics may have prevented their marriage. In 1923, her husband divorced her, naming Pound as the co-respondent in the petition.

Marking Pound's entrée into the formal, if slightly dreary, world of the London literary establishment was his participation in the Poets' Club, where the Irish poet, Joseph Campbell, read Pound's 'The Ballad of the Goodly Fere' in bardic robes. Pound, himself, read a passage on Arnaut Daniel from his about-to-be released *The Spirit of Romance*. Accepting an invitation to join meant his acknowledgment but not acceptance by these literary elders. Earlier, even *Punch* took satiric notice of the young poet, mentioning 'the new Montana [sic] (USA) poet, Mr Ezekiel Ton ... the most remarkable thing in poetry since Robert Browning' (*Punch* 136 [23 June 1909] 449). Pound soon found a more sympathetic group of listeners in the spring of 1909, when a secessionist body, which had broken away from the Poets' Club, met in a Soho restaurant on Thursday evenings. This group sought improvements in poetry and had as their titular head T.E. Hulme, a young writer who had been sent down from Cambridge, went briefly to Canada and then returned to audit some classes in philosophy before drifting to London. There he fell in with several radical writers, including F.S. Flint, who contributed to the *New Age* and who would soon attack the conservatism of the Poets' Club where Hulme had been honorary secretary at its founding in 1908. Edmund Gosse and Henry Newbolt were among the original members.

Hulme, with Flint and others such as F.W. Tancred and Edward Storer, broke away in 1909 from the Poets' Club; Pound joined them at their third meeting in April 1909 and recited 'Sestina: Altaforte' with such force that the cutlery vibrated on the restaurant tables according to Flint who would soon review *Personae*. In that review, he celebrated Pound as 'a rebel against all conventions except sanity;' there is 'something robustly impish and elfish about him' (*CH* 46). Talk of the French symbolists among this group and genuine interest in Pound's metrical experiments created a welcoming circle for the young poet, although he was at times incapable of maintaining the quick repartee and conversational wit, preferring letters or social monologues for his barbs (*SCh* 117).

Expressing something of his comic, if uncritical, admiration of Hulme, Pound appended to his volume *Ripostes* (1912), 'The Complete Poetical Works of T.E. Hulme' which consisted of five poems. Pound's prefatory note congratulates Hulme for setting 'an enviable example to many of his contemporaries who have had less to say' (*C&R* 58). However, as a kind of literary insurance, Pound also maintained his membership in the original Poets' Club. But at last, Pound had a community of artists in a variety of groups, something he had earlier lacked which his poem 'In Durance' (1907) lamented. In the few years since his arrival in London, he had more memberships than he could reasonably handle.[5]

But money was still a problem. To make ends meet, Pound did private tutoring and translations of some Italian and French songs. An unexpected windfall of £15 from Ford for publishing three canzoni, however, made it possible to take a quick trip to Italy, leaving for Paris first, in late March 1910. During that short visit, he stayed with his pianist friend Walter Morse Rummel and met Margaret Cravens who studied piano with Ravel. She admired Pound's work and carefree manner. Pound had received only a modest fee from the Polytechnic for his lectures which was determined by attendance but Cravens, who was fascinated by Pound's poetic efforts and literary enthusiasms, soon provided a regular subsidy for Pound plus occasional 'gifts,' allowing him to complete *The Spirit of Romance* and plan new projects. By April 1910, Pound no longer needed to ask his father for a regular remittance to meet his living expenses, telling his parents that his sudden acquisition of wealth originated with his editors and publishers. He never once told them of the real source.

Several months later, when Pound went to see Henry Hope Shakespear about marrying his daughter Dorothy – October 1911 – he mentioned that beyond his anticipated writing income was an additional £200 from an unnamed source. He was refused, the patronizing Shakespear adding, 'I also return the book of counterfoils from which I am glad to see that you have a balance to your credit' (*EP/DS* 74). It was likely that Pound counted on Cravens to support him financially – up to nearly $1000 a year (*EP/MC* 6). She continued to assist him until her death in June 1912. Such treatment was not unexpected because Pound believed that private patronage was one of the necessary steps for an American 'Risorgimento' which he celebrated in a 1912–13 series, 'Patria Mia,' a study of the artistic potential of America. He implicitly understood that economics would determine the quality of one's available time and work.

Later visits to Cravens in Paris united their friendship and he consulted her while working on a translation of Cavalcanti in the winter of 1910. In the spring of 1911, Cravens actually commissioned an American painter in Paris to do portraits of both of them. But Cravens unexpected suicide on 1 June 1912, shortly after learning that her close friend and possible lover Walter Morse Rummel was engaged to Cravens's former piano teacher, shocked everyone. (see H.D., *CST* 19). Pound, trying to come to terms with her loss, stood with a shaken H.D. in Paris and waved his 'Whistlerish stick towards the river, the bridge, the lights, ourselves, all of us' and 'said what we couldn't: "And the morning stars sang together in glory"' (H.D., *CST* 19). His Imagist poem, 'His Vision of a Certain Lady Post Mortem' (1914) records a dream about Cravens, although he cut the original opening line: 'They call you dead, but I saw you' (Longenbach 53).

During his 1910 trip to Italy, Pound visited Verona where he praised the Church of San Zeno and settled in Sirmione on Lago di Garda near the ruins of Catullus' villa. Sirmione, jutting out into an immense lake bordered by jagged mountains, would become one of the most important sites for him in Europe, not only for its literary past, physical beauty and intersection of northern and southern Italy but as the place which inspired Dorothy's own artistic ambitions and where he would meet

Joyce for the first time. To John Quinn, New York lawyer and art patron, Pound would write that Lago di Garda 'is where I always go to refit' (in Rainey 241). And it would be at Sirmione in June 1922 that he would relaunch work on *The Cantos*, recalling visits to the Hotel Eden in Sirmione in *The Pisan Cantos*. In 1910, he corrected proofs of *The Spirit of Romance* and wrote several poems there, but he did not remain alone for long. Olivia and Dorothy joined him in April, Dorothy as an artist, particularly enamored by the visual splendor of the lake and the surrounding mountains. All three went on to Venice in May, Pound returning alone to Sirmione before making his way back to London. Then on, 18 June, he journeyed to Liverpool and the *Lusitania* bound for America. He had decided to return: while literary notice was growing, his bank account was shrinking.

Pound's American visit – from June 1910 to February 1911 – was a period of reassessment. Would he resume an academic career and remain, or return to the uncertain literary life of a poet/critic in London? Would he find steady income as a writer or could he survive in less costly Europe? After a brief time with his parents in Philadelphia, he moved to New York. H.D. followed, seeking some form of literary employment and attachment but found nothing except that Pound was more interested in himself than her. She returned to Philadelphia, still fixated on Pound, who said nothing of his new love interests in London. At the same time, Pound was also in contact with Viola Baxter and Mary Moore, although each were pursuing other relationships. Mary, however, promised to visit Pound in Europe which she did in 1912. Kitty Heyman was also in New York at this time and Pound saw her on several occasions but thoughts of acting as her manager faded. Visits to Williams in Rutherford, New Jersey, where he was practicing medicine, deepened their friendship.

Pound also looked up John B. Yeats, the poet's father, who was then living in New York. Yeats elder, in turn, introduced Pound to the lawyer and art patron, John Quinn. At first, the two did not get on because of what Pound detected as Quinn's imperious manner and misunderstanding, five years later, when Pound criticized in an essay collectors who purchased only old masters (and possibly fakes) rather than contemporary painters. An exchange of letters occurred, Quinn erroneously thinking that he was the subject of the article. The matter was cleared up and the two became close friends, Quinn visiting Pound in Paris in 1923 where several memorable photographs were taken in Pound's studio showing Joyce, Pound, Ford Madox Ford and Quinn together. Pound even placed Quinn in Canto XII under the alias of 'Jim X' and recalled an evening with Quinn, Jack Yeats and others at Coney Island in Canto LXXX. Quinn's premature death in 1924 startled everyone. In the summer of 1910, Walter Morse Rummel toured the US, joining Pound for two weeks in Swarthmore, PA where he met H.D. Music and musicians were fast becoming an important subject for Pound (and by writing about them, a means to some income) who, on his return to London, would begin to publish music criticism under the pseudonym of William Atheling. Although his own early efforts at performing were amateur at best, Pound had a profound respect for the talent of musicians, which may have led to his admiration and involvement, some years later, with the classical violinist, Olga Rudge.

Originating in his study of the Troubadour tradition, Pound understood the crucial relationship between music and poetry, writing in 1918 that 'poetry is a composition of words set to music' (*LE* 437). Pound established, and would continue, close and lasting relationships with a series of musicians and composers beginning with Kitty Heyman and extending to Rummel, Arnold Dolmetsch, George Antheil and, of course, Olga Rudge – and through her, the music of Vivaldi. One of his early encounters with music was his discovery that Arnaut Daniel included music in two of his canzoni as seen in a manuscript Pound examined in Milan in 1911. It surprisingly accorded with his own theories of Troubadour music. Song appears early in Pound's own poetry, 'A Dawn Song' (1906) or 'To the Raphaelite Latinists' (1908) two early examples. In his 'Credo' of 1912, he highlights rhythm, what in poetry 'corresponds exactly to the emotion or shade of emotion to be expressed' (*LE* 9). Pound's focus on metric is a focus on music, while 'song clarifies writing as long as they stick together' (*ABCR* 158). Before he journeyed to Europe, Rummel invited Pound to join him in Paris to work on setting several troubadour translations to music and creating musical accompaniments to a number of Pound's poems.

Before he decided to return, Pound gave New York a chance. He spent time at a literary book shop run by Laurence Gomme where he met a series of writers including Joyce Kilmer and Harry Kemp. He liked none of them. He attended the opera and visited the Metropolitan Museum of Art and tried to establish a literary magazine. However, visits to relatives to secure funding for his ventures brought little success and even Aunt Frank couldn't help: she had lost a great deal of money on her hotel venture and was living in seclusion in New Jersey. At the end of eight months in America, Pound made only £14, 'my exact fare from Philadelphia back to Paris' he wrote Quinn. (*EP/JQ* 14). He did publish his first book in America, however, *Provença* (1910), with the Boston firm, Small, Maynard and Company, introduced to them by Witter Bynner. The volume contained a selection from *Personae* and *Exultations*. In 1912 they would publish Pound's *Sonnets and Ballate of Guido Cavalcanti* on which he was working.

New York did not charm nor even intrigue Pound. In his lyric 'N.Y.,' he writes that the city will not listen to him, foregoing its chance to gain 'a soul' (*Per* 58). The architecture of New York also seemed inauthentic to him and its culture overwritten by commerce. He expanded these views in a series of articles in the *New Age* between 1912–13 and collected in his book *Patria Mia*, first published in 1950. Even membership in the Barnard Club and involvement with the nascent Poetry Society of America did not alter Pound's view that poetry in America would find no audience and that a poet would be isolated. After many discussions with his parents (and a bout of jaundice), he lobbied and succeeded in returning to Europe – with the financial assistance of his parents once again. On 22 February 1911, he boarded the *Mauretania* for the journey across the Atlantic.

Pound returned to London but stayed briefly. Paris was his destination, music and Walter Rummel his purpose. Rummel would not arrive for another month but Pound occupied himself at the Bibliothèque Nationale with its manuscripts of the troubadours, continuing Pound's love of European libraries which the Royal Library in Madrid, the British Museum with its library and the Ambrosian Library in Milan would sustain. Indeed, among modernist poets, Pound is perhaps the most library-centered, archival poet, constantly researching, reading and writing in libraries which provided the source material and references for his many poetic allusions and details in *The Cantos* and other poems.

In Paris, Pound spent time with Rummel's brother, a cellist, and Margaret Cravens who would become his secret patron. By September 1911, his *Three Songs of Ezra Pound for a Voice with Instrumental Accompaniment* with music by Rummel would appear in London, Arnaut Daniel the basis of the work. In March 1913, Pound and Rummel would issue *Hesternae Rosae: Serta II* (Yesterday's Roses : Garland II), a collection of nine troubadour songs for piano and voice with English translations by Pound and music by Rummel. Yeats turned up in Versailles for a rest and the two visited Notre Dame, recalled in Canto LXXXIII. He also met Arnold Bennett, satirized as Mr Nixon in a sequence of Pound's 1920 work, *Hugh Selwyn Mauberley*. But while in Paris, Pound principally focused on his rendering of Cavalcanti and completing his publication *Canzoni* (1911), a work dedicated to Olivia and Dorothy Shakespear.

The poems in *Canzoni* were an unsuccessful mix of troubadour and Renaissance styles, attempting to blend Cavalcanti, Dante and the earlier work of Arnaut Daniel. Rhetorical flourishes and echoes of a rhetorical past mask Pound's voice, as in the opening of the first canzoni, 'Canzon: The Yearly Slain':

> Ah! red-leafed time hath driven out the rose
> And crimson dew is fallen on the leaf
> Ere ever yet the cold white wheat be sown
>
> (*CEP* 133)

The most modern section of the volume Pound cut: 'Redondillas, or Something of That Sort,' which would not be published until 1968 in a deluxe, signed edition of 110 copies. The work contains several powerful passages including this parodic self-indictment:

> I am that terrible thing.
>   the product of American culture,
> Or rather that product improved
>   by considerable care and attention.
> I am really quite modern, you know,
>   despite my affecting the ancients.
>
> (*CEP* 220)

To Dorothy Shakespear, who was a part of its production, Pound explained that 'artistically speaking it[']s supposed to be a sort of chronological table of emotions: Provence; Tuscany, the Renaissance, the XVIII, the XIX, centuries, external modernity (cut out) subjective modernity. finis' (*EP/DS* 37–8).

Following a period in Sirmione, where he had gone to work further on his translations, Pound went briefly to Milan and then to on to Freiberg to visit Professor Levy the foremost Troubador scholar (Canto XX). He then went to Giessen to visit Ford where the famous roll on the floor – 7 August 1911 appears to be the date – occurred when Ford read a portion of *Canzoni* (*P/F* 172). Pound returned to London by late August 1911 with a new mandate to sharpen his poetry and rid it of archaic excesses, regular meter and abstract images. His effort to transform romantic philology into contemporary poetry needed to be rethought. Pound knew that Provençal's possession of an exoticism akin to Yeats' Celtic twilight, based on its remoteness and hieratic rites of love, was no longer germane to the new requirement that poetry be precise and exact. The spirit of romance was giving way to experiment.

Nevertheless, Arnaut Daniel and Cavalcanti still held sway, Pound trying to master their ability to be precise and yet poetic. He embarked on an edition of *The Canzoni of Arnaut Daniel*, a companion volume to the forthcoming *Sonnets and Ballate of Guido Cavalcanti* (1912). Ten translations of Arnaut's canzos with erudite analyses of this art appeared in a seies of essays in the *New Age* (1911–12) but the edition did not materialize until 1920 when it appeared in abbreviated form as a chapter of *Instigations*. Pound's attraction to Arnaut's *motz el son* (strict relation of word and tune) led to Pound's reading an Arnaut ms. in a Milan library, the only one with musical notation for two poems. Working with Walter Morse Rummel in Paris led to his research into troubadour *melopoeia*, poetry as music (see 'How to Read,' *LE* 25). But as he recounted his absorption with Cavalcanti to T.E. Hulme, Pound explained that the Italian 'thought in accurate terms; that the phrases correspond to definite sensations undergone' (*LE* 162). In two sentences, Pound actually outlined his own program:

> What we need now is not so much a commentator as a lexicon. It is the precise sense of certain terms *as understood at that particular epoch* that one would like to have set before one.
>
> (*LE* 162)

Pound needed to grasp this before he could articulate his first major school, Imagism. But Hulme had another role, introducing Pound to the editor A.R. Orage who would begin to publish the poet extensively in his journal the *New Age*.

Originally involved with the Fabians, including George Bernard Shaw, Orage managed to borrow enough money to purchased a moribund paper, the *New Age*, and turn it into a socialist voice to further the arts. He maintained it for all liberal causes, publishing, in addition to Shaw and Hulme, H.G. Wells, Katherine Mansfield, Herbert Read and John Middleton Murry. He also entertained Pound's poetical and social rebelliousness. And it was through Orage's friendship with Major C.H. Douglas that Pound became introduced to Social Credit with its fixation on the destructiveness of banks and their control over society. In late 1911, Orage commissioned Pound to write a twelve part series on '"The New Method" in scholarship,' to quote the editorial statement. He titled it 'I Gather the Limbs of Osiris' (*EPCP* I: 43), referring to the Egyptian god of vegetation murdered by his brother and the efforts of Isis, his sister and wife, to gather up his scattered parts and reassemble his body into what became the first mummy. The first part of the series appeared on 30 November 1911 and was Pound's translation of the Anglo-Saxon 'The Seafarer;' other parts contained translations of Arnaut Daniel. Soon, Pound published music criticism, printed under the pseudonym of William Atheling, and then art criticism using the name B.H. Dias. Orage's role in promoting Pound's prose cannot be overestimated providing him with a platform and a voice.

'The Seafarer,' one of Pound's important early works, begins with a distinctively Poundian tone: 'May I for my own self song's truth reckon,/ Journey's jargon, how I in harsh days/ Hardship endured oft' (*EPCP* I: 43). Although scholars later criticized Pound's liberalism with the original, the translation stands as a distinctive, vigorous rendering of the text, although he also made unauthorized emendations, a habit that would characterize his later treatments of Propertius, Cavalcanti and the Confucian Odes – and upset purists, although not readers. Translation transformed original texts, a persistent feature of Pound's poetic project based on the principle: 'don't bother about the WORDS, translate the MEANING' (in Reck 99). For Pound, translation became a model for the act of poetic representation.

Another important editor for Pound at this time was Harold Monro whose conservative journal, *The Poetry Review*, soon included the outspoken Pound; his revealing 'Credo' appearing in the 12 February 1912 issue (*LE* 9ff). In it, Pound sets out his poetic beliefs including two statements that anticipate the next stage of his poetic development: Imagism and *vers libre*. The first statement emphasizes the character of imagery, declaring that the natural object is the perfect symbol. The second recognizes that a 'vast number of subjects cannot be precisely, and therefore not properly rendered in symmetrical forms' requiring freer poetic forms (*LE* 9). Pound sought a 'passionate simplicity' (*LE* 53) which Imagism provided.

By 1912, Pound was called 'a small but persistent volcano in the dim levels of London literary society' (Aldington, *Life* 105). Steam and ash were constantly spewing forth. Within three years, he had become a force in literary circles, disrupting the preciousness of the Georgians and their aesthete tendencies. 'With vastly less fuss than a Georgian affronting the perils of the Cotswolds,' Pound would fly off to Paris or Venice to reconnect with a European literary tradition and return with fresh ideas and new energy (Aldington, *Life* 111). But 'like other American expatriates, Ezra and H.D. developed an almost insane relish for afternoon tea' Aldington, soon-to-be the husband of H.D., complained (Aldington, *Life* 134).

Ironically, it was the tea room of the British Museum that would be the location of Imagism's birth. There, in the early fall of 1912, Pound read H.D.'s poem 'Hermes of the Ways.' Rapidly, he wrote 'H.D. Imagiste' at the bottom of the typed sheet 'now slashed with his creative pencil, "Cut this out, shorten this line"' he declared as he prepared to send it off to Harriet Monroe's journal *Poetry* where he had become Foreign Correspondent (*End* 18, 40). Authoritative and direct, Pound became, in Aldington's words, 'a bit of a czar in a small but irritating way,' although they listened because Harriet Monroe in Chicago usually published what her correspondent in London sent (Aldington, *Life* 135).

Imagism, of course, did not just whimsically happen one fall afternoon in London. Pound had been led to this concept through his study of Arnaut Daniel, Cavalcanti and Dante, writers of precision and detail. By late April 1912, he had formulated the term 'imagist' when he was reworking the proofs of *Ripostes*: he uses the term and designates the movement in his introduction to the five poems of Hulme appended to the end of the book (*C&R* 59). Pound's introduction to the French Symbolists through Hulme (who imitated their work) and F.S. Flint, whose essay on contemporary French poetry appeared in the *Poetry Review* for August 1912, further directed Pound's thinking.

Soon, Pound took it upon himself to be the spokesperson of Imagism and began to publish on the movement, his 'A Few Don'ts by an Imagiste' appearing alongside Flint's note, 'Imagisme,' in *Poetry* for March 1913. Pound actually drafted Flint's contribution which laid out the few principles of the movement:

1. Direct treatment of the 'thing' whether subjective or objective.
2. To use absolutely no word that does not contribute to the presentation.
3. As regarding rhythm: to compose in the sequence of the musical phrase, not in sequence of a metronome.

Pound's 'A Few Don'ts' begins with this definition: 'An "Image" is that which presents an intellectual and emotional complex in an instant of time.' The instantaneous presentation of such a 'complex' gives a sense of 'sudden liberation,' adding 'it is better to present one Image in a lifetime than to produce voluminous works.' He concludes with this directive: 'go in fear of abstractions. Do not retell in mediocre verse what has already been done in good prose' (*EPCP* I: 119–20; *LE* 3–5).

A movement is often best served and confirmed by an anthology and Pound soon prepared *Des Imagistes* published in New York in 1914 by Albert and Charles Boni. This 63 page volume contained selections by

Aldington, H.D., Flint, Pound, William Carlos Williams, Ford, James Joyce and Amy Lowell, soon to become Pound's Imagist nemesis. The thin volume in blue boards with gold lettering quickly became an important document of the new movement, but was soon challenged by Lowell's own gathering, *Some Imagist Poets*, which appeared in 1915. Lowell disagreed with almost everything Pound said, noting that in *her* anthology, the poets chose their own work, not an editor. But the politics of the movement was complex, since several of those in Pound's anthology were also in Lowell's: Aldington, H.D., Flint and herself. A set of principles she provided (little different from Pound's) united the contributors.[6]

When she arrived in London in July 1914 with her maroon Pierce-Arrow motor car and current lover, Amy Lowell was disappointed to learn she was late: Imagism had been superceded by Vorticism. Nevertheless, she hosted a dinner to celebrate, belatedly, the publication of Pound's *Des Imagistes*. in which she had a single poem. The dinner was a disaster, Pound satirizing Lowell's determined efforts to get to the secret of the Imagist doctrine by disappearing into the kitchen when she asked the question and returning with a large galvanized tub, challenging her to display her own whiteness by bathing, an allusion to the final line in her poem, 'In a Garden' from *Des Imagistes*: 'Night and the water, and you in your whiteness, bathing' (*Des Imagistes* 38). Insulted, Lowell planned another dinner *without* Pound but with H.D., Aldington, D.H. Lawrence and John Gould Fletcher, left out of Pound's collection; she also planned her own anthology.

Pound satirized this effort as 'Amygism' and responded in a 1915 essay, noting that the term Imagism has been misunderstood to mean Hellenism or to designate any poem in *vers libre*. This was wrong. Its origin was in intense emotion which created what he labels a 'pattern-unit' which, when repeated, establishes an arrangement of forms which in turn creates the Image which can be either subjective, arising within the self, or objective, coming from outside. Crucially, 'the Image is more than an idea. It is a vortex or cluster of fused ideas and is endowed with energy' (*SP* 344–5). Additionally, Pound believed that 'poetry to be good poetry should be at least as well written as good prose,' and that emotion is the organizer of visible and audible form. Poetry, he asserts, is 'a composition or an "organisation" of words set to "music"' (*SP* 345). These fresh ideas he summarized when in Canto LXXXI he wrote, 'To break the pentameter, that was the first heave' (LXXXI/538).

But overtaken by Amy Lowell – whose anthology sold better than Pound's and was followed by two further volumes – Imagism became

diluted and distilled. Pound disliked its sloppiness and Lowell's willingness to include any *vers libre* work in her collections. Pound now felt
insulted and told Harriet Monroe that his problem was 'to keep alive a
certain group of advancing poets, to set the arts in their rightful place as
the acknowledged guide and lamp of civilization.... Artists first, then, if
necessary, professors and parsons' (*SL* 48). Pound had, furthermore,
moved ahead into the converging forces of Vorticism (See Chapter. 3).

At the end of April 1912, Mary Moore from Trenton appeared but
Pound had little time for her. He was off to Paris to be with Rummel
and read the proofs of *Ripostes*. Aldington and H.D., now in love, joined
him in Paris. Pound visited Margaret Cravens briefly and then headed
south on a walking tour of France to trace the route of the troubadours.[7]
Shortly after starting, he learned of Cravens' suicide and hurriedly
returned to Paris to a shaken Rummel and a depressed H.D. Cravens
would linger in Pound's mind, appearing in *The Cantos*. After some
time, Pound resumed his journey and when he returned to London in
late August, he found a letter from a Harriet Monroe of Chicago
announcing an international magazine of poetry and asking him to
contribute. She had bought *Personae* and *Exultations* in Mathews' London
bookshop in 1910 and after reading them on a train journey across
Siberia, felt she had to contact the American poet then living in
London. He accepted immediately, offering to locate new work by
Americans in Europe and sent two poems which appeared in the first
issue: 'To Whistler, American' and 'Middle-Aged.'

In early 1913, Pound made another discovery: Robert Frost. Struck at
once by Frost's natural imagery and voice, Pound enthusiastically wrote
to Monroe telling her of his 'find' (*SL* 14). He reviewed Frost's first book
for *Poetry* and promoted his later work, although the two never quite
became friends, Frost resenting Pound's 'improvements' to his verse.
When Pound told him he changed a poem of fifty words to one of
forty-eight, Frost angrily replied that he 'spoiled' his metre, idiom and
idea (*SCh* 201). Their cool relationship improved, however, when Frost
actively sought Pound's release forty-five years later. Politicians listened
and he, with others, succeeded.

Pound's association with Harriet Monroe and *Poetry*, which lasted on
and off for some four years, was anything but tranquil. Pleased to locate
important new work in England for American audiences, he was also
absolutely clear in his preferences and disgust at Monroe's misjudgments.
In the autumn of 1913, for example, when *Poetry* was about to award its
first annual prize for the best poem printed in the year, Monroe favored
Vachel Lindsay's 'General William Booth.' Pound was appalled and

insisted that the $250 go to Yeats for 'The Grey Rock.' After argument, dispute and debate, she agreed but when Yeats wrote to thank Monroe, he said that the majority of the money would go to a young American writer. It was Pound, who received £40 from Yeats, although Yeats told him he was not in favor of his metrical experiments, despite showing 'a vigorous creative mind' (*SCh* 214). Pound used the money for a new typewriter and two statuettes from the young sculptor and new friend, Gaudier-Brzeska. But the dashing young poet who spoke in a pseudo rustic *patois* was thought to be more operatic than literary among the London *cognoscenti*, a cross, it seemed, between Puccini's *La Bohème* and his *La Fanciulla del* West (*The Girl of the Golden West*).

Frequently angered by Monroe's publication of poets Pound thought second-rate and 'soft,' he bombarded Monroe with letters that reflected his bristly energy, his first letter to her actually stabbed several times through by his pen in his agitation. Her resistance brought out his vigor. In response to her objection to the strident tone of his 'Status Rerum,' which she published in January 1913, he wrote:

> I've got a right to be severe. I'm not a masked reviewer – a non-producer – I'm not shielded by anonymity. For one man I strike there are ten who can strike back at me. I stand exposed. It hits me in my dinner invitations, in my week-ends, in the review of my own work. Nevertheless it's a good fight....
>
> (*DE* 49).

With acerbity, he offered to Monroe his own creed in May 1915:

> Objectivity and again objectivity, and expression: no hindside-beforeness... no Tennysonianness of speech; nothing – nothing that you couldn't, in some circumstance, in the stress of some emotion, actually say
>
> (*SL* 49).

Disagreement between the two was intense, yet their exchanges caused Pound to articulate many of his critical principles. And he never stopped pointing out her errors to her.

Pound's connection at *Poetry* became Alice Corbin Henderson, Assistant Editor, who moved from Chicago to Santa Fe, New Mexico in 1916 to battle tuberculous. She became Pound's first and most admiring reader. She then sent his submissions on with advice to Monroe in Chicago. A minor poet, Henderson impressed Pound with her critical sensibility towards his own work and to those of others he recommended. She shared principles similar to his own, notably a rejection of the effusive and sentimental. He also found her more akin to his own thinking about experiment in verse, while Monroe remained often hostile to new work. In January 1914, however, Pound quit in disgust as Foreign Editor, the immediate cause the editing of his prose without his permission. But Monroe asked him back and he agreed, although he knew it would be temporary. Nonetheless, *Poetry* became a forum for Pound who took full advantage, publishing poetry and prose often extreme in its tone and argument. 'Status Rerum' (January 1913), for example, was dogmatic, praising Yeats, dismissing the Georgians and provoking anger among readers. In his correspondence with Monroe, he constantly challenged her in his best, abrasive manner:

> My GORD! but this stuff of Mrs. Van Rensselaer's is *twaddle*. . . . Surely this good lady should shine as a patron rather than as a contributor . . . . you aren't fostering Am. letters by printing her. . . she is utterly unprintable.
>
> (*DE* 54).

In another letter, he asks 'how are we to be two decades ahead of the country and cater to news stands at the same time? We've simply GOT to lead. . . . We *can't afford* to give the public what it wants' (*DE* 56). Monroe, in turn, became defensive, telling Pound that, indeed, a lot of her contributors 'think they must talk in Tennysonian or Elizabethan . . . [but] we are trying to train them out of that. And frequently our suggestions for emendations result in distinct modernizing of the tone and general improvement' (*DE* 59). But Pound cultivated reaction: speculating about a forthcoming book, he tells Monroe that he will probably be attacked when the book appears 'but they may have the cunning to ignore it. I am getting even that much disliked' (*DE* 63)

During this period, Pound was renewing and strengthening his ties with Yeats. Beginning in the winter of 1913, the two poets went to Stone Cottage on the edge of the Ashdown Forest in Sussex for three successive winters. Pound would act as Yeats' part-time secretary. Yeats, whose eyesight was deteriorating, needed Pound to write for him and, in the evening, to read to him. Yeats also had a civil list pension and could actually employ Pound. But having just received the papers of Ernest Fenollosa, Pound began to examine Chinese literature and revise Fenollosa's draft translations of Japanese Noh plays. Yeats, who read the translations, found inspiration for his own drama. At the same time, Pound became interested in Yeats's occult studies and started to read widely in esoteric literature. Yeats then began his autobiography with Pound's assistance, reconsidering his early days with the Rhymer's Club. Pound also read Browning's *Sordello* aloud to Yeats and initiated steady work on his long poem, *The Cantos*. They also wrote war poems, while Yeats introduced Pound to the work of Joyce, and Pound introduced Yeats to the work of Eliot. Stone Cottage also began to shape not just the literary but the social and political attitudes of the two writers.

At the outset, however, Pound was sceptical, writing to his mother that although he detested the countryside, he was going with Yeats to Stone Cottage but it won't be profitable: 'Yeats will amuse me part of the time and bore me to death with psychical research the rest. I regard the visit as a duty to posterity' (*SL* 25). Written with the confidence of a writer twenty years younger than Yeats, Pound's remarks were only partially inaccurate, although not in all of its predictions.

The collaborators lived in a six-room cottage perched on the edge of a heath, not far from a crossroads known as Coleman's Hatch, Sussex. Yeats selected the cottage partly because he had been to the area to visit Olivia Shakespear who had rented another home nearby. Pound used the time productively, finding the isolation helpful not only in forging his union with Yeats but in forwarding his own art. Writing, translating and reading, Pound would recall this period positively in *The Pisan Cantos*. Yeats also found the time beneficial, although he was also urged by Lady Gregory and Olivia Shakespear to consider another topic: marriage. Both women thought it was time for the poet to find a wife. The solitude of the two – although Yeats would regularly go into London for his Monday evening soirées and Pound once a week to send and receive mail – also satisfied Pound's desire for a poetic aristocracy avoiding the demands of an inferior public. He sought respite from what he told Joyce in an early letter was the endless 'whirl of a metropolis' and the 'endless calls on one's time and endless trivialities of enjoyment (or the reverse)' (*P/J* 44). Pound referred to the two poets, freed from any club, movement or circle, the 'Brothers Minor' and thrived in their mutual support (*EPCP* I: 190).

During the summer of 1914, as the war began to threaten Pound's hoped-for community of artists, Pound polished his adaptations of Fenollosa's translations, at the same time he (Pound) lamented the passing of the Vortex. That same summer, the first issue of BLAST had appeared with Pound satirizing his own wish to establish a brotherhood of artists in the poem 'Fratres Minores' which opens with lines the publisher insisted be blotted out (line one and the last two):

With minds still hovering above their testicles
Certain poets here and in France
Still sigh over established and natural fact
Long since fully discussed by Ovid.
They howl. They complain in delicate and exhausted metres
That the twitching of three abdominal nerves
Is incapable of producing a lasting Nirvana.

(*Per* 78)

The myth that Pound influenced the development of Yeats' later style, especially in *Responsibilities*, Pound himself corrects. The statement, outlining the impact of Synge, not Pound, on Yeats's transformation from the *Wind Among the Reeds* to his later work, occurs in a passage written by Pound for an unpublished work, *This Generation*. What Pound did *do* was make minor revisions to a set of poems Yeats offered to *Poetry* in late 1912. Yeats referred to them only as corrections. He actually began the process of modernization long before Pound began to 'tinker' with his verse (Longenbach 19, 276n). Nevertheless, Yeats acknowledged Pound's importance for him in a letter to Lady Gregory written 3 January 1913:

> He is full of the middle ages and helps me to get back to the definite and the concrete away from modern abstractions. To talk over a poem with him is like getting you to put a sentence into dialect. All becomes clear and natural.
>
> (Yeats in Jeffares 167)

Pound, in turn, continued to champion Yeats.

A transition in Pound's own poetic development at this time resulted from a bequest. In late 1913, Pound received a packet of manuscripts from the widow of the historian of Oriental art and student of Oriental literature, Ernest Fenollosa. At his death in 1908, Fenollosa had been translating a number of classic Chinese poems plus Japanese and Noh dramas, while writing an essay on the Chinese written character as a medium for poetry. In it, he emphasized how Chinese words contain pictographic concreteness and how the syntax of Chinese possessed a dynamic word order. These ideas paralleled Pound's Imagist concepts stressing concrete speech and natural images. Although he knew virtually no Chinese, Pound forged ahead and completed the Fenollosa translations, publishing them in a small volume of thirty-one pages containing nineteen poems, later expanded to twenty-three. Yet *Cathay* (1915), incorporated into *Lustra* (1916), was perhaps his most important early book, Pound, in the words of Eliot, 'the inventor of Chinese poetry for our time' ('Intro,' *SPP* xvi).

'The River-Merchant's Wife,' an understated love poem, and the war poems, 'Song of the Bowmen of Shu' and 'Lament of the Frontier Guard,' have often been anthologized. In the poems, image and tone unite as in Pound's version of Rihaku's 'The Jewel Stairs' Grievance:'

> The jewelled steps are already quite white with dew,
> It is so late that the dew soaks my gauze stockings,
> And I let down the crystal curtain
> And watch the moon through the clear autumn.

> (*Per* 136)

The entire book alternates between tranquility and violence, embodying the almost schizophrenic mood of England at the time, caught in the horror of the first World War, while a certain tranquility resided at home. Some, however, found that Pound's lack of Chinese impeded his 'translations,' which he defended as appropriately conveying more of *his* poetry than exact representations of a foreign literature. Purists objected but readers of poetry regarded the volume highly because Pound showed that a single line could be a unit of composition and that a poem could build its effect from things. Ford in *Outlook* praised the book, as did Orage in the *New Age*.

Pound's education in the Chinese style and its ideograms, however, actually predates his encounter with Fenollosa. It began at the British Museum with its 1910 exhibition of Chinese and Japanese Paintings which ran until 1912, the year Fenollosa's posthumous *Epochs of Chinese and Japanese Art* appeared, Imagism was born and *Poetry* was started. Pound's earliest contact with Chinese art occurred in Philadelphia, beginning with his parents who had a Ming vase in their suburban parlor (Qian 4). A magnificent display of Chinese ceramics, ink paintings and wood-carvings opened when he started college. And during a visit to Aunt Frank in New York in his last years in America, Pound saw a screen book with waterscape scenes alongside manuscript poems in Chinese and Japanese. The screen book would become a major source of the 'Seven Lakes Canto,' Canto XLIX.

But it was in London between 1909 and 1914, under the informal tutelage of Laurence Binyon, art expert and curator of the Prints and Drawings section of the British Museum, that Pound expanded his appreciation and understanding of Chinese visual culture which prepared him for his work with the Fenollosa material. Binyon's *Paintings in the Far East* (1908) and lectures and articles on the subject, plus his curatorial role in the British Museum Oriental exhibition of 1910–12, made him the leading Orientalist in London, providing serious attention to Oriental art for its aesthetic instinct and imagination. Pound met Binyon, also a poet, in February 1909 through Elkin Mathews and the two remained friends the rest of their lives.

Pound brought Fenollosa to Yeats. Although he received the notebooks and manuscripts of the writer in the fall of 1913, he did not begin to study the material until the autumn of 1914, eager to accept the charge from Fenollosa's widow to complete the work partly because he believed a study of Chinese writing might advance Imagism. His publication of 'The Chinese Written Character as a Medium for Poetry' (1919) was an influential essay that confirmed for Pound the value of the ideogrammic method. But *Cathay* (1915) was the instrumental work, initiating a vogue for Chinese translations. Pound based his bold translations on the incomplete notes and efforts of Fenollosa which in turn led to the metrical innovations of *The Cantos*. In his essay, 'Chinese Poetry' (1918), Pound argues for the harmony between Chinese poetry and the principles of Imagism: vivid presentation and non-moralizing of subject. He, furthermore, relates the short, obscure poems of Chinese to the traditions of Provençal and Tuscan poetry and their mutual goal of extreme clarity and directness of expression. The impact of nature, simplicity and stress on the human completes Pound's link between the two traditions.

Once Pound discovered the Chinese material, there was no stopping him and soon both Yeats and Pound were deeply involved in the Orient, adapting Noh drama for English readers. *Certain Noble Plays of Japan* 'chosen and finished by Ezra Pound with an Introduction by William Butler Yeats' (1916) was one result. With an eighteen page introduction and forty eight pages of text, the work presented four Noh dramas with notes by Pound. Without the Yeats introduction, the volume was reprinted as *Noh or Accomplishment* by Pound in the following year with an added subtitle: 'a study of the classical stage of Japan by Ernest Fenollosa and Ezra Pound.' This was a greatly expanded edition which included the four plays from the earlier volume, plus two introductory prose pieces written by Fenollosa but 'polished' by Pound.

The importance of these volumes was not only to introduce Western readers to the Japanese dramatic tradition but as a shaping influence on Yeats' own late dramatic efforts. This intensified when Yeats realized that one translation of 'Noh,' offered by Frank Brinkley in his *Japan and China: Their History, Arts and Literature*, a work Pound studied, was 'accomplishment,' interpreted to mean works limited to the aristocracy. Noh theatre required neither a mob, nor a public theatre to support it. To Yeats, this resolved his dilemma with the Abbey Theatre's controversial dramas: he would write his late works as a new 'form of drama, distinguished, indirect, and symbolic and having no need of mob or Press to pay its way – an aristocratic form' (Yeats, *E&I* 221). Pound, in turn, would show connections between Japanese and Irish folk traditions. The Noh translations strongly influenced the later plays of Yeats. But Pound did not forego Imagism entirely as his volume *Lustra* (1916), with its combination of the Vorticist drive and reliance on traditional modes of satire, shows.

But if Pound brought Fenollosa, Yeats brought Joyce. In November 1913, Yeats told Pound about the difficulties an unknown Irish writer was having in finding a publisher. Pound wrote to Joyce from Stone Cottage to offer assistance, adding that he was 'informally connected with a couple of new and impecunious papers,' adding that 'W.B.Y. says… we have a hate or two in common.' In his next letter, he asked for permission to print 'I hear an Army' in his Imagist anthology (*P/J* 17–18). Joyce replied positively and sent along a letter he circulated in the Irish papers in 1911 which Pound published in the 15 January 1914 issue of *The Egoist*. It dealt with the aborted attempts to publish *Dubliners*. Joyce also sent a copy of *Dubliners* and the first chapter of *A Portrait of the Artist as a Young Man*. Pound immediately set to have *Portrait* published in *The Egoist* and a lifetime's relationship began.

But if Pound continued to introduce Yeats to new ideas, Yeats did similar service for Pound, extending his early exposure to the occult. At first this was through G.R.S. Mead, former secretary to Madame Blavatsky and then founder of the Quest Society devoted to the study of comparative religion, philosophy and science. His journal, *The Quest*, was a publication of theosophists and it was to the Quest Society that Pound lectured on 'Psychology and Troubadours' in 1912, reprinted in *The Spirit of Romance*. In the lecture, he developed the idea of the *phantastikon*, or the seeing of visions, stronger than reality. The term came from the Greeks but the concept from the visionary experiences in the early Yeats and his essay 'Magic' in *Ideas of Good and Evil*. The arrival of the Bengali poet Tagore in London in the early summer of 1912 led to Pound and Yeats celebrating his ethereal poetry. Pound wrote an introduction to six of Tagore's poems which appeared in *Poetry* in December 1912.

The visionary was, however, embedded in Pound's thought and writing. In 'Ikon,' a prose poem of December 1913, he wrote that 'in art the highest business [is] to create the beautiful image.' The order and profusion of images furnish 'the life of our minds with a noble surrounding,' he explained, answering, it seems, Yeats' notes to the *Wind Among the Reeds*: 'the Image... is an eternal act; but our understandings are temporal and understand but a little at a time' (*EPCP* I: 203; Yeats, 807). Pound's esoteric theories of the Image and interest in the occult were drawn from the example and inspiration of Yeats and he recalled many of these moments from his first winter with Yeats in *The Pisan Cantos*, retelling, in particular, Yeats's composition of 'The Peacock' (LXXXIII/553–4).

The next two winters at Stone Cottage were equally productive, although a change was occurring: Pound was adopting some of the social criticism and posture of Yeats and feeling that the poet should, indeed, speak out on political and social issues of the day. The 2 February 1914 issue of *The Egoist*, for example, contains 'The Bourgeois' by a certain 'Bastien von Helmholtz,' an aggressive if slightly disguised attack on George Moore who had pummeled Yeats for his pretensions to an aristocratic ancestry and disdain for the middle class. Rather than criticize the bourgeoisie, which Pound and Yeats argued was a state of mind, Pound claimed that Yeats was attacking the aristocracy. Furthermore, the bourgeois is the intestine of the body politic: the artist is the nostrils and 'the invisible antennae' (*EPCP* I: 220). Importantly, with the exception of his 1912–13 articles on America, later published as *Patria Mia* (1950), 'The Bourgeois' is the first work of explicit social criticism from Pound exhibiting the exaggerated arrogance which would obscure portions of his work for the next thirty years.

Pound's aggressive personae, which came into full form at Stone Cottage, would soon take further root in his 'SALUTATION THE THIRD,' a set of poems written in direct and forthright language. Deriding the smugness of *The Times* and their 'gagged reviewers,' he rebukes them as 'slut-bellied obstructionist[s],' the 'sworn foe[s] to free speech and good letters.' 'You fungus, you continuous gangrene' he rails (*EPCP* I: 254). Yeats, uncomfortable with Pound's unrestrained language, nevertheless admired his unreserved tone. In two articles written during his first winter at Stone Cottage, 'Ferrex on Petulance' and 'Porrex on Ferrex,' Pound further outlined the tension between two generations of English writers, the elder expressing criticism in lofty indifference, the younger attacking, parrying, and thrusting (much like fencing, of course) against wrongs. As Yeats summarized in a celebratory speech on Wilfred Blunt – honored by a peacock dinner organized by Pound and attended by Yeats, Aldington, Flint, Plarr, and Sturge Moore – 'Ezra Pound has a desire personally to insult the world,' although he often does it with charm: 'he corrupted us all to his way of thinking' wrote Frances Gregg, lover of H.D. (Yeats in Aldington, 57; Gregg 84). This quality would last throughout Pound's prose and poetry.

Although Yeats and Pound would later diverge on their poetic roadway, Pound would repeatedly celebrate his debt to Yeats, not only in their shared belief that a poem should attain some degree of intensity but in their conviction 'that one should make NO compromise with the public' (*EPCP* IV: 265). But those close to Pound frequently commented that his aggressiveness seemed unnatural, Aldington disclosing that in person Pound was 'modest, bashful' and kind: 'I cannot help thinking that all this enormous arrogance and petulance and fierceness are a pose' (Aldington, '*Blast*' 273). But Pound, 'the cowboy songster ... in a ten-gallon hat,' quickly grew into this personae, which he would ride forward for the remainder of his career.[8]

3

'The Noble Crested Screamer':
1914–20

I appear to be the only person of interest left in the world of art, London.

(Pound, 1916)

Pound became a figure London could not avoid. Suddenly, he was everywhere: *Punch*, the papers and the public took notice. His enthusiasms dictated his friendships, while his ideas decreed his behavior as he hunted for new talent to promote in his role as literary advisor to *The Egoist* and Foreign Correspondent of *Poetry*. With 'exuberant hair' and flying clothes, Pound descended upon literary dinners, lectures or appointments with an air of purpose and controversy, projecting a persona that could ignite a room with conversation and controversy (Barry 165). He epitomized the Crested Screamer, a South American bird he would soon celebrate in a review of a book by the writer, W.H. Hudson.[1] Vocal and visible, Pound perched on numerous London branches, it seemed, at once.

Vorticism followed Pound's first winter at Stone Cottage and it began with a burst of energy. More interdisciplinary than Imagism, Vorticism also lacked easy imitators, the problem with Imagism. Non-representational painters like Wyndham Lewis and Edward Wadsworth, and sculptors like Henri Gaudier-Brzeska and Jacob Epstein, formed the early cadre under the Vorticist banner. Cubism, Futurism and Expressionism influenced their aesthetic which celebrated abstract formalism and the dynamic nature of creativity. A Vortex was the creative energy within the artist, ready to burst forth.

Fashioning the term to distinguish Lewis' paintings and the sculptures of Gaudier-Brzeska from Cubism, and to distinguish it from what was being done in *avant-garde* circles on the Continent, Vorticism contained energy. In his short statement 'Vortex,' Pound declared that 'the vortex is the point of maximum energy' and represents 'in mechanics, the greatest efficiency.' The Vorticist artist relies on 'the primary pigment of his art,' whatever that might be. Sounding like a Futurist, Pound explained that:

All experience rushes into this vortex. All the energized past, all the past that is living and worthy to live. ALL MOMENTUM, which is the past bearing upon us, RACE, RACE-MEMORY, instinct charging the PLACID, NON-ENERGIZED FUTURE.

(*EPVA* 151)

Futurism is no more than 'the disgorging spray of a vortex with no drive behind it' Pound announces (ibid.). The 'primary pigment' of the Vorticist poet is the image, expressed through dynamic form: 'vorticism from my angle was a renewal of the sense of construction... vorticism...was an attempt to revise the sense of form' (*EPVA* 153n.4). Vortographs supplemented these ideas, experimental photographs by Alvin Langdon Coburn, the American photographer who provided photo-frontispieces to the New York Edition of Henry James and for whom Pound wrote an introduction to a catalogue of a 1917 exhibition at the Camera Club in London. The concentration on the arrangement of form and color is the essential principle of the Vorticists, what Pound, in referring to the paintings of Edward Wadsworth, called 'radicals in design' associated with the Vorticist's search for precision (*GB* 116–17). Coburn's own Vortograph of Pound, showing his face from two contrasting but joined angles as if emanating from a frame whose border surrounds the image, creating its reflection below, emphasizing its construction, is one example. A Vorticist, whether painter, photographer, sculptor or poet presents 'a beautiful arrangement of forms on a surface' but energy below (*EPVA* 155). Yet as Pound added, 'every inch of the surface is won at the point of the chisel' (*GB* 31). An arranged impact is one of the Vorticist goals.

As an *avant garde* movement, Vorticism adopted an aggressive if not antagonistic stance towards the public which perfectly suited Pound. In 1914, he attempted a history of Vorticist art, more specifically Vorticist poetry. Imagism, he began, is a stylistic movement, 'a movement of criticism rather than creation.' He then explains that the image is 'the furthest possible remove from rhetoric' and is definitely not symbolism which deals with allusion and almost always is associated with 'mushy technique' (*EPCP* I: 275–7). 'The image is the poet's pigment' he argues, adding that Browning's *Sordello* is 'one of the finest *masks* every presented' but that 'Dante's "Paradiso" is the most wonderful *image*' (*EPCP* I: 279). He then tells the story of how he wrote 'In a Station of the Metro' and the difficulty of finding words to convey his emotions when seeing a series of beautiful faces. Splotches of color not words came to him. And after he read a tract by the artist Kandinsky, he understood that pleasure can come 'in an arrangement of planes or in a pattern of figures' (*EPCP* I: 279). 'Vorticism,' he argues, 'is art before it has spread itself into flaccidity, into elaboration and secondary applications.' Imagism 'does not use images as *ornaments*. The image is itself the speech' (*EPCP* I: 280). In an image poem, one idea is 'set on top of another.' He wrote a thirty line version of his metro poem and destroyed it; six months later it became a fifteen line poem and a year later it became his famous two line '*hokku*-like sentence:'

> The apparition of these faces in the crowd:
> Petals, on a wet, black bough.

> (*EPCP* I: 281)

This sort of poem, he explains, tries to record the 'precise instant when a thing outward and objective transforms itself, or darts into a thing inward and subjective' (*EPCP* I: 281) but even its later publication will alter its appearance as Pound changed its spacing to emphasize the breaks and imagist thought. Futurism, descended from impressionism, contrasts with Vorticism which is 'expressionism, neo-cubism, and imagism gathered together in one camp...vorticism...is intensive,' supported by his claim that great works of art 'cause form to come into being.' Finally, the image is 'a radiant node or cluster...a VORTEX, from which, and through which, and into which, ideas are constantly rushing' (*EPCP* I: 282, 283).

From this energy came Vorticism, the term to describe the action. Paintings and sculptures are similar: through shape and color they create planes in relation; the organization of forms is energetic and creative. Romance and sentiment and description detract from the Vorticist energy which Wyndham Lewis and Picasso possess (*EPCP* I: 285). In a note to the essay, Pound argues that it is possible to write a long vorticist poem, a work gathered about one image, although 'no artist can possibly get a vortex into every poem or picture he does.' And in remarks that prefigure the structure of *The Cantos*, Pound adds that 'certain things seem to demand metrical expression, or expression in a rhythm more agitated than the rhythms acceptable to prose' (*EPCP* I: 285).

Pound and Wyndham Lewis, tyro painter and writer, first met in late 1908 in the company of their respective mentors: Laurence Binyon (Pound) and Sturge Moore (Lewis). At first, it was mutual suspicion between these two self-promoting artists but by late 1913, they were partners in a program to revolutionize art. At a tea party, they formulated lists of people and institutions which their editorial policy would support and those it would attack. The lists were headed 'BLESS' and 'BLAST' (O'Keeffe 143). They selected the name *BLAST* for their typographically irregular (or bold) journal which borrowed the techniques of advertising to polarize a mass public. In a letter to Joyce, Pound tells him that Lewis is starting 'a new Futurist, Cubist, Imagiste Quarterly...it is mostly a painters magazine with me to do the poems' (*P/J* 26). The first of the two issues appeared in June 1914; the second, in July 1915.

Preceded by Pound's lecture on 30 May on 'Imagisme' at the Rebel Arts Centre – exhibition and lecture space established by Lewis for art and ideas that would overthrow the conventional in culture – *BLAST'S* first issue was a remarkable compendium of visual originality and provocative prose. The title, all caps, appeared diagonally and page 1 was a typographical assault on the unsuspecting reader; it began with these lines:

> **BLAST First (from politeness) ENGLAND**
> **CURSE ITS CLIMATE FOR ITS SINS AND INFECTIONS**
> **DISMAL SYMBOL SET round our bodies,**
> **of effeminate lout within.**
> **VICTORIAN VAMPIRE, the LONDON cloud smoke**
> **The TOWN'S heart.**

The varying fonts and point sizes suggested a belligerence to the eye with each page distinguished from the next through stark contrasts of dark type separated by gaping white spaces making each page distinctive. Every page was, in fact, an abstract composition. Manifestos made up a good deal of the two issues with an emphasis on the mechanical and geometric rather than the organic and naturalistic in art. The metaphor of the machine, in fact, provided Vorticism with the vocabulary of their artistic idiom. Lines which are clear-cut, clean and mechanical were favored, while engineer's drawings became the newly admired form.

The first issue of *BLAST* (June 1914) contained a one-act play by Lewis, fiction by Ford and Rebecca West, a discussion of Kandinsky's 'On the

Spiritual in Art' and twelve poems by Pound, plus his statement on the Vortex. The second issue, July 1915, had eight poems plus a prose contribution by Pound and contributions by T.S. Eliot, Gaudier-Brzeska and others. But immediately after Gaudier-Brzeska's piece was a note on his death on 5 June 1915. Issue No.1 was loud, stimulating and offensive; issue No. 2, 'The War Number,' was more subdued, the cover an angular woodcut based on a sketch by Lewis of three soldiers with rifles ready. Although there was less striking textual material, there were more woodcuts and illustrations emphasizing the Vorticist ideals of severity and geometrical clarity. Among the illustrators was Dorothy Shakespear. Lewis, busy with his novel *Tarr*, did not remain much involved with *BLAST* No. 2, although he contributed an editorial note.

Aggressive, uncompromising and in its way alarming, *BLAST* was the reaction to the artificiality and convention of 'Wardour Street,' at the end of the 19th century a street in Soho known for its antiques and theatre costume shops reflected in language that was artificial, stilted and masking true emotion or feeling. The new poetry was all action and energy and *BLAST* a challenge to the commonplace: 'BLAST alone has dared to show modernity its face in an honest glass' Pound trumpeted (*PD* 147).[2] But by participating in this short-lived but vocal movement, Pound may have overplayed his hand, his work no longer accepted by prestigious but conventional journals like the *Quarterly Review*. Soon, Pound was shunned, his work hardly published, his books neglected. His sense of combat and belligerent tone immediately removed him from the vestiges of the genteel Georgian literary world. This was vitality turned on its head at the same time he championed the view that art is never estranged from the world.

Pound had met Gaudier-Brzeska, a Polish–French sculptor, in London in 1913. He and Dorothy Shakespear visited the Allied Artists exhibition at Albert Hall and in front of a statuette in the so-called Futurist style, Pound began to imitate its form by dancing about. Suddenly, a gaunt man with long hair rushed up and threatened violence if he did not stop. It was Gaudier-Brzeska and the two soon became friends, Pound encouraging the work of this penurious artist whose sculpture studio was an arch under the Putney train bridge but who admired Pound's combative poetry, especially 'Sestina: Altaforte.' Pound's celebration of the artist's work during and after his death in 1915 in battle led to Gaudier-Brzeska's recognition. His profile drawings and 'Hieratic Head' of Pound, carved from a block of white marble, have long been signature images of the poet. In his 'Affirmations' of 1915, Pound praised Gaudier-Brzeska as a complete artist who can arrange 'not only the planes and volumes which are peculiarly *of* his art, but an ability for historical synthesis, an ability for bringing order into things apparently remote from the technique of his art' (*EPVA* 18). Mass, not line, conveyed the energy of art for him, while the arrangement of surfaces expressed emotion. The large type and flaring cover of *BLAST* expressed the Vorticist concentration on arranged forms to create impact. Earlier, in his essay on the sculptor Jacob Epstein, Pound praised Gaudier-Brzeska's 'Vortex' in *BLAST* and in 'Affirmations' praised the way his work creates a 'definition of masses' expressive of 'emotional and intellectual forces' (*EPVA* 21).

Pound quickly grasped how the sculpture of Gaudier-Brzeska could metaphorically illuminate a way of writing. A Gaudier-Brzeska work Pound purchased that he woke up to each morning in his room gained shape by building up plane upon plane as the light hit it. This suggested a method Pound soon employed in his own work, especially in 'Homage to Sextus Propertius,' *Hugh Selwyn Mauberley* and *The Cantos*: one of accumulated lines, references and images that almost stand one upon the other. The beauty of the statue was there first in its mass and then its details (*EPVA* 21). The new form is 'an arrangement of masses in relation . . . energy cut into stone' or, in Pound's case, energy cut into verse (*EPVA* 22). As Pound would later state, 'kulch is language, and melody and stone' (*EP* to G. Bing, 10 October 19[37?]). Pound, himself, seemed to take on this chiseled quality. Donald Hall recorded that when Pound greeted him in Rome in February 1960, 'his face was large and jagged, constructed in sharp triangular sections, like modular architecture.' To Hall, Pound's face was, itself, cubist (Hall, 114). The shocking death of Gaudier-Brzeska on 5 June 1915 in the trenches was a blow Pound had difficulty recovering from. As a tribute, Pound published *Gaudier-Brzeska* (1916), a memoir, which included the published writings of the sculptor and a selection from his letters with illustrations. As late as 1959, Pound could declare that 'Gaudier was the most absolute case of genius I've ever run into, and they killed off an awful lot of sculpture when they shot him' (Bridson 161).

Following his first winter with Yeats, Pound's personal life dramatically changed. He intensified his pursuit of Dorothy Shakespear winning over her mother and then grudgingly her father shortly after his return from Stone Cottage in the early months of 1914. They married on 20 April 1914 in St. Mary Abbots' Church, Kensington. Pound wanted a civil ceremony but Dorothy's father insisted it be in a church. He won. He reluctantly agreed to the marriage despite Pound's precarious financial situation.

On several earlier occasions, Pound had asked Mr. Shakespear permission to marry Dorothy but the lawyer always rejected him because it was clear that Pound could not support himself. However, armed with a new contract from a British publisher showing that his Cavalcanti and new collection *Ripostes* would appear, Pound again approached Dorothy's father, only to be rebuffed. The marriage would again be postponed. In September of 1912, a perturbed Olivia Shakespear sternly wrote to Pound telling him to see her daughter less, adding that she didn't know if Dorothy still considered herself engaged to him 'but as she obviously can't marry you, she must be made [to] realize that she can't go on as though you were her accepted lover – it's hardly *decent*.' Olivia then complained that her daughter '*must* marry' noting that the two of them 'can't possibly go on living this feminine life practically *a deux* for ever & we haven't money enough to separate.' 'You *ought* to go away' she implored Pound: 'Englishmen don't understand yr American ways,' adding, however, that 'if you had £500 a year, I should be delighted for *you* to marry her...' (*EP/DS* 153–4).

Pound and Dorothy treated this directive nonchalantly and continued to see each other, Dorothy attending his talks, reading his work and corresponding with him when he traveled. She also began to draw regularly and did the cover of *Ripostes* (1912), a series of strong black and white intersecting planes beneath the title across the top of the cover; another of her works appeared in *BLAST* No. 2. By 1914, Mr Shakespear may have realized that his twenty-seven-year-old daughter was no longer young and that she was, indeed, in love with the poet, who was nonetheless carrying on flirtations and other relations with various women. Olivia Shakespear was also now urging their union.

In preparation for married life, Pound moved out of his cramped, No. 10 Church Walk to an oddly shaped two room apartment at 5 Holland Park Chambers across the hall from where H.D. and Aldington lived. H.D. recounts how one day she found the door open to that flat before Pound was married and asked what he was doing there? 'He said he was looking for a place where he could fence with Yeats. I was rather taken aback when they actually moved in' (*End* 5). Few attended the wedding service, while the war prevented the newlyweds from going to Spain for their honeymoon; instead, they went to Stone Cottage. As a gift, Olivia settled £150 a year on the couple easing their need for an income. Dorothy, in fact, would do little or no cooking for them, even when they returned to London (indeed, she did none until forced to do so during World War II); in fact, she was thought by many to be 'cold' and very English: unbearably critical and lacking warmth. H.D., admittedly somewhat jealous, wrote in 1924 that the general consensus was that 'Mrs E [Dorothy Pound] has not been "awakened"' (*Guest* 64). But Dorothy immediately fit in with Pound's circle and found herself party to activities at South Lodge, the Rebel Art Centre and Yeats' Monday evenings.

Another figure of importance from this period was the young American poet T.S. Eliot, introduced to Pound by Conrad Aiken, another American living in London at this time. Their friendship grew, despite differing backgrounds: Eliot, born in St Louis, came from a wealthy family and graduated Harvard. He had come to England on a traveling Fellowship to study philosophy at Oxford. The war prevented him from taking a summer course in philosophy in Germany and in September 1914, he visited Pound through Aiken's introduction. The pedantic and tactful Eliot differed from the far-ranging and out-spoken Pound but Pound sensed a warmth beneath the shy and formal exterior of Eliot.

An affinity quickly emerged between the two young writers and in a few weeks Pound would tell Harriet Monroe that Eliot is 'the only American I know of who has made what I can call adequate preparation for writing. He has actually trained himself *and* modernized himself *on his own*' (*SL* 40). In the same letter, he reports to her that Eliot has 'sent in the best poem I have yet had or seen from an American' – 'Prufrock.' He mailed it to her in October and urged her to publish it, although the hesitant Monroe would not print it until June 1915. Indeed, throughout 1914 and into 1915, Pound defended Eliot's work, telling Monroe that he will not 'ask Eliot to write down to any audience whatsoever,' while prodding her to get on with publishing *Prufrock* (*SL* 44, 57). He would continue to defend, promote and even – looking ahead to *The Waste Land* – edit Eliot who in turn would shortly offer a defense of Pound's own work in an anonymous brochure to accompany the American publication of *Lustra* (1917).

Pound's poetic evolution at this stage, ca. 1914/15, might be outlined as follows: from his study at university of French, Spanish, Italian and Provençal, he developed a verbal and perhaps mental identity with the Troubadour tradition defined by polite diction and poetic speech that relied on antiquated forms. His earliest books reflect this influence in works that were historical and imitative with only flashes of the linguistic originality that would later dominate his poetry. 'Sestina: Altaforte' or 'The Seafarer' illustrate this new energy which appears to derive from three sources: Imagism, Vorticism and Chinese poetry via Fenollosa. Suddenly, in *Cathay* (1915) and his work with Yeats on Noh drama, Pound realized that a new authority can be achieved in the focused, intensity of poems that used the ideogrammic method and framework of a strong narrator, borrowed from Browning.[3] Coupled with the experimental metrics and form that Pound was beginning to employ in 'Three Cantos,' and then in 'Homage to Sextus Propertius' and *Mauberley*, the stage was set for the expansion of *The Cantos*, mixing fragmentary voices, historical themes and new ways of expression which united his work on Noh drama, Fenollosa and the understanding of 'luminous detail.' All of this appeared to erupt from a vortex. The arranged planes and lines of Gaudier-Brzeska had made their way to the page.

Pound's progress might also be measured geographically. As he moved about London, his literary orientation shifted. Editorial meetings at the offices of the *New Age* on Cursitor Street, continuing at the ABC teashop nearby in Chancery Lane, marked a kind of institutional if slightly formal schooling counter-balanced by his Kensington social life beginning with visits to Brunswick Gardens where the Shakespear's lived and then, a few minutes away, South Lodge, the haunt of Ford Madox Ford and his 'wife,' Violet Hunt. Dinners in Kensington at Lady Low's home with the likes of Maurice Hewlitt, May Sinclair and George Prothero, editor of the *Quarterly Review*, galvanized Pound's desire to belong. He told Dorothy Shakespear from Paris in June 1912 that he wanted to 'entrench himself behind' the *Quarterly's* covers (*EP/DS* 125). His marriage to Dorothy in April 1914 solidified his Kensington foundations but the pull of the Rebel Art Centre and then *BLAST* lifted him from the conservative activism of Kensington into a world of literary extremism. Soho, not South Lodge, became the new beacon.

At the Voricist dinners at the Eiffel Tower Restaurant and Dieudonnés, and Vorticist dances at London's first night club, the Cave of the Golden Calf off Regent Street, Pound found a new circle. Readings at Lady Low's no longer held sway and the older poets gave way to figures like the young poet Iris Barry, found working in the Birmingham Post Office. Pound soon orchestrated evenings at Belotti's in Old Compton Street in Soho to which Symons, Waley, Yeats, Ford, Lewis, Aldington, Dorothy Pound, H.D. May Sinclair, Harriet Shaw Weaver, Violet Hunt and others came.

Barry would become the mistress of Wyndham Lewis (introduced to him by Pound), although Lewis would try to hide this and the two children she had with him. Barry's account of the period, however, provides one of the most detailed views of Pound's Soho life.[4] Importantly, the gendered nature of the Soho group, where the sexes freely mixed, was very different from the 'Edwardian' or Kensington group. The

Freewoman and *New Freewoman* were at the centre of the developments, extended under Pound's leadership to a campaign against censorship. If the *Egoist* represented literary modernism, the *New Freewoman* embodied feminism but uniting both was an awareness, if not focus, on sexuality. Throughout these worlds and locales, Pound maintained his bohemian personae, melding the brashness of an American with the dress of an aesthete: Whitman and Whistler in one.

Pound hadn't forgotten his cantos in the midst of this activity. He told Donald Hall that he first conceived of a work like *The Cantos* while at Hamilton College in about 1904. 'It was a question of dealing with material that wasn't in the *Divina Commedia*' he explained (*RP* 223). This may have occurred during his many talks with his favored professor, Ibbotson, the Anglo-Saxon specialist. It wasn't until September 1915, however, that Pound, after working on *Noh or Accomplishment*, began to compose 'Three Cantos,' a work he conceived to be both epic and modern drawing equally on tradition and history, yet with a radical pattern in its design, relying on what one early critic called anecdote rather than narrative (R.P. Blackmur in Bush 6). Inclusivity of content and form became Pound's keynote, supported by a rejection of poetic decorum for a new colloquial speech linking the *enfant terrible* with the social satirist which began to emerge in his work of 1914. Kandinsky, translated in *BLAST 1*, argued that harmony was not a rounded or united beauty but depended on interesting dissonances, an idea that would soon define *The Cantos*. The unity of *The Cantos*, however, derives from patterns of imagery or a recurrent series of metaphors that hold the poem together. Juxtaposition and recurrence become the structural motif of the work.

'Three Cantos' went first to Alice Corbin Henderson, Assistant Editor of *Poetry*, then living for health reasons in Santa Fe, New Mexico. Pound felt her more sympathetic to his work and after she read them, she sent them on to Harriet Monroe in Chicago. The poems arrived in Santa Fe in early February 1917 and Henderson's response was immediate and positive, beginning with an eleven line poem of her own alluding to Canto II and then 'Your cantos are very beautiful and I long for more to come.... You've explored worlds beyond worlds, and it's a pleasure to follow you' (*EP/ACH* 190). But Henderson warned Monroe in her letter accompanying the cantos that 'they are erudite – but there is life – and a poet's life – in it & through it all.' Harriet Monroe responded with less enthusiasm: 'I read two or three pages of Ezra's Cantos and then took sick – no doubt that was the cause. Since then I haven't had brains enough to tackle it.' A month later – she let Robert Frost take them

East – she finished them, although she wasn't happy with the direction his writing was taking: 'a hint from Browning at his most recondite, and erudition in seventeen languages' she complained (*EP/ACH* 194). Monroe wanted to published each Canto separately and Henderson concurred. They appeared in *Poetry* in June, July and August 1917.

'Three Cantos' is an original work, summarizing what has influenced Pound, while outlining what is to come in his writing. Canto I, with its opening criticism of Browning's looseness with fact, discusses why progress is inadequate as a subject for a modern poem. In the second part of the first Canto, Pound introduces motifs that expand in the later 'Three Cantos' and in subsequent sections of the long poem, emphasizing the avoidance of 'speech figurative:' 'set out your matter/ As I do, in straight simple phrases' the poet urges (*Per* 232).

The second of the 'Three Cantos' marks a departure from lyric poetry for the epic journey across the vastness of the work, opening with an imagistic leave taking and turn to history:

> Leave Casella.
> Send out your thought upon the Mantuan palace –
> Drear waste, great halls,
> Silk tatters still in the frame, Gonzaga's splendor
> Alight with phantoms! What have we of them,
> Or much or little?
>
> (*Per* 234–5)

Myth, history and autobiography blend. The canto is also more sophisticated, building its theme around the nature of 'drear waste' using the technique of layering the rich past over the empty present. Classical, Renaissance and religious figures begin to appear, often quoted, anticipating what Pound will do in the later *Cantos*. The disappearance of worship ends the canto, the gods forgotten in the rush of commerce.

Canto III takes one into the world of Homeric primitivism and introduces Andreas Divus whose 16th century Latin translation of Homer becomes a focal point. The narrator is soon:

> Caught up his cadence, word and syllable:
> 'Down to the ships we went, set mast and sail,
> Black keel and beasts for bloody sacrifice,
> Weeping we went.'
> I've strained my ear for *-ensa*, *-ombra*, and *-ensa*
> And cracked my wit on delicate canzoni –

> Here's but rough meaning:
> 'And then went down to the ship, set keel to breakers,
> Forth on the godly sea.

(*Per* 243)

These revisions, which Pound performs before the reader, become the revised opening of Canto I in *A Draft of XVI Cantos* published in 1925 and set the tone for the entire long work. 'Three Cantos' ends with a return to a lyrical Homer, mixing Latin with English and such lyrical lines as 'Light on the foam, breathed on by zephyrs,/ And air-tending hours' (*Per* 245).

Borrowing initially from Browning, who believed that a work must forego narrative continuity to present the fragmented consciousness of the modern mind, Pound also draws from a new interest in the energy of primitivism seen in Nietzsche, Hulme, Sir James Frazer and Picasso, plus Wyndham Lewis and Gaudier-Brzeska. Pound applies these approaches to his own form, cutting from scene to thought and back again without connections, although within an overall epic structure borrowed from Dante. Vorticism's interest in primitive abstractions and vitality added to Pound's understanding of the value of geometric art.[5] The obtrusive narrator, taken from Browning, adds to the singularity of Pound's voice in 'Three Cantos,' as Pound prepared for the ritual journey through history. Dante's structure, Browning's voice – they, and the theories of Vorticism, shape the 'Three Cantos' and their later revision.

But Pound's move from the 'showman' narrator crisscrossing history in the 'Three Cantos' to the more focused narrative structure of the revised *Cantos* presented in *A Draft of XVI Cantos* was not direct. He first returned to classicism with 'Homage to Sextus Propertius' and then to modernism in his critique of the London *avant garde* and its failed culture in *Mauberley*. But from those two encounters he was prepared to re-engage his *Cantos* and shape them into the evolving form that came to dominate their structure. The ironic tonalities, as Hugh Kenner has called them, of 'Propertius' prepared the way for the satire of *Mauberley* and cleared the pallette for Pound's new casting of his long work (Kenner, *PE* 162–3). His impasse with the narrative structure of 'Three Cantos' led to his revisions but only after he reconciled the seemingly contrasting state of narrative poetry and prose realism in the novel. Flaubert, James and Joyce, plus Remy de Gourmont, all influenced his approach and suggested ways of overcoming the stalemate between self-expression and realism (Bush, *Genesis* 144–151; *LE* 340).

In the summer of 1917, Pound reviewed Eliot's *Prufrock and Other Observations* and began to grasp a new realism. He also began to read Laforgue, the source of Eliot's satiric irony and his essay 'Irony, Laforgue and Some Satire' is the result, an analysis by Pound that shows that Laforgue's realism is actually satiric (*LE* 282). He also called Laforgue's technique and irony 'verbalist,' a form of poetry equal to lyricism and Imagism which anticipates Pound's later term, *logopoeia*, which he defined in *How to Read* as 'the dance of the intellect among words' (*LE* 283, 25). Pound's critical formulations anticipate a poetic break-through. In 1917, the year he reviewed Eliot and read Laforgue, Pound also began to write 'Homage to Sextus Propertius,' attempting to show the modernity of a Roman poet. A discursive style devoted to the movement of a historical consciousness defines the work. Propertius is both deeply in love and aware of his folly and the challenge for Pound is to give 'a feeling of the reality of the speaker' and then to gain 'any degree of poignancy in one's utterance' (Pound in Bush, *Genesis* 175). What he also learned was that poetry did not need verbs as much as 'a syntax that could incorporate their actions and relate it to other actions,' an idea he attached to Fenollosa's 'Chinese Character' essay when it appeared in December 1919 in the *Little Review* (Bush, *Genesis* 179). Earlier, in the summer of 1919, he finished Canto IV in a revised narrative style, avoiding verbs and rendering activity by using the techniques of participial construction favored by Henry James.

In 1916, Pound had published *Lustra*, appearing the following year in the States with the subtitle *with Earlier Poems*. To enhance its reception, Eliot anonymously wrote *Ezra Pound; His Metric and Poetry*. The 31pp pamphlet also contained a bibliography by Pound and a large frontispiece of Pound in profile by Gaudier-Brzeska. Beginning with the notice Pound had already earned as a poet, Eliot admits that his work is little known in America. He then argues that Pound is more of an artist than a scholar, translator or journalist. Eliot then provides a 'summary account of ten years' work in poetry' (*Metric* 4), providing a detailed account of Pound's output with little comment, although occasional remarks reveal Eliot's sympathetic understanding of Pound's work. 'Pound's verse,' he explains, 'is always definite and concrete, because he has always a definite emotion behind it' (13).

Eliot especially praises the way Pound adapts metre to mood, something he can skillfully do because of his intensive study of metre, yet he has 'always been ready to battle against pedantry' (8). What his poems require 'is a trained ear, or at least the willingness to be trained' (9).

Saddled with the term *vers libre*, Eliot argues that Pound uses it only when the material requires it. His skill is technical: 'few have studied the forms and metres which they [other poets] use so carefully as has Pound' (12). Eliot then raises a comparison between Pound and Mallarmé suggesting that Pound's imagery will 'appear always sharp in outline, even if arbitrary and not photographic' (14–15).

Praising 'The Seafarer' and 'The Return,' Eliot contradicts the notion that Pound is a propagandist for any of the current 'isms' and then cites the parody of him from *Punch* to indicate his impact on literary London. And then, through quotation, he shows Pound's use of discipline and form in his work. If he has experienced any disapproval, it may be more from his praise of certain contemporary poets he likes rather than his theories, or, to be more accurate, from those poets he does not praise. In continuing with his summary, Eliot then celebrates *Cathay* (which will rank with 'The Seafarer' among 'Pound's original work') and *Lustra* before talking about influences which have freed rather than bound Pound: Catullus, Gautier and Laforgue are three. *Noh or Accomplishment* also receives accolades. The final paragraph cites 'Three Cantos' which appears in the American edition of *Lustra* and Pound's attraction to the epic, noting that when one has 'mastered "Lustra" and "Cathay," he is prepared for the Cantos – but not till then' (28). Failing to like them means that you've 'omitted some step in his progress, and had better go back and retrace the journey' (28). Eliot, making the case for the progress of Pound's work, convinces readers that it is crucial to understand what is valuable about contemporary writing. But Eliot was ready to expand the readership and reception of Pound's work in America. England, however, was not.

Pound was finding London increasingly unsympathetic to his programs. Despite his usually frantic activity, especially his editorial work for the feminist *New Freewoman*, the modernist *Egoist*, the American *Poetry*, the adventurous *Little Review*, the socialist *New Age* and the conservative *Dial*, while promoting such writers as Joyce and Eliot, Pound was meeting with little success. Notoriety yes, but literary recognition, no – complicated by such acts as challenging a *Times* reviewer to a duel because of his high opinion of Milton (Ford, *Return* 357)! His work as a critical propagandist became clear in March 1917 when he became the London editor of the *Little Review* edited by Margaret Anderson and Jane Heap, and used the occasion of his first contribution to condemn *Poetry*, even though he still remained their Foreign Correspondent. The journal was never the instrument of his 'radicalism' he writes but the *Little Review* could fill that role and become a regular outlet for

Joyce, Lewis and himself. In fact, he managed to serialize a portion of *Ulysses* in the *Little Review* in 1918.

Pound's increasing work for the *Little Review* required assistance and in the summer of 1918 he hired Iseult Gonne as a typist to work three days a week. Pound and the attractive 23-year-old daughter of Maud Gonne (Yeats's former great love, although he married Georgie Hyde Lees in October 1917 with Pound acting as his best man) soon began an intense love affair. This lasted until Iseult returned to Dublin after the Armistice to join her mother who had evaded surveillance and snuck back into the country. From Ireland in the winter of 1918, Iseult would frequently write to Pound, ending her letters with impassioned expressions of love in French. In December 1918, for example, she wrote 'Ezra chaque jour je t'aime un peu plus que la veille malgré que j'ai oublié la façon dont tu ris . . . sans courage je t'embrasse' ['Ezra, every day I love you a little more than the day before in spite of the fact that I have forgotten how you laugh . . . without courage, I embrace you.'] (Gonne 144, 237). Their secret affair (she signed her letters to him 'Maurice') prompted Pound to consider leaving Dorothy, although he did not. Still affected by the affair in 1925, Pound wanted to name his daughter with Olga Rudge, Iseult; she refused (Gonne 137). Several critics have speculated, however, that the increased eroticism of Pound's poetry during the 1918–20 period might have originated in his affair with Iseult (Gonne 236). Pound was discrete about his affair, however, and, apart from telling Olga and then his daughter Mary in 1943, denied that he had any contact with Iseult after her return to Ireland despite letters that have recently come to light that indicate they likely met in 1919 (Gonne 138).

Pound at this time soon turned to anthologies to shape literary taste and publically demonstrate his principles. Following *Des Imagistes* of 1914, he edited *The Poetical Works of Lionel Johnson* (1915), and the *Catholic Anthology* (1915) with five poems by Eliot, two by Williams and ten by himself. Several years later, *Profile* (1932), *Active Anthology* (1933) and, finally, *Confucius to cummings* (1964) appeared. Anthologies were vehicles for getting his ideas of poetry and new writing into the hands of readers as he demonstrated in *ABC of Reading*: almost half the book is made up of 'Exhibits,' an anthology of key writings. Pound constantly admonished publishers for not printing cheap anthologies because they were, he was convinced, effective, cheap and useful for reminding a culture of great literature it had forgotten and new literature it should know. Pound, at the beginning of this period, also returned to the classics, writing 'Homage to Sextus Propertius' (dated 1917) in-between such works as his memoir of Gaudier-Brzeska (1916) and a collection of prose essays, *Pavannes and Divisions* (1918). But soon, Vorticism was blowing over and *BLAST* was ending as the war and general cultural depression overshadowed new movements and new energy.

Between 1916 and 1918 Pound began to find himself culturally isolated: Joyce was in Europe, Lewis was at the front and Gaudier-Brzeska had been killed. He could not get Lewis' novel, *Tarr*, published and had difficulty placing Joyce's *Portrait*. His own volume, *Lustra*, was meeting obstacles because Elkin Mathews felt some works in it were obscene. However, the poems displayed a new assertiveness in language that finally went beyond his influences, possessing a directness and precision only preceded by *Cathay*. Pound also continued to busy himself in establishing the reputations of others, while completing his study of Gaudier-Brzeska's sculpture, writing reviews, puffing others and quarreling. Iris Barry described Pound's frantic activity: 'no one was ever busier, gayer ... seeing everything, meeting everybody, full of the latest gossip ... making strange sounds and cries in his talking but otherwise quite formal and extremely polite.' In 1916, his name 'stood in England, along with that of the sculptor Epstein, for all that was dangerously different, horridly new' (Barry 165, 159).

But by the war's end, Pound had become disenchanted with commercial publishing and the resistance of the public to the new. The absence of any sustained literary culture disturbed him. He needed a vibrant metropolitan culture which London no longer provided. When Richard Aldington visited Pound just after his return from the war, he found the poet still in his Kensington apartment with its pentagonal living room, tapping his Adam's apple and assuring Aldington that 'the English stopped short there' meaning that they no longer had any brains. He related this in part to their lack of appreciation of his own work (Aldington, Life 216).

But Pound still retained his flamboyant pose. H.D. remembered him in 1919 with his beard, black hat, ebony stick and 'something unbelievably operatic – [a] directoire overcoat, Verdi;' his image was thoroughly bohemian (*End* 7). He 'seemed to beat with the ebony stick like a baton ... [and] there is a sense of his pounding, pounding (*Pounding*) with the stick against the wall' (*End* 8). He had banged that stick like that once before 'in a taxi, at a grave crisis in my life. This was a grave crisis in my life. It was happening here. "But," he said, "my only real criticism is that this is not my child"' (*End* 8). Pound was visiting H.D. in hospital for the anticipated birth of a child but he couldn't stand still: he talked and stamped the length of the room. He hurtled himself into the nursing home in Ealing demonstrating again that he could not be contained (*End* 7–8). But despite Pound's fall in popularity, as Carl Sandburg reluctantly admitted, 'all talk of modern poetry, by people who know, ends with dragging in Ezra Pound somewhere' (Sandburg in Tytell 131).

In this transitional period, 'Propertius,' and 'Three Cantos' are his most important works, capped by *Mauberley*. 'Propertius' is ironic, however, beginning with its title: it is a 'Homage' not a translation, what Hugh Kenner labels a 'rescription' of the original. To the elegies Pound brought a sensibility, Kenner adds, 'alert to elegant cynicism' as he began to fashion the first of what would be his sequence poems: 'Propertius,' *Mauberley* and then *The Cantos* (Kenner, *PEP* 148, 147).

'Propertius' is the bridge between Pound's Imagist program, the influence of Fenollosa and his later works, presenting his last, major single *persona*. Like *Cathay*, the poem is a free translation of ancient lyrics relying on the convention of a single unifying speaker. Pound selects and arranges the Latin elegies of the Roman poet Propertius to develop a complex portrait of the man. Yet the themes contain many of the concerns of the first World War: death, love, war and the ability of poetry itself to express these crises. Disillusionment is the controlling mood, paralleling Pound's own distemper over the 'ineffable imbecility of the British Empire' with that of Propertius over the decline of the Roman Empire (*SL* 231). Yet the poem suggests hope and the possibility that eternal values will survive.

Rather than celebrate war, Propertius celebrates love and private life which, of course, contains their own conflicts. Most interestingly, the poem treats its readership as a casualty of war, a victim of the corruption of the cultural values that prolong the conflict. To denounce that corruption is Pound's aim through the *persona* and poetry of Propertius:

Annalists will continue to record Roman reputations, . . .
But for something to read in normal circumstances?
For a few pages brought down from the forked hill unsullied?
I ask a wreath which will not crush my head.

begins the narrator (*Per* 205). Retreating from heroic poetry that celebrates battle, Propertius turns to love, not barbarism. 'Now if ever it is time to cleanse Helicon' he announces at the opening to the fifth section of the poem and declares that 'It is noble to die of love, and honourable to remain uncuckolded for a season' (*Per* 212, 214). Grafting myth with history through a historical *persona* of the Roman Empire gives the poem depth and originality, prefiguring the structure and tone of *The Cantos*. But the publication of 'Propertius' was controversial because it appeared to be a translation, but one riddled within accuracies according to the Latinists. Pound tried to justify these 'mistakes' at the same time he defended the work as original but to no avail. Yeats, however, told Bunting that in 1918 Pound had created the greatest *vers libre* structure yet done in English. It was, Bunting said, 'in the *Homage* that Pound discovered how to organize a poem on the model of music so that every line grows out of the line before by modification. The effect is very much like the sonata form' (Laughlin, *PWuz* 97). But very little that Pound wrote at this time met with praise. *Quai Pauper Amavi* (1919), a collection of his most recent work, was panned except for a review by Eliot in *The Athenaeum*. Even his prose was finding a very small audience. He explained to Williams in September 1920 that 'there is no longer any intellectual *life* in England save what centres in this eight by ten pentagonal room.' 'Have I a country at all ...' he wondered in the same letter (*SL* 158–9). Insecurity and restlessness fed each other and prompted a search for another home.

Hugh Selwyn Mauberely (1920), the second sequence poem of this period, extends the form and disenchantment of 'Propertius' with the added belief that art must be instrumental to social practice. Challenging the 'art for art's sake' aesthetic is the counter view that art must have a social purpose, an idea originating in Pound's reading of Ruskin and exposure to the doctrine of Social Credit outlined by its founder, Major C.H. Douglas. The pages and offices of A.R. Orage's *The New Age* introduced him to these new ideas. An engineer turned economist, Douglas believed that there was never enough money in circulation to acquire the goods needed by society. The only solution was to issue more currency. Poverty and war result from the unfair distribution of purchasing power, the effect of the control of credit by the banks and the excessive interest charges imposed on people. Goods are always priced higher than available purchasing power. Credit must be nationalized in the public interest. If that is not done, war and poverty are inevitable.

Douglas' first article appeared in January 1919 in the *New Age*, his first book published serially in June that year and entitled *Economic Democracy*. These ideas deeply affected Pound who likely attended the *New Age* teas held at the Chancery Lane ABC shop where Douglas held forth. In an interview in the *New York Herald* (Paris edition), reprinted in the *New Age*, Pound is reported to have said that 'he looks upon credit control as the focus of power and that he can see no economic improvement without revision of the credit system' (Martin 273). In the years to come, Social Credit would become Pound's over-riding obsession.

Mauberley, Pound's poetic farewell to England, embodies a largely embittered social vision. After twelve years, Pound no longer found England conducive to the arts which the Latin epigram to the poem suggests: '*Vocat æstus in umbram;*' translated, it means 'The heat calls us into the shade.' In a challenging structure and uncompromising style, Pound condenses imagery and allusion but *without* a central speaker. The tone of each section also shifts, as juxtaposed material appears on every page without apparent logic. The general movement of the poem follows this division: the first twelve sections analyze the false values of modern civilization by showing their impact on the market for art. The title character is a fictional poet who ironically doesn't even appear until the second part of the poem which opens with 'Mauberley 1920.' Part one features a critique of the age and its impact on a series of minor artists rather than a single protagonist. They form a heritage for Mauberley but a confusing one since Pound's voice adopts irony, detachment, rage and impersonality. No illusion of a single dramatic character emerges. The predominant tone is diagnostic and satiric with a series of social languages reproduced in the text, complicated by shifts in voice and tense.[6]

The first four poems of the second section of *Mauberley* are written in the third person and in the past tense with the pronoun 'he' assumed but not named as Mauberley. 'Medallion,' the fifth poem, is written in the present tense. By contrast, the first part of the entire work begins with a mock obituary of 'E.P.' and some of the poems are written in the first person. Such narrative uncertainty reflects the confusions of the age and the problematic nature of poetry Pound now promotes, which a letter of 1922 slightly elucidates: 'Mauberley is a mere surface. Again a study in form, an attempt to condense the James novel' (*SL* 180). The poem is Pound's attempt to write a condensed Jamesian novel but instead of a coherent, linear text, the narrative focuses on the 'atmospheres, nuances, impressions of personal tone and quality,' features he declared to be Jamesian subjects (*LE* 324). *Mauberley* might actually be thought of as an experimental verse novel; its printed subtitle in the first edition reads 'Life and Contacts.'

In the poem, Pound condemns the philistine privileging of money over life and art, condemning a world where profit is more important than beauty. He also criticizes artists who escape the responsibilities of the age. More explicitly, after the opening Ode, sections II–V focus on Pound's critique of British values, unflinchingly requiring that 'The age demanded an image/ Of its accelerated grimace.' 'Better mendacities/ Than the classics in paraphrase!' he exclaims (*Per* 186). Decreeing beauty in the market place scurrilous because it becomes mechanical, not artistic, he condemns the replacement of the lyre with the pianola. The Great War of 1914–18 is the outcome of displacing life with money, while those who left idealistically, returned disillusioned, coming home:

> to a lie,
> home to many deceits,
> home to old lies and new infamy;
> usury age-old and age-thick
> and liars in public places

(*Per* 188)

A great deal of the concentrated and complex poem concerns itself with how artists of a previous generation responded to economic and social pressures. And his diagnosis is always unsentimental. The list of failed or compromised artists begin with one 'E.P.', a version of Pound in his early London years. 'E.P.' fails to modernize his style and becomes trapped in an old-fashioned ideal of beauty. The 'Yeux Glauques' section, alluding to Théophile Gautier's poem *Émaux et Camées* [*Enamels and Cameos*, 1852], provides a condensed portrait of the Pre-Raphaelite period, proceeding chronologically from Ruskin, Rossetti, Swinburne and Burne Jones to the Rhymers of the 1890s, Max Beerbohm, Arnold Bennett ('Mr. Nixon') and Ford Madox Ford. But in Sections XI and XII of *Mauberley*, Pound shifts from the artists to the audience, satirizing numerous representations of popular taste.

'Mauberley 1920' begins the second part of the sequence, replacing the active Pound with the aesthete. It traces the effect of such forces upon the career of the English poet, Hugh Selwyn Mauberley, who begins as an Imagist but drops off into a kind of hedonistic impressionism. Beginning with his admiration of Gautier, Pound models the quatrains and cameo technique of the poem on the hard surface technique of Gautier's *Émaux et Camées*. Visual art soon begins to define the nature of Mauberley's work. Pound then gives two versions of the same event offered in 'Envoi' and 'Medallion.' In the first, Pound responds to a woman singing by offering his own song and showing the collapse of the English lyric, while in 'Medallion' Mauberley offers his response, something that reminds him of art objects in books and museums before drifting into an aesthetic analysis of the singer's face, a profile portrait.

But Mauberley's talent soon fades and he does not yield to the demands of the age. He withdraws into a private world of 'selected impressions' passively received. Delighting him is no more than the 'imaginary/Audition of the phantasmal sea-surge' (*Per* 200). Yet his terse final note summarizes the compression that characterizes the poem, although Pound incorporated lengthy lines of tedious abstraction to define Mauberley's earlier style (see Part II, 'The Age Demanded'). In his note, Mauberley writes:

> 'I was
> And I no more exist;
> Here drifted
> An hedonist.'
>
> (*Per* 201)

The interplay of voices instead of a clearly established narrative structure defines the quality of *Mauberley* with its bleak critique of the age. Pound, however, rejected such cultural and poetic *malaise*, turning away from minor forms of poetry which had characterized his earlier work to a remarkable, major undertaking of epic proportions: *The Cantos*. But to do so, he had to free himself of London.

Despite his rejection of England and its hostile, postwar literary climate, Pound did praise four British writers whose influence was inescapable: Robert Bridges, who warned him against homophones; Thomas Hardy, who stressed concentration on subject matter rather than technique; Ford Madox Ford, who insisted on the freshness of language; and Yeats who by 1908 had written simple lyrics in which 'there were no departures from the natural order of words' (*RP* 227). Pound also used this period of change to reconsider his own work and life. 'A Retrospect' (1918) allowed him a poetic summing up and a chance to glance ahead. After surveying the emergence of Imagism and then a critique of how *vers libre* 'has become prolix and as verbose as any of the flaccid varieties that preceded it,' he reprints his 'A Few Don'ts' for Imagists, including the admonition, 'Go in fear of abstractions,' followed by earlier critical pieces: 'Prologomena,' and 'Re Vers Libre' (*LE* 3, 5). In this last, he states that his 'blasts and essays have done their work,' focusing the gaze of the audience on new work (*LE* 13).

In 'A Retrospect,' Pound also reaffirms the value of anthologies because they make great work accessible to many. In the final section, 'Only Emotion Endures' (anticipating several final passages in the late *Cantos*) love remains, recalling those poems that have remained with him 'these things [that] have worn smooth in my head' adding 'I am not through with them' (*LE* 14). 'Technique' is 'the test of a man's sincerity' he writes, noting that he would rather create than analyse, preferring to lie on 'what is left of Catullus' parlor floor and speculate the azure beneath it . . . than discuss any processes and theories of art whatsoever' (*LE* 9). But, to write in an atmosphere and culture which would encourage such new work, Pound had to make his way to Paris.

Encouraging his departure was more disappointment: a promised position at the *Athenaeum* fell through largely because of his scathing review of a favored actress. Preceding the review was a disclaimer from the Editor that the woman had more talent than the reviewer understood. Preceding this setback was the denial of publication in the *Quarterly Review* by its editor, George Prothero, because of Pound's involvement with *BLAST*. His negative comments on British imperialism did little to consolidate his popularity and his comments on the reading public hardly endeared him to his former audience, Pound's sense of 'the incredible stupidity, the ingrained refusal of thought!!!!!!' of the English made what he perceived to be the open-mindedness, intellectual self-confidence and individualism of the French all the more appealing (Wilhelm 1:248; *LE* 357). In *Who's Who*, Pound listed his recreation as 'searching *The Times* for evidences of almost incredible stupidity' (Tytell 131). 'The British literary episcopacy' clearly prevented one from 'writing what one thinks' he declared, an attitude and culture he would excoriate in Canto XIV (*LE* 357). 'How people hate him,' John Butler Yeats wrote to Quinn, 'but hatred is the harvest he wants to gather' it seems.[7] Pound's only escape was France where he anticipated a period of excitement, punctuated by bursts of promotion (largely for Joyce) until till two other 'isms' gripped him that he could not shake: anti-Semitism and Fascism. But as Pound wrote in 1915, 'the best artist is the man whose machinery can stand the highest voltage' (*SP* 346).

4
'Bring Order to Your Surroundings': 1920–29

> I am perhaps didactic... [but] it's all rubbish to pretend that art isn't
> didactic. A revelation is always didactic.
>
> (Pound, 1922)

Pound was in Paris when *Mauberley* appeared in London. He and
Dorothy had stopped there in June 1920 on their return from Sirmione
and stayed for almost six weeks, waiting in part for Joyce to arrive so
that Pound could arrange for his apartment. Their spring sojourn to
Italy and France prefigured their soon-to-be permanent departure from
England which Pound reconsidered in a passage from 'Indiscretions:'

> speculation as to... whether in one's anthropo- and gunaikological
> passion one were wise to leave London itself – with possibly a paren-
> thetical Paris as occasional watch-tower and alternating exotic *mica
> salis* (3).

Years later, he was more positive, telling an interviewer that the art scene
alone was reason enough to go to France. Léger, Brancusi, Cocteau,
Picabia and Picasso were there. And so were the musicians: Ravel,
Stravinsky and Virgil Thomson, while Aaron Copeland, as well as
George Antheil, an experimental composer from America, were soon to
arrive. Paris, Ford announced, 'gyrated, seethed, clamoured, roared with
the Arts.' Artists so crowded 'the boulevards that you could not see the
tree-trunks' he exclaimed (*Nightingale* 282).

In Paris Pound would soon meet the American violinist who would
become a crucial and lasting part of his life: Olga Rudge. And while
Joyce continued to be a presence, arriving in the city on 9 July 1920,
another figure of importance emerged: Ernest Hemingway who became

one of Pound's closest friends and boxing instructor (*AMF* 108). 'Why Paris?' Pound would ask in the Dadaist publication *391*; Paris, he answered, was the center of the world. No other place was as stimulating, exciting, or provocative; its cultural adventurousness gave Pound a new self-confidence which became apparent in a letter written a year after his move to France. In it he announces the end of the Christian Era and the beginning of another: the Pound Era (*SL* 174; *EPLR* 282).

Mauberley, Pound's 'envoie' to England and its literary life, prepared him for his turn to a Euro-centered world marked first by his January 1921 move to Paris and then his resettlement in Italy in 1924 where he lived until his arrest in 1945. Returning in 1958, Pound remained in Italy until his death in 1972. After England, France and Italy became Pound's chosen homes, although he still maintained his American citizenship, reiterating his American identity throughout his life and especially during the period of his radio broadcasts of 1942–43. Preceding his permanent move to Paris, in fact, Pound briefly reconsidered a return to America and, in a search for his roots, wrote the autobiographical and quasi-mythical account of his family and youth published as *Indiscretions*. A forceful letter from Quinn in 1920, however, told Pound why he should *not* return to America: there was no Eliot, Lewis, Joyce or Yeats and 'no art that would interest you except imported art. No first rate man of letters. No pleasant coterie. You would find much in the country to irritate and annoy you' which would only cause distraction. Quinn added that Pound was too fine an artist to bother with such criticism which Mencken does well: 'that's not the work of a poet. And you are a poet' Quinn concluded (*EPJQ* 174). In the twelve years since he departed New York, America had not grown; while there may have been little left for Pound to do in London, America offered nothing.

Earlier, Pound had met Joyce. After numerous false starts and confusions concerning trains, thunderstorms and timetables, complicated by a train crash and strike, Joyce hesitatingly made his way from Trieste to Sirmione (*EP/JJ* 167–9). They had been corresponding for six years and when he learned that Joyce had finally arrived at Desenzano, a short distance from Sirmione, Pound rushed to the station. The two immediately fell into literary talk, Pound impressing Joyce as 'a large bundle of unpredictable electricity,' Joyce impressing Pound with first a 'shell of cantankerous Irishman' but then, underneath, a man of sensitivity: 'the rest is the genius' with 'a concentration and absorption passing Yeats.' 'He is, of course, stubborn as a mule or an Irishman, but I failed to find him at all *unreasonable*' Pound noted (*EP/JJ* 178). Pound then convinced Joyce that he could live more comfortably and in a better intellectual climate if he moved to Paris. As insurance, Pound would be there to greet him and help the family get settled.

Returning to London after the summer of 1920 in Paris, Pound realized that England no longer held sway. It dismissed his work and sustained only stale ideas, while Paris seemed to contain promise. London became a city of separate cultural tables – literally, as Osbert Sitwell described in his memoir. On Thursday evenings, he and his brother would dine with several other writers including T.S. Eliot, Lewis, Herbert Read and Pound in a restaurant at Piccadilly Circus. Each writer sat at his own table, back to the wall: 'the distance helped to make conversation self-conscious or desultory. Ezra Pound was inclined to mumble into his red beard.... He was particularly a type the English do not understand or appreciate' (Sitwell 32). Overcoming this isolation would be Paris, providing 'the triple extract of literature for export purposes ... a poetic serum to save English letters from postmature and American telegraphics from premature suicide and decomposition' (EPCP IV: 102). Paris, he later wrote, 'wanted the dead things cleared out even if there was nothing to replace them' (JM 49).

Many thought Pound's departure from London arrogant and disdainful, and some, like Eliot, were shocked: 'This is a blow ... what happens to the Dial?' he asked (Lett 46–7). Others could hardly forgive him, Marianne Moore writing in 1925 that she herself loved 'the dust of London' and had 'long look[ed] askance at Ezra Pound's apostasy' (MM, SL 217). Countering this view was A.R. Orage's quasi-obituary on Pound's departure published in the New Age which praised Pound's 'exhilarating influence for culture in England,' while leaving his mark on more than one of the arts. 'Quite a number of men and movements owe their initiation to his self-sacrificing stimulus' but like many who sought to advance intelligence and culture, Pound made more enemies than friends: 'Taken by and large, England hates men of culture until they are dead' Orage concluded (CrH 200). He would, himself, soon follow Pound to France where he would enter the Gurdjieff Institute and, after a year's study, go to New York to teach the Gurdjieff system.

In December 1921, an exhilarated Pound wrote Eliot from Paris that 'it is after all a grrrreat littttttterary period,' summarizing the excitement and vigor of the artistic life. He was also elated by the musical as well as literary work he had newly undertaken (SL 170). The musical project was principally an opera, Le Testament de Villon, Pound composing the music and libretto, the latter drawn from Villon's lengthy poem, Le Grand Testament. The poem was a comic catalogue of the poet's supposed will, interrupted by lyrical ballads and songs. The text was to be a mixture of 15th century French with some sections translated into English. Agnes Bedford, an English friend and musicologist, would be his adviser. His nearly decade-long research into troubadour music gave him the confidence but not the musical knowledge nor the voice to fully compose the work. Yeats recognized this early, telling Lady Gregory that when Pound sings 'it is like something on a very bad phonograph' (*Lett.* 543). Pound also lacked a keyboard yet attempted to notate the music himself and orchestrate the accompaniment. Pound's lack of musical theory and almost tone deaf ear made composition almost impossible. Yet he possessed a strong sense of rhythm – when composing poetry at the typewriter, he often hummed, sounding out the rhythm of the words – and enjoyed dancing, although his rhythm was often oppositional: the rhythm of individual words, for example, would be contrary to the rhythm of the structure of individual stanzas as in *Mauberley*.

These drawbacks did not stop Pound who wrote the one act opera, set in a brothel next to a cathedral, in several days working at break-neck speed. Using only the C major scale, he created a work of limited complexity without conventional harmony or structured melodies, one critic calling it 'nearly tuneless' (*SCh* 389). In striving for archaism, as Pound told Agnes Bedford, he sacrificed harmony, con-structing a work percussive, disjointed and seemingly arbitrary in character. Determined to push through with the work, despite Bedford's hesitancy, Pound told her 'RIEN that interferes with the words, or with the utmost possible clarity of impact of words on audience.' Even counterpoint 'would presumably bitch the words' and they were key, their linguistic rhythm shaping the music (*SL* 169). The orchestration is 'simply an emphasis on the consonantal and vowel sounds *of the words.*' he explained (in Bricknell 81). His attachment to the opera remained strong and it was in his hand when he went to visit Olga Rudge for the first time. When he read it to Cocteau, however, the poet/painter giggled the entire time, finding everything medieval comical (*SCh* 392).

The opera met with mixed if critical success, rarely being played, but after the 1926 premiere, Virgil Thomson offered praise: 'The music was not quite musician's music, though it may well be the finest poet's music since Thomas Campion' (Thomson 83). In the audience at this performance were Cocteau, Joyce, Eliot, Ford, and Hemingway. In a statement for the BBC which was preparing an adaptation for broadcast in 1931 with the subtitle 'A Melodrama,' Pound expressed his inten-tions. His aim, he declared, was '"to take the world's greatest poetry out of books, to put it on the air, to bring it to the ear of the people, even when they cannot understand it . . . . the meaning can be explained but the emotion and beauty cannot be explained"' (in Fisher 20).[1] While working on the opera in 1921, Pound was also writing Canto IV which focuses on myth, Vidal, Cavalcanti, song and imagist treatments of light.

Pound flourished in Paris, a city that encouraged his multiple interests which his dress reflected, adopting a large velvet beret and flowing tie 'of the Latin Quarter artist of the 1830's' according to Margaret Anderson. Ford described Pound in full Parisian flight:

Look at his slouch hat, his forked beard, his spectacles. And his extraordinary tie. His malacca cane certainly contained a sword-stick. What else could make you carry anything so out of date as a malacca cane . . . [at one point] Ezra dashed into the traffic, still waving his cane as if he had been Bertran de Born about to horsewhip Henry II of England.

(*Nightingale* 305, 288)

Sylvia Beach recorded a similar impression, referring to his outfit of a 'velvet jacket and the open-road shirt' as that 'of the English aesthete of the period. There was a touch of Whistler about him; his language, on the other hand, was Huckleberry Finn's' (Beach 26). At this time, Pound boasted not about his poetry but his carpentry. Swept up by the artistic *milieu* of the city, Pound even became – temporarily – a sculptor in the style of Brancusi. Ford's description of him at work was brief: 'Mr Pound fiercely struck blocks of granite with sledge hammers' (*Nightingale* 283).

One of Pound's favorite haunts was the salon of Natalie Barney, an American exile who lived in a mansion on the rue Jacob. Barney, a seductive lesbian, reputedly enticed some of the most beautiful women in Paris to her home with a neo-classical temple in the garden. Pound had corresponded with Barney for several years and when he and Dorothy first moved to Paris, Barney introduced him to Anatole France, André Gide, Paul Valery, Francis Picabia and Jean Cocteau. Soon, he was well connected: a photo from the opening of the Jockey Club shows Pound standing with Tzara, Man Ray and Cocteau. At a new year's party, he met Picasso. Visitors soon appeared: in the summer of 1921, Quinn came to Paris from New York. A picture from a second trip of 1923 shows Quinn standing in front of Pound's studio with Pound, Joyce and Ford Madox Ford. Margaret Anderson and Jane Heap of the

Little Review were early arrivals, eager publishers of *Ulysses*. Pound quickly arranged a meeting for them with Joyce.

Pound had been guiding the publication of *Ulysses* since 1917, telling Nora Joyce in September that year that the *Egoist* would be serializing the novel and that the *Little Review* would likely publish portions in America (*EP/JJ* 125–6, 129). Masterminding these publications, and the purchase of a portion of the manuscript by Quinn in New York, occupied Pound throughout his last years in London and early days in Paris as he praised Joyce's progress, worried about his getting paid and considered how the entire novel might be published. But he immediately recognized Joyce's achievement.

In turn, Joyce respected Pound's acumen, sending him episodes of the novel for more than three years for comment. This continued through the 'Circe' section of the novel up to 1921. The *Little Review* published thirteen portions from March 1918 until December 1920, before it was suppressed for printing supposedly obscene portions of 'Nausicaa.' The *Egoist* printed five sections before it was enjoined. Pound, incensed by America's suppression of the novel, began a series of criticisms and ridicules against the obscenity laws of the states, criticizing a judge's remark that free expression is acceptable in the classics because they are little read but not in popular literature. Nevertheless, in his letters to Joyce, Pound freely comments on changes to the text and its reception. Of 'Calypso' he candidly says 'certain things [are] simply bad writing...bad because you waste the violence. You use a stronger word than you need, and this is bad art, just as any needless superlative is bad art' (*EP/JJ* 131). Joyce did not always agree and frequently demanded that excised lines be restored. Pound, however, was carefully balancing standards of art with the need for free artistic expression.

To mark the important second edition of *A Portrait of the Artist* in March 1918, Pound wrote a column on Joyce in *The Future* perceiving the publication of the novel as a new phase of English publishing. The book is clearly literature and introduced a new style exhibiting 'the metallic cleanness of Joyce's phrasing,' although the power of Joyce's writing is in its scope – from fig seeds to Aquinas, from 'subjective beauty' to 'external shabbiness, squalor, and sordidness....' These are, he adds, 'the bass and treble of his method' (*EP/JJ* 134, 135). *Chamber Music*, also just republished, receives similar praise in the article which ends with admiration for the incomplete *Ulysses*, a work he describes as 'obscure, even obscene, as life itself is obscene in places' (*EP/JJ* 139). With Pound's direction, Harriet Shaw Weaver's finances and Sylvia

Beach's determination to publish all of *Ulysses*, Joyce found the champions he needed to see his work in print. When finally given the 'Circe' and 'Eumaeus' episodes to read, Pound wrote in April 1921, that 'Circe' was 'Magnificient, a new Inferno in full sail' and that 'Eumaeus' was 'enormous – megaloscrumptious-mastodonic' (*EP/JJ* 189; *SL* 166). But while he delighted in the publication of the novel in February 1922, Joyce began to think of Pound less as a poet/critic and more of an impresario. Valery Larbaud, critic and friend of Beach, became Joyce's official, public voice for the novel. Nevertheless, Joyce proudly told his English patron, Weaver, that he began *Ulysses* on 1 March 1914, Frank Budgen's birthday, and ended it on 30 October 1921, Pound's. But while authority of interpretation rested with Larbaud and later Budgen, authority of publication remained Pound's.

By December 1921, Pound finally moved to a ground-floor studio at the rear of 70 *bis*, rue Notre Dame des Champs in Montparnasse approached via a quiet courtyard populated with a few trees and surrounded by peeling, drab stucco walls. After retrieving books, Gaudier-Brzeska sculptures and even his fencing foils from London, Pound and Dorothy settled in, Pound undertaking the construction of two tables (painted red) and several armchairs with canvas seats. From Holland Place Chambers he brought his strangely shaped triangular typing table designed to fit its unusual London layout.

A month before, Eliot stopped in Paris on his way to Lausanne for a rest cure and showed Pound a long poem he had been working on for most of the year. Originally titled 'He Do the Police in Different Voices,' by November 1921, it was called *The Waste Land*. Pound likely offered some criticism of the work which Eliot took with him and then revised, adding the section 'What the Thunder Said.' Leaving a revised draft of what he thought was the finished poem with Pound on his return, Eliot continued on to London. Pound now got to work editing the typescript. In a letter of January 1922, Pound told Eliot it was much improved but still wanted cuts. The 19 page length was more than enough; don't prolong it with three more pages, he advised (*SL* 169). A series of short poems at the end must be placed at the beginning if Eliot wanted to keep them and the work had to end with the 'Shantih, shantih, shantih' passage. Excised was a passage dealing with an Arctic shipwreck and the original opening of 'The Fire Sermon,' a pastiche of *The Rape of the Lock* in couplets. In another section of the poem, Pound dismembered Eliot's regular, Gautier-style quatrains, pruning images and statements that softened juxtaposition and fragment. Impersonation was gone as he replaced a diffuse narrative with isolated lines displaying what Pound had earlier labeled in his writing about Imagism, the 'Ideogrammic Method.'

Eliot submitted the terse, final work to *The Dial* where it received the annual *Dial* award of $2000, although Eliot felt the award should have gone to Pound. The recovery of the typescript, made public in 1968, and published with Pound's excisions and criticism in 1971, offers documented proof of Pound's role and why Eliot inscribed the Boni & Liveright first edition to Pound with 'for E.P./ miglior fabbro/ from T.S.E./ Jan. 1923.' The Italian phrase, 'the better craftsman,' alludes to Dante's praise of Arnaut Daniel in Canto 26 of *Purgatorio*. Pound had used the tag as the title for his chapter on Arnaut in *The Spirit of Romance*. The achievement of *The Waste Land*, he told Quinn, was 'about enough ... to make the rest of us shut up shop' – but of course, the determined Pound did not: 'knocked out another Canto (not in the least *à la Eliot*, or connected with "modern life")' he shortly told Quinn (*EP/JQ* 206). He hadn't done so for two years. He referred to it as the VIIIth Canto in 1922, but it was eventually renumbered the second.

Pound's complex relationship with Dante is worth a pause. He studied his poetry in university and early commentators of *The Cantos* sought easy parallels between the three part structure of the *Divine Comedy* and Pound's progress through hell, purgatory and, finally, a form of paradise. Yeats and even Eliot were early readers eager to link the *Commedia* and *The Cantos* stressing Pound's quest 'to make Cosmos' (CXVI 815). And early fragments from 1906–7 show Pound's shift from the high song of Whitman to a more fragmented, Dantesque voice (Moody 67).

Pound's 1909 lectures in London, which became *The Spirit of Romance*, reflect his knowledge of Dante in his reading of *La Vita Nuova* and *The Divine Comedy*. In further essays, reviews and talks, Dante was present but in Pound's orbit Dante was closer to the *avant garde* rather than Renaissance writers. Initially, *The Cantos* reflect the structural journey of Dante, Pound's 1928 essay 'Medievalism' an evocation of a Dantescan 'world of moving energies' (*LE* 153–4) which the first thirty Cantos illustrate. The clarity of image, precise terminology and unity of thought and object, all embodied by Dante, also became Pound's goals (*LE* 215). Admiration of Dante's language increased throughout Pound's career; in *Guide to Kulchur*, for example, he noted that Dante's words 'grow ever more luminous as one's own experience grows' (*GK* 317). Dante remained Pound's guide to ethics, economics and paradise.

The events of the 1940's, beginning with the war, however, established a contested view of Dante for Pound which Pound's earlier work on

Cavalcanti anticipated. An alternative to Dante, Cavalcanti provided a counter weight through what Pound believed to be his modernity: 'the tone of his mind is infinitely more "modern" than Dante's;' he is dangerous to 'the peace of the medieval mind' he added (*LE* 159). There is a gulf between the two, Cavalcanti willing to challenge and be sceptical, Dante willing 'to take on any sort of holy and orthodox furniture' (*LE* 159).

Cantos 72 and 73 illustrate the contrast. Canto 72 is written in language and metre imitative of the *Commedia* and incorporates the use of a Dantesque vision, while Canto 73 has Cavalcanti appearing in person and is drafted in short lines and rhymes that echo Cavalcanti's style. If Pound intended to write an analogue to the *Commedia* as he began *The Cantos*, that altered as his own experiences and encounter with history affected his poetic outlook. All of Dante, especially the *Convivio*, a work crucial to the development of Dante's philosophical thinking, became the model for Pound's project (see Dasenbrock). Dante furthermore becomes a political not visionary thinker for Pound as seen in Canto XCIII. Paradise becomes a civic not theological construct as Pound drops the Dantean sense of convergence or sequential order in the late cantos, replacing it with fragments that do not cohere. Pound, through this move, manages to gain a paradise without confession. Too simple is the view of a Dantean ascent in *The Cantos*; for Pound it is more complex. Pound's requirement for paradise is humanity.

In 1932, Pound wrote that for forty years he schooled himself 'to write an epic poem which begins "In the Dark Forest" crosses the Purgatory of human error, and ends in the light, and "fra i maestri di color che sanno"' (in Dasenbrock 212). Roughly translated, the Italian reads 'master of those that cut apart, dissect and divide' (*GK* 343). Dante took the fragments of his culture and put them back in order. Pound tried to do the same – seeking a form 'elastic enough to take the necessary material' (*RP* 222). But as his career and work evolved, Pound questioned his ability to achieve Dante's vision: 'it is difficult to write a paradiso when all the superficial indications are that you ought to write an apocalypse. It is obviously much easier to find inhabitants for an inferno or even a purgatorio' (*RP* 241). The times did not permit paradise:

I was not following the three divisions of the *Divine Comedy* exactly. One can't follow the Dantesquan cosmos in an age of experiment. But I have made the division between people dominated by emotion, people struggling upwards, and those who have some part of the divine vision.

(*RP* 242).

A postscript to the Pound-Dante connection, however, is Pound's impact on later Italian poets and translators of the Italian poet.[2] At this moment, March/April 1922, Pound, jealous of Eliot's recognition and ability to find money for a new review, the *Criterion*, nevertheless informed Eliot of a plan to free him from his job at Lloyd's Bank and allow him to devote himself to writing full-time. The scheme called for thirty donors to guarantee Eliot £10 per year for life or as long as he would need. Natalie Barney named the plan 'Bel Esprit' and Pound had circulars printed, with an image of the Greek temple in Barney's courtyard on the cover, to announce it. Hemingway campaigned for the project which collapsed when Eliot refused to take the money. Nevertheless, Hemingway dreamt that he and Pound freed Eliot who had come to live in the temple where he and Pound would regularly visit to crown Eliot with a laurel 'any time Ezra had gone over the manuscript or the proofs of another big poem like *The Waste Land*' (*AMF* 112). Ironically, Hemingway lost the money he collected betting at the steeplechase at Enghien. Nonetheless, these and other activities justified Hemingway's claim that 'Ezra was the most generous writer I have ever known and the most disinterested. . . . He worried about everyone' (*AMF* 110). But it was time for Pound to return to *The Cantos*.

Between 1917 and 1919, Pound had done little work on his epic, but by 1919 he discovered the right tack when he wrote Canto IV. Up until then, the original 'Three Cantos' displayed a kind of faith in a Sordello-type narrator who could seemingly hold together the disparate allusions, references, mythical elements and literary history that Pound felt should be the material of the poem. But in a pattern that would characterize his career, Pound's later work reinterpreted his former, sometimes repudiating what he had done or his treatment of earlier material. Pound's *Cantos*, in their sequence, actually interrogate themselves. The orderly structure of *The Divine Comedy* could not accommodate the torsions and fragments of history Pound confronted which disrupted narrative unity. Modernist models limited the form of the work, while 'making language look like pictures' (part of the Futurist agenda) became unworkable (Albright 61). Meaning could not be seen; it had to be read and Pound began to think that a central consciousness, animating and integrating with various narratives in the text, would be the answer. But his dislocative style quickly found such a controlling element too limiting. 'You had one whole man?' the narrator asks Browning in 'Three Cantos I?' 'I have many fragments' worth no less, he replies (*Per* 230). Only in his dialogue 'Aux Etuves de Wiesbaden' (1918) did Pound find a voice and posture that made sense. The figure of Poggio admits that 'I myself am a rag-bag, a mass of sights and citations, but I will not beat down life for the sake of a model' (*PD* 102). The challenge was to avoid chaos, while not restricting the work to a single persona who could never be sufficiently inclusive.

Pound's aesthetic at this time was shifting, no longer centering on the artist writing to sustain an audience but to the artist sustaining a voice: 'The question of survival of personality,' more metaphysical than ethical, replaced the artist's need to refashion society. Pound joined this to a revivified interest in the possibility of sustaining a long poem in an age that seemed to have little time for literature (*EPCP* IV: 187). Canto IV provided a way to move forward, essentially offering a flat field where events, allusions and the poet co-exist on the same plane. And providing the means for Pound to reshape his poem is the Orient, both the world of Noh theatre and that of *Cathay*. In theatre without drama, Noh, Pound located a form that dismantled time and space, allowing distant images to unite. In Canto IV, Pound learned how to take a series of disparate narratives, ranging from the story of Baucis and Philemon to Actaeon and Peire Vidal, and turn them into a shape that establishes a single, unified action that is beyond time and space. Glint by glint, Pound reassembles the shards of the mythical and historical past to splice together a new whole.

Canto IV provided a new beginning for Pound who in December of 1919 – the canto appeared in October – wrote Cantos V–VII, although they were not published until 1921. Canto V also had a new element: a secondary conjurer to do his (Pound's) summoning so that in the finished and revised set of *A Draft of XVI Cantos* (1925), Tiresias's ghost is raised up by Odysseus who is raised up by Homer, who is raised up by Andreas Divus, who is raised up by Pound. The Florentine historian, BenedettoVarchi, plays the role of 'magus' in Canto V which marks a break with Canto IV which had focused on mythic metamorphosis. Canto V enters history with the anxieties and uncertainties of events, while elaborating voices other than the poet's. Pound will enlarge this device through the remainder of the poem which will prove to be one of its most striking qualities. The troubadour poet Bernart de Ventadour's song and voice fill Canto V confirming not only the Italian meaning of canto, song, but embodying Pound's desire to reactivate voice through music. By Canto VII, however, this has dissolved, the sounds of the old

men in the canto transformed into a kind of muttering: 'Dry casques
of departed locusts/ speaking a shell of speech.... The words rattle'
(VII/26–7). But *The Cantos* overall might be thought of as the re-anima-
tion of voice transmitted from a series of unexpected sources. 'Ghosts
move about me/ Patched with histories' as Pound wrote in 'Three
Cantos' (*Per* 229).

Pound did not yet have an overall structure for *The Cantos*, only
fragments of an approach but by the summer of 1922 a working plan
emerged with Homer, not Browning, as his guide. This change was
partly inspired by Joyce's use of the classical poet for his novel. Pound's
'Paris Letter' of June 1922 summarizes how Joyce incorporates Homer
and how Joyce is the successor to Flaubert; such an application of the
mythic to the modern, in turn, sets the foundation for the revised
Cantos (*EP/JJ* 194–200). Not only does Pound praise the use of dialect in
the essay, allowing Joyce to enter the minds of his characters more
rapidly and directly, but it allows for a multiple range of voices that
comes to dominate his and Pound's work. Size also matters: in its scope,
Ulysses demonstrates how prose fiction successfully becomes epic in
range, subject matter and language.

But other interests of Pound's competed with writing more cantos:
completing *Mauberley*, translating Remy de Gourmont's *Physique de
l'amour*, finishing his opera *Villon*, continuing with the 'Paris Letter'
series for *The Dial*, promoting *Ulysses*, confronting George Bernard
Shaw (over his failure to subscribe to the edition) and publishing essays
on Major Douglas' Social Credit. However, reading Joyce, editing Eliot
and re-reading Flaubert (1922 was the centenary of his birth and Pound
published several essays on him) stimulated Pound to restart his long
poem. In August 1921, for example, Cantos V, VI and VII appeared in
The Dial and then in his *Poems 1918–1921* edited by Eliot.

Working with Joyce and Eliot, while reconsidering the work of
Flaubert, not only changed the future of *The Cantos* but Pound's
relationship to cantos already written. *The Waste Land*, indeed, might
be said to follow Cantos V–VII's 'ragged textual surfaces imprinted with
voices juxtaposed,' although its piecemeal construction predates, or at
least coincides with, Pound's writing (Albright 69). Both works lack
a coordinating sensibility, yet search for an authentic voice through
history and myth to rectify the modern world. The polyvocal style of
the entire poem was also the style of Pound speaking, as Iris Barry,
among others, recorded: Pound talked in a series of accents with
'strange cries and catcalls, the whole very oddly inflected, with dramatic
pauses and *diminuendos*' (Barry 159).

But in the Cantos of 1922, then numbered VIII–XII but renumbered in 1925 as II and VIII–XI, two sustained voices emerged: Acoetes in renumbered II and Sigismundo Malatesta in VIII–XI. Pound was breaking away from *The Waste Land* and history became his key – but not before he fully treated myth. Borrowing a tale from Ovid, the 1922 Canto VIII describes Dionysus' kidnap and deposit on a ship piloted by Acoetes who narrates the strange metamorphosis that takes place on their journey to Naxos during an attempted hijack when Dionysus reveals his powers. Pound wrote the canto while reading *Ulysses* in book form and it may have influenced his use of humor in this section. So pleased with the canto was Pound that he renumbered it and moved it from VIIIth to IInd place. He also considered starting the entire poem with Acoetes narrating his travels with Dionysus. Pound briefly thought the entire poem might be a single voyage and throughout *The Cantos* sailors noticeably dominate: Odysseus, Acoetes, the Honest Sailor (XII), Hanno the Navigator (XL). But he moved from water to land in the 1922 Cantos VIII–XI, the so-called Malatesta Cantos.

The 15th century ruler of Rimini and patron Sigismundo Malatesta (1417–68) fascinated Pound who spent three months visiting Italy in the spring/summer of 1922 studying his life and accomplisments. Malatesta's Tempio Malatestiano, actually the incomplete Church of San Francesco, designed by Leon Battista Alberti, and built as a monument to Malatesta and his mistress, Isotta (later his third wife), epitomized for Pound the fusion of Renaissance art and power. Originally a 13th century church built in accordance with Franciscan traditions, stressing a simple, spare style, Alberti transformed it into an architectural achievement, the first building to adapt the composition of the Roman triumphal arch to ecclesiastical architecture. A further innovation was the use of seven deeply arched niches divided by piers creating an austere yet harmonious rhythm along one side of the building. Alberti, furthermore, constructed a shell around the exterior of the older church. War and economics, however, prevented the building's completion (Rainey 10–14). Sigismundo could not afford it, although he did complete a magnificent tomb for Isotta. Nevertheless, the inscriptions and decorations that celebrate the building's sponsor, the interior sculptural decorations with neo-Platonic and Pythagorean allusions and the tomb of Isotta degli Atti all attest to the intricate, complicated and fascinating history of the space which absorbed Pound when he visited it in May 1922. The impact on Pound's work and imagination was profound, resulting in the first sustained and harmonious section of the poem, the Malatesta Cantos (VIII–XI).

One of the most intriguing elements of the Tempio for Pound was the interpretation of the Church as both a monument to Isotta and to paganism. The architectural mix of achievement and failure (the building, of course, remained incomplete) and discovery that in an exterior niche Malatesta interred the ashes of a neo-Platonist philosopher, Gemisthus Plethon, who helped to revive Greek learning and sought to synthesize Plato and Christianity, confirmed this. Malatesta, himself, was understood as both cultivated and treacherous and Pound studied his character in a 19th century biography written by C.E. Yriarte, concluding, however, that Malatesta was 'POLUMETIS,' many-minded, a Homeric epithet for the versatile Odysseus (IX/36). The Renaissance ruler became the first of many cultured but authoritative leaders Pound admired.

Significantly, the composition of the Malatesta Cantos, which would take ten months and require another visit to the site, became the 'decisive event of the Paris years for Pound's career as a writer' according to one critic (Rainey 27). The set of four cantos, written in an accessible, colloquial style, allowed Pound to crystallize his entire poem, while underscoring a change in his poetics. In the four cantos, he turns from Symbolism to a montage 'of the documentary surface upon which dislocated fragments are juxtaposed.' Pound discovers a new model: Dadaism, as his work resembles 'a flat surface as in a Cubist or early Dada collage, upon which verbal elements, fragmented images and truncated bits of narration . . . are brought into collision' (Perloff, *Poetics* 157, 181). Pound's reading of the layered history of the unfinished Tempio and the story of Sigismundo results in a new aesthetic. The most distinctive feature of the Malatesta Cantos is the conspicuous use of quotation from historical sources establishing an intertexuality that dislodges earlier forms of modernism.

In telling the story of Malatesta, which Pound studied in the Bibliothèque Nationale and in Rimini, he produces the most coherent and chronological sequence in the poem until the later Chinese Cantos (LII–LXI). This sequence is also one of the earliest cantos to include actual documents, as Pound allows history to speak directly to the reader juxtaposing the surface of documents and allowing them to speak. Mixing third person narrative with a first person plural, Pound annexes the voice of the subject as if it were his own:

> And we beat the papishes and fought
> them back through the tents . . .
> And it went on from dawn to sunset

And we broke them and took their baggage
and mille cinquecento cavalli

(XI/ 48)

However, Pound was also aware that he needed a figure of rebelliousness and energy: 'If I find he was TOO bloody quiet and orderly it will
ruin the canto. Which needs a certain boisterousness and disorder to
contrast with his [Malatesta's] constructive work' he explained to
Quinn (*EP/JQ* 217). But Pound sympathized with Malatesta, especially
when he outlined the conversation between the ruler and the Papal
librarian when Malatesta visited Rome to plan, perhaps, the murder of
Pope Paul II. When asked what they talked about, the librarian replied
'books, and fighting, and unusual intelligence, both in the ancients,
and in men of our own time;' this was clearly Pound's own agenda –
except for murder (*EP/JQ* 217). Pound wrote the Malatesta sequence
almost immediately after his opera, *Le Testament de Villon* and in some
ways it forms an opera without music. A contemporary of Villon,
Malatesta's life of action, heroics and art symbolizes a kind of action
and completeness Pound admired and would attempt to recognize in a
new set of heroes soon to appear in his poem: Confucius, Jefferson and
Mussolini.

Completing the Malatesta quartet in 1923, it soon appeared in Eliot's
new magazine, the *Criterion* in July as 'Cantos IX to XII of a Long Poem'
(although they are now numbered VIII to XI), Pound then quickly
finished the five cantos that followed, revised all the previously published cantos and assembled the whole into *A Draft of XVI Cantos*. But
Pound could not let the Tempio Malatestiano go: over 100 references to
events or personalities related to the Malatesta story appear in the
remaining cantos including the recently incorporated Cantos 72 and
73, the 'Italian Cantos' written in 1944.

By 1922, Pound realized that his project had outgrown its early form,
especially the 'Three Cantos' : 'up to now it has been mainly hash' he
wrote to Ford Madox Ford (*P/F* 63). But by the summer of 1923, he had
revised the beginning of his poem and wrote a series of new Cantos,
although they would not appear until *A Draft of XVI Cantos* in 1925.
Canto VI was substantially re-written, while Canto III of 'Three Cantos'
was reduced to the translation of Odysseus's descent into the underworld which became the new Canto I. The original Cantos I and II were
almost entirely eliminated. A letter to Felix Schelling, his former Shakespeare professor at the University of Pennsylvania, describes the revised
structure and energy: 'the first 11 cantos are preparation of the palette.

I *have to* get down all the colours or elements I want for the poem. Some perhaps too enigmatically and abbreviatedly. I hope, heaven help me, to bring them into some sort of design and architecture later' (*SL* 180). He also vigorously defends the didacticism of his work: 'a revelation is always didactic. Only the aesthetes since 1880 have pretended the contrary, and they aren't a very sturdy lot.' And as to the hell he might describe in his poem, he argues that 'if the poets don't make certain horrors appear horrible who will? All values ultimately come from our judicial sentences' (*SL* 180–81).

Soon, a shape for the early Cantos emerged: Canto I began with Homer, Canto II (the former Canto VIII) dealt with mythical meta-morphosis and Acoetes; III–IV, more myth; V–VII, the troubadours and the Middle Ages plus Eleanor of Aquitaine; VIII–XI, Malatesta and the Renaissance; Canto XII, a reprieve to the New World and honest sailors; Canto XIII detours briefly to China and Confucius in preparation for, or by contrast with, the Hell Cantos, XIV and XV, which display hell not as corrupt politicians or usury (two themes that will be excessive in later Cantos) but the degradation of language and the corruption of the printing press. This led to Canto XVI, the Purgatory of the Great War with its reminiscences of those who fought: Gaudier-Brzeska, T.E. Hulme and Wyndham Lewis, anticipating his much later recall of many past figures in *The Pisan Cantos*. In these early Cantos, what begins in myth ends in contemporary history, as Acoetes comes to Bayswater, the task Pound set for himself in a letter to Ford (*P/F* 67).

But another transition soon occurred. It was at Natalie Barney's salon in 1923 that Pound met Olga Rudge, the young violinist from Ohio. The night they met in Barney's Turkish drawing room following one of Olga's recitals, Pound entered with the soprano Raymonde Collignon on his arm (he had often taken to escorting women about Paris) and throughout 1921/22 had had an affair with Nancy Cunard, friend of Cocteau, Aragon and Janet Flanner. She would later found the Hours Press and publish *Draft of XXX Cantos* (Cunard felt Dorothy somewhat reserved and later said her classic looks were 'a beautiful picture that never came to life' [*O/E* 5]). At Barney's, Pound was struck by the dark haired, vibrant American with whom he discussed Théophile Gautier – she had attended his daughter's salon as a child – and the American composer and friend of Pound's, George Antheil who lived above Shakespeare and Company, Sylvia Beach's bookstore. A few days later, Pound visited Olga alone, arriving at her rue Chamfort apartment with the score of his opera. He was thirty-seven; she was ten years younger.

Pound first heard Olga Rudge play in London at the end of 1920 but was indifferent to her music and charms. She was unaware of him until she gave a 1923 Paris recital and he caught her attention in the concert hall thinking that in his brown velvet jacket he must have been a painter. After they met, a friendship quickly developed starting with an interest in Antheil and compositions for the violin. At Pound's urging, Antheil soon wrote two violin sonatas for Olga. Admiringly, she wrote that Pound 'didn't talk about things – He wanted something *done*' (*SCh* 433). Unlike the remote Dorothy, Olga possessed an 'Irish adrenal personality' according to Antheil (*SCh* 434). Born in Youngstown, Ohio, she was taken to London at nine months by her independently minded mother and brought up in Catholic schools in Paris and London. She began a career as a solo violinist, performing in London for the first time at twenty-one. A confident conversationalist with a strong understanding of music, her energy and good looks appealed to Pound and a difficult romance began that lasted a lifetime despite Pound's marriage to Dorothy.

Pound's absorption with music at this time was complete. A December 1923 recital by Olga and Antheil contained two contributions by Pound: his transcription of a 12th century piece for an unaccompanied violin, a work he found in the Ambrosian Library in Milan in 1911, and an original composition of his, 'Sujet pour Violon (resineux).' At a May 1924 recital in London, Olga and Antheil played Pound's 'Fiddle Music, First Suite.' In July that year in Paris, a fanfare by Pound was performed. and one evening in Montparnasse, Pound noisily accompanied Antheil on percussion for a 'Sonata for Drum and Piano' (*SCh* 435). He also wanted his opera improved and believed that if Antheil added proper time signatures, as well as some enigmatic notations, this would occur. To entice Antheil and aggravate some noisy tenants above his Paris studio, Pound obtained a piano and encouraged Antheil to practice in his rooms. At the same time, Pound continued his loud hammering at stone which he called sculpting.

But in spite of his composing, editing, promoting, performing and writing, Pound was becoming disenchanted with Paris. He increasingly felt left out, perhaps because he felt Parisian artistic circles no longer took him seriously, or perhaps because he felt there were too many cliques, none of which he started. Individual friendships with Cocteau, Brancusi, Léger, Breton or Aragon helped but he was not a part of Gertrude Stein's circle, nor even the one that circulated around Sylvia Beach and Adrienne Monnier. Unlike Joyce, who was caught up in the artistic excitement of Paris, exuberantly telling his brother Stanislaus that Odysseus is 'very much in the air here' and then listing a series of new works by Anatole France, Fauré, Giraudoux and Apollinaire that dealt with Homeric figures or themes, Pound found no similar enthusiasm or confirmation of his work (*P/J* 185). He felt neglected.

At the same time, Pound found economics more important than aesthetics as he promoted Major Douglas's ideas of Social Credit in *The Dial* and elsewhere. His reputation among American writers in Paris became ambiguous, a figure more admired than read. Hemingway and e.e. cummings remained friends, but his stature altered. In 1922, Pound felt he was the one fixed point in the *mêlée* of artistic life, but by 1924 he had been surpassed (*EP/JQ* 216). A dream Joyce had in 1922 in which Pound appeared as an American journalist presaged the role Pound himself was beginning to fulfill: no more than a reporter for modernism. He sought to refute this and thought he could do so if he removed himself from the 'scene,' giving up his role as impresario and freeing himself from the responsibilities of promoting he felt Paris imposed on him (*EP/JJ* 191). He would also be able to concentrate on his own work.

Pound's quick-tempered manner did not help, his corrosive behavior offending many. 'Inflammable Ezra' Iris Barry called him in her 1931 reminiscence (Barry 171). Pound could be difficult and irascible and freely offered his unsympathetic opinions: 'glittering Paris' soon became 'everyman's Paris. Picabia gone to hell, Brancusi universally recognized by the cognoscenti. Cocteau in *Vogue* and finally Léger's photo in *Vanity Fair*' (Barry: 171; Ackroyd 69). The *avant garde* and the elite character of Paris had dissipated and with it, its artistic importance for Pound. Paris was no longer special and no longer cultivated a distinctiveness. With this attitude, it was no wonder that the new and younger French poets, including the Surrealists, ignored Pound. Ford Madox Ford's launch of the *Transatlantic Review* occupied him briefly but by October 1924, he was ready for change.

Recovering from appendicitis, Pound went with Dorothy to Rapallo, south of Genoa, in February 1924. They did not stay long, moving on to Assisi and Perugia. That spring he was back in Paris and saw a great deal of Olga, while Dorothy went to England. When Dorothy returned in October, they left almost immediately for Italy, a decision taken as much to remove Pound from Olga as to meet his wish to be free of Paris. The first goal, however, failed: Olga and Pound would soon be together.

Rapallo was again their first stop in the fall of 1924 but this time Pound had his essentials: 'racquet, typewriter, bassoon;' only his clavichord was missing (*SCh* 438). He spent his 39th birthday in the relaxed atmosphere of the seaside town of sun-whitened buildings on the gulf of Tigullio. But by December, the restless couple moved on to Palermo in Sicily, wondering if that might be their new home but they opted for Rapallo where they returned by February 1925 and selected an apartment on the top floor of a six-story, seafront building with a terrace that overlooked the promenade. Enhancing the beautiful setting were mountains covered with woods, vines and olives, rising steeply from the edge of the sea. Near the summit of one, Pound would later lease the upper floor of a house in the village of Sant'Ambrogio for Olga. As a guide book from the period celebrated, the bay, city and surrounding hamlets appear 'in perfect perspective, but almost as if there was no atmosphere to lend to distance a softening veil' (*Rapallo* 113).

Pound and Dorothy ate out daily, Dorothy's income the main source of their finances. In his study in the apartment Pound invented what he called his active filing system, a network of strings from which hung envelopes, manuscripts, pens, scissors and a pair of pince-nez. Dorothy's studio was in another room (*SCh* 440). When he did acquire some funds, Pound often passed them on to other, more needy writers who in 1931 included Ford Madox Ford. When Pound received the annual *Dial* award of $2000 in January 1928 (Marianne Moore was then editor of the magazine), he immediately invested the money and gave away the interest.

At the time Pound became upset with Paris, he became more fascinated by economics. 'The life of the mind doesn't stay in one department fixedly' he told D.G. Bridson: 'after 1924 it wasn't in literature. It was in thinking about civic order, and nobody was doing any of that' (Bridson 170). Yet Pound took little interest in the 1926 copyright controversy over the pirated printing of *Ulysses* by Samuel Roth in New York, appearing in the magazine *Two Worlds Monthly*. He even refused to sign a letter of protest, despite signatures from Eliot, Yeats, and Wyndham Lewis. Joyce, he believed, was creating too much fuss about a particular case; energies should be concentrated on changing the entire copyright law to prevent all piracies he thought. And when Joyce sent to Pound some chapters from 'Work in Progress,' later to be named *Finnegans Wake*, he was dismissive, as he was of some poems Joyce had written and which would appear in *Pomes Penyeach*. The breech between the two was never repaired, Joyce expressing criticism when he told Harriet Shaw Weaver that Pound 'makes brilliant discoveries and howling blunders' (*EP/JJ* 229).

Soon, however, a complicated personal life began to entangle Pound. Olga, who was in Venice at a conservatory in October 1924 when

Pound left Paris for Italy, invited Pound to join her but he declined, largely because his mother-in-law was visiting in Rapallo. A month later, they did meet in Genoa with Olga then going on to London where she likely realized that she was pregnant. This was not entirely a surprise: as early as 1923, she had written in her notebook that she 'would like a child by EP' partly because after nearly ten years of marriage, it was clear that his wife did not want children (*O/E* 56). Once Pound had some assurances that the child would be cared for and possess some financial security, he agreed. As the time for the birth grew closer, Olga moved from Rome to Sirmione and then on to Bressanone (Brixen), a small town in the Italian Tyrol near the Brenner Pass where on 9 July 1925 she gave birth to a daughter named Maria Rudge, the father listed as Arthur Rudge, Olga's deceased brother, to avoid any embarrassment. Pound was with her at the time of the birth (*SCh* 448). But because of Olga's unsure life as a concert violinist, unmarried state, and belief that the child would be healthier if she stayed at one location, the baby was to be brought up by a farm family in Gais. By August, Olga went to Florence and, by November, after a visit with her daughter, she prepared for a concert in Paris. In the interim, Pound was sending Olga portions of *The Cantos* for comment and criticism.

During this period, Dorothy went to Cairo, sailing from Genoa in mid-December 1925 and not returning until 1 March 1926. Olga took her place and it was she who was there when T.S. Eliot arrived for a short visit and she who went down to see Mussolini when he spoke in Rapallo. Pound avoided him, 'not interested enough to leave his desk and go down to see the procession' (*O/E* 64). Earlier, while awaiting the birth of her child, Olga sent Pound a clipping about Mussolini who had captured Rome in the bloodless coup of 1922 and had installed a new government. Pound approved of the new leader (*O/E* 58) and this would be the beginning of long admiration of il Duce whom Pound would briefly meet in January1933, which would feature strongly in Canto XLI. Soon, Olga herself would meet and perform for Mussolini.

In June 1926, Pound and Dorothy, joined Olga in Paris for the premiere of Antheil's *Ballet Mécanique*, a remarkable orchestral work involving eight grand pianos, several electric bells and two airplane propellers. The audience was uproarious and divided into two groups: supporters and opponents. Yelling, punching and pushing occurred in the hall until the propellers drowned out the sounds and blew the wig off the head of a man sitting next to Joyce's friend Stuart Gilbert.[3] Ten days later Pound premiered his own *avant garde* work, *Le Testament de Villon*. Some three hundred attended the ornate Salle Pleyel for the expanded concert version which included Olga on violin and a five foot *cornet de dessus* (medieval horn). Brancusi, Joyce, Hemingway, Djuna Barnes, Robert McAlmon and Eliot attended. To Agnes Bedford, Pound reported that 'it went fairly well: no riots or departures' (*O/E* 66, 67). After another performance of the opera in July, the Pounds stayed on in Paris. Dorothy was expecting and wanted to have the child at the American Hospital. The father was Egyptian; after fourteen years of marriage, the thirty-nine year old Dorothy had decided to become pregnant. On 10 September 1926, Hemingway, not Pound, accompanied her to the hospital, although Pound went the next day to sign the birth certificate identifying himself as the father. Afterwards, he wrote to his parents to report that a male had arrived. They named him Omar but he was taken almost immediately by Dorothy to London to be brought up by her mother, although Dorothy would remain with him until the following autumn when she returned to Rapallo. She would then visit her son every summer, although Pound would not see the boy until he was twelve years old. He visited his daughter frequently in Gais, however, starting in November 1926. Alluding to these complicated arrangements, Pound wrote to his parents that 'life is stranger than fiction, and imagination always gets left behind' (*O/E* 69).

Olga performed throughout 1927, establishing a reputation as the leading interpreter of Antheil's work, as well as that of Vivaldi. In Rome at a reception at the American Embassy in February, she met the *New York Herald*'s Rome correspondent who arranged a private performance by her for Mussolini at his residence. On the 19 of February, Olga performed Beethoven's *Romanza*, Mozart's Sonata opus 15 and a Veracini sonata. Mussolini complemented her on her musical feeling, and displayed a large assortment of violin music on his desk, along with five carefully arranged violins according to a report in the *Herald*. In conversation, Mussolini and Olga agreed on the singular importance of Vivaldi (*O/E* 71). Olga's international reputation was growing and she was soon invited to play at the art critic Bernard Berenson's Villa I Tatti and to give a recital at the estate of Gabriele d'Annunzio.

In the midst of these developments, Pound's parents decided to visit Rapallo in the fall of 1928 and, to everyone's surprise, decided to stay. They wanted to be closer to their only child and the extroverted Homer, who had his pension from the US Mint to support them, found Rapallo pleasing. His wife, somewhat aloof, did not. During their first Christmas in Rapallo, Pound revealed to his father that he had a four-year-old daughter. Pound reported to Olga that his father was 'duly and properly pleased at nooz of his granddaugher,' although they both agreed that

Pound's mother was not ready for such information (*O/E* 90). Pound, at this time, did not identify the mother of his daughter. Olga came to Rapallo from Paris after Christmas and met Yeats then vacationing there. That same year, Olga gave up her Paris apartment and moved to the 'hidden nest' just off the Dorsoduro at 252 calle Querini in Venice, mentioned by Pound in Canto LXXVI. Her father purchased the small house in which Pound would later find refuge.

By early 1930, however, Pound was finding the relationship with Olga difficult and was, himself, becoming lethargic and depressed. Olga was similarly upset, realizing that she would have to bring up her daughter alone, while maintaining an active concert career largely because her father's allowance had to be curtailed because of business reversals in Ohio caused by the Depression. Despair overcame her, which Pound tried to counter by convincing her of his love even if they spent little time together. As the art critic Adrian Stokes, one of Pound's followers, told her, 'You are necessary to Ezra, of that I am certain. You've only got to hold on' (*O/E* 93). Yet, she was too proud to accept any money from Pound except for what he contributed to the upbringing of their daughter. When Olga visited Rapallo in January 1930, Pound located a small cottage for her above the bay in the village of Sant'Ambrogio. He rented the top floor for her and it would remain his second home, overlooking the sea, until he was arrested in 1945. She could descend the footpath (*salita*) to Rapallo and be with Pound in less than an hour.

Rapallo at this time had a circle of English and European writers including Max Beerbohm, the Nobel Prize winner Gerhart Hauptmann, Yeats and, for a short time, Peggy Guggenheim. Basil Bunting, another young disciple of Pound's, visited, as well as Louis Zukofsky, American poet, and James Laughlin, later to become Pound's American publisher. Society was removed from the troubling economic and political issues of the day, although Pound was also isolated from the active literary circles of Paris, London or even Rome. For Olga, who did not enjoy nor participate in this crowd, Pound set her a literary task: translating Cocteau's *Mystère Laïc*, a secular mystery play. Pound was well-ensconced in Rapallo in the thirties and recognized with affection as 'Il Signor Poeta,' partly because he often prowled the promenade in a swirling cape and wide-brimmed sombrero, with yellow scarf and cane, and partly because he had had Gaudier-Brezska's head of himself shipped from Violet Hunt's front garden at Campden Hill to him in Rapallo. Too cumbersome at first to lug up the six flights of stairs to his apartment, it for some time overlooked the entrance of the Albergo Rapallo, although it later made its way up to the terrace to reign outside his study window.

When not climbing the path to Sant'Ambrogio, dining with friends or playing tennis, Pound was writing – not only new cantos, but translating and editing. Shortly after his arrival in Rapallo, he prepared what was to be his 'Collected Poems,' excluding *The Cantos*. It quickly became a selection, however, as he discarded material he thought inferior, although he retained a good deal of poetry from his earliest volumes. He re-used the title *Personae* for the collection which appeared in December 1926. In 1928 his translation of the Confucian *Ta Hio or The Great Learning* appeared, as well as *A Draft of The Cantos 17–27* published in a deluxe edition by John Rodker in London with illuminated initials by Gladys Hynes. In November that year, his *Selected Poems*, edited by T.S. Eliot, appeared in London. One of his more interesting undertaking was the editing of his own magazine, which lasted only four issues, *The Exile*.

A venue for his political and social views, *The Exile* (1927–28) was entirely Pound's: he was editor, publisher and backer. However, the contents was uneven: a novella by John Rodker, verse by Cheever Dunning and a confession by a woman who turned out to be by a literary hack from Chicago. Many of the items were written by Pound. However, 'Poem Beginning "The"' by the young American poet, Louis Zukofsky, appearing in issue number three, warranted attention as did Yeats's 'Sailing to Byzantium' (#3) and Williams's 'The Descent of Winter' (#4). Throughout the four issues, Pound was also making increasingly more reckless statements on public issues and American politics. His interest in America was unusual given that he expressed little concern for US domestic matters for almost two decades. But now, Prohibition, passports, politicians and presidents all came under fire. Additionally, Pound began to link Mussolini and Lenin in *The Exile*, writing in issue number one that the fascist and Russian revolutions were equally important phenomena. In the final issue, Pound celebrated not Lenin's style but his 'new medium, a sort of expression half-way between writing and action' (*Exile* 4: 6). This, too, became Pound's goal. When his letters and articles began to appear in the communist *New Masses*, Pound was identified as '"the leader of the most vital wing of the younger American writers. He formulates the unformed political creed in their minds"' (Redman 73).

But not everyone agreed nor was happy with Pound's European bias. In his 1928 'Open Letter to Ezra Pound and Other "Exiles"' in *transition*, the critic Matthew Josephson berated Pound for his neglect of America and its cultural progress. With a touch of cynicism, Josephson wrote:

> Keeping in mind your 'old world views,' perhaps you had best return to your Cantos, with their odd mixture of classical and modern tags? Was this not the best of you?...Then return, to America, whom you long for, no doubt in the jealous way of lovers! Return!
>
> (Josephson 101–2)

Pound, of course, dismissed the challenge.

Pound's attraction to politics soon affected his poetics. Rather than concentrate on style or rhythm, content became his new concern. In a letter of December 1926, he dramatized this need: 'the lasting vitality of SUBJECT, and yet again subject...Hell yes, the rhythm has to be, but it must be the content; it must be so much the content' (*SCh* 459). But it was political not literary content that began to dominate his thinking and writing. Some of his friends tried to advise him otherwise. Richard Aldington, for example, told him to reissue his collected poems, produce some new work and stop engaging in polemics: 'you manage to hit yourself and your friends more than your adversaries when you wield your Excalibur. Leave the polemics to Tom Eliot, who has a genius for it' (Aldington, *Auto in Letters* 80–1).

Social Credit and the work of Major C.H. Douglas were the principal sources of Pound's new politics. From his early acquaintance of Douglas at the offices of Orage's the *New Age* and subsequent readings of Douglas's works, Pound became convinced that Social Credit remedied the exploitation of prices, people and economic damage occurring in Europe. Opposition to the gold standard and banks was endemic to Social Credit and Pound soon lobbied against both. The arbitrary nature of credit also infuriated Pound. The foundation was the belief that credit had a social, not private, base and that the individual should determine the economic direction of his society. Financial control should be taken out of the hands of the bankers into that of the community. The basis of economic reform is in the state but rather than borrow money to re-establish employment, one must reform or revalue the state's currency. The first edition of *Social Credit* (1924) was read and re-read by Pound who shared with Douglas a conspiracy theory of banking. and hope in a 'Just Price' theory for goods. Douglas also believed that artists or creators should be freed in society from having to contribute to it economically. This had extraordinary appeal for Pound who increasingly began to use his poetry and prose to discharge these ideas.

During his first five years in Rapallo, Pound also re-considered the structure of *The Cantos*, writing his father just before he arrived that the eventual shape of the poem would be 'rather like, or unlike subject and response and counter subject in fugue:

A. A. Live man goes down into world of Dead
C. B. The 'repeat in history'
B. C. The 'magic moment' or moment of metamorphosis

(*SL* 210)

In his short work, *A Packet for Ezra Pound*, Yeats contradicted this view, stating that Pound 'is not trying to create forms because he believes, like so many of his contemporaries, that old forms are dead, so much as a new style, a new man' (in Ackroyd 74). Unsure and resistant to a strict structure or form, Pound continued to label his later volumes of the poem *A Draft of the Cantos 17–27* (1928) and then *A Draft of XXX Cantos* (1930) suggesting their unfinished state.

Pound's 'tale of the tribe,' however, was taking shape and the appearance of Cantos I–XVI in 1925, in the deluxe edition printed in Paris by William Bird's Three Mountains Press with large initials designed by Henry Strater, marked the poem's formal entrance into hands of readers (*SL* 294; *GK* 194). As he continued – writing the next seven Cantos by March 1925, although they would not be published until 1928 – Pound shifted imagery and theme. Venice begins to play a role as soon as Canto XVII, appearing as an elegant world of artifice not Paradise. But after the Purgatory of XVI, the search for Paradise emerges, continuing until Canto XXIII. Economics and the exploitation of people by industrialists and arms manufacturers also begin to appear as subjects.. The life of Niccolò d'Este looms large, starting in Canto XX. Niccolò d'Este, a Renaissance contemporary of Malatesta, had his wife and illegitimate son murdered when he found they were sleeping together. In a delirium after their deaths, d'Este mixes past tales of beautiful wives running off with men as Helen of Troy and others suddenly appear. d'Este's travels through the Mediterranean form part of Cantos XXIV–XXVII with Venice and elements of the seacoast surrounding Rapallo emerging in the idealized Mediterranean landscape of the poem.

Between 1927 and 1928, Pound offered more explanations of his work in an effort to understand it better himself. In 1927 he admitted to his father that he was 'afraid the whole damn poem is rather obscure' and then presented his fugual structure (*SL* 210). But the poem did not exactly fit this form, since, among other things, it lacked the required set of arranged, carefully organized, overlapping notes or themes. But in February 1928, Pound persisted in explaining the work in fugual terms, which Yeats adjusted to other comments he remembered by Pound:

> There will be no plot, no chronicle of events, no logic of discourse, but two themes, the Descent into Hades from Homer, a Metamorphosis from Ovid, and mixed with these, mediaeval or modern historical characters.

Yeats then provided sets of letters in fugual form Pound had scribbled on the back of an envelope, the entire structure 'set whirling together' (*AV* 3–5).

The description stuck but Pound objected, complaining of the wasted ink spent on his explanation. But if he rejected his own fugal suggestions, Pound began more and more to rely on music for the poem, Canto XXV, for example, a concentrated vector of sound and image where music seems to freeze in the air:

> 'as the sculptor sees the form in the air...
> 'as glass seen under water,
> 'King Otreus, my father...
> and saw the waves taking form as crystal,
> notes as facets of air,
> and the mind there, before them, moving,
> so that notes needed not move.
>
> (XXV 119)

Instead of following the formality of a fugue, Pound essentially relied on a constative method drawn from Ford and Flaubert. This approach, a precursor to Pound's imagist technique, demands the presentation of observed concrete or historical details registered as exactly, unemotionally and unrhetorically as the mind perceives them. The work (or poetic line) embodies, or becomes, the detail, some constructed out of literal registers of fact or statement without authorial exposition or comment. Constation is the means of creating impersonality and detachment. The focus is on exact detail and presentation in the exact word, Flaubert's *le mot juste*.

Such a method balances or alternates with the 'mapping of recurrences in time ... as if history were an endless troubadour song, a huge *canto*' that forms the thematic structure of the poem (Albright 82). This structure is more musical and lyrical, allowing for the flow of images and expression of emotion to counter the impersonal record of history or event. Accompanying the musical, however, is the satiric and as Pound moves to the final canto in the sequence, XXVII, supplanted by three new Cantos, to give an even thirty, he almost begins to parody his earlier work as destruction, rather than construction, rules. Light and mud, represented by Artemis and Hyle, Greek for wood or matter, contend with each other in Canto XXX. Lucidity battles opacity, but ironically the final element of the thirtieth Canto is a document, not a god, a document registering the development of cursive typeface at the beginning of the 16th century, the means for making printed books into works of art. Pound turns to historical means to control the appearance of his book and structure of design.

By 1930, Pound decided to gather *A Draft of XVI Cantos, A Draft of the Cantos 17–27* and three new Cantos into a single volume to summarize fifteen years worth of work. He turned to the innovative Paris printer (and his former lover), Nancy Cunard, and her Hours Press to produce the elaborate and costly *A Draft of XXX Cantos* printed in only two hundred copies, with an additional ten signed by the author. It was the embodiment of the very art he chose to celebrate at the end Canto XXX where he declared 'here have I brought cutters of letters/ and printers not vile and vulgar' (XXX 148). Art and economics now joined in a limited edition of high quality defined by linen boards, exquisite paper, initials by Dorothy Pound and, for the ten signed copies, red-orange leather boards lettered in gold. Not only were *The Cantos* complex poetry but they now existed in a form that equaled their artistry, ironically appealing more to book collectors and connoisseurs than to readers. Pound's desire for a wider readership did not seem to matter. Politics, however, did, supported by constant attempts to link social action and literature as one of his most influential critical works, *How to Read* (1931), demonstrated.

In this book, Pound reiterates many of his ideas on precise thought and exact language but through the figure who will now influence many of his concepts on writing, government and history: Confucius. In his first systematic attempt to define the role of art in a well-ordered state, Pound predicates the proper order of the state and its laws on the behavior of artists, as did Confucius: they alone have the care of words and understand, *a priori*, that their value rests on their precise definition and use. When language becomes imprecise, society disintegrates. Through his use of clear language, the writer unquestionably contributes to the welfare of the state. In *How to Read*, Pound abandoned his belief in the self-justifying nature of art. Its function was now to sustain the state through the ethical application of language. Not surprisingly, politics, economics and language would quickly envelope his writing, encouraged by the example of Italy, Mussolini and the triumph of fascism. But another idea entered to embrace these concepts: *paideuma*, a term he borrowed from Leo Frobenius, a German anthropologist and explorer who wrote extensively on Africa and whom Pound first read in 1929. *Paideuma* essentially means the total expression of any culture manifested in all of its forms, or in Pound's words, a concept 'implying a tangle of ideas, mental habits, predispositions which make the mind of an era.' In *Guide to Kulchur*, he defines it as 'the gristly roots of ideas that are in action' (*EPCP* 7:77; *GK* 58). In other words, the art of a period or culture can reveal the nature of that society's economic and moral system. Good art will prevail when a good economic system exists. Taste for Pound became the unity of the aesthetic and economic, suggested earlier by the accomplishments of Sigismundo Malatesta. Pound discerned such unity of culture through the concept of *paideuma*, an ideal he hoped *The Cantos* would demonstrate and the political economy he found in Italy would confirm.

5
'The Indifferent Never Make History': 1930–40

Europe belongs to Dante and the witches' sabbath, not to Newton.

(Yeats, 1933)

In 1931, Pound offered an explanation for his move to Rapallo. Citing his absorption with the 'high peaks of culture,' he emphasized Italy's double civilizing of Europe: 'each time a strong, live energy is unleashed in Italy, a new renaissance comes forth.' 'English stupidity and French imbecility' also drove him to Italy where the only viable comparison to its leader, Mussolini, is Jefferson. Furthermore, 'without a strong Italy, I don't see the possibility of a balanced Europe' (Redman 76–7). He also quipped, on another occasion, that the trains between Paris and Rome always stopped in Rapallo so it was easy for friends to drop in (Laughlin *P. as Wuz* 9).

Hoping for a return to the 15th century, when science and culture functioned to their maximum, Pound found in Italy a 'new virility.' Fascism, which meant for him 'DIRECT action coupling an active past with a new order, also meant a feeling of freedom greater than he had ever experienced in England or France (Redman 77; *J/M* 70, 74). Politics now reflected his aesthetics as he found a country and government that embodied his own literary agenda of enacted history via effective change. Italy was also a country of fact, not illusion, and where 'NOTHING IS WITHOUT EFFICIENT CAUSE' to quote his epigram to *Jefferson and/or Mussolini* (1935). Mussolini's statement that 'the indifferent have never made history' confirmed Pound's own belief in the need for commitment and action (*J/M* viii). The policies of Mussolini's government coincided with the political, cultural and ideological identity Pound projected on the Italy of the past and his plan of immediate literary action in the present.

Pound's writing in the thirties and forties concentrated on political and economic matters with prescriptive titles like the *ABC of Economics* (1933); *Make it New*, (1934); or the *ABC of Reading* (1934). His preference for primer-like titles was likely drawn from A.R. Orage who titled an early work *An Alphabet of Economics* (1917). Politics also dominated Pound's poetry, the so-called Jefferson Cantos, appearing in *Eleven New Cantos* (1934), praising the rationality of the American Founding Fathers (similar to what Pound saw in the rationality of fascism) in contrast to the irrationality and darkness that shaped most of Europe (Cantos XXXI–XXXIV). Canto XXXVI refocused itself on Renaissance Italy with its successful translation of Cavalcanti's 'Donna mi prega.' *Eleven New Cantos* concludes with a comparison between Mussolini's *virtu* challenging the monopolists and then Jefferson's ideas of democracy. Economics initially controls *The Fifth Decad of Cantos* (1937) with its focus on monetary reform in Siena in the 18th century and the anathema of usury (Canto XLV), although China soon gains prominence as Pound prepares *Cantos LII–LXXI*, the so-called Chinese Cantos (1940). This work encapsulates Pound's absorption with Confucius, a figure of immense power for him. In fact, when Pound was arrested on 3 May 1945 by Italian partisans, he was at his desk working on an English translation of Confucius. The only two books he took were a Chinese dictionary and the Confucian text.

Pound found the study of Confucius and Chinese poetry endlessly engaging on literary as well as moral and political grounds: 'when I did *Cathay*, I had no inkling of the technique of sound, which I am now convinced *must* exist or have existed in Chinese poetry' he told Katue Kitasono, Japanese poet and editor of the Tokyo literary magazine, *Vou*. 'Only Kung [Confucius] can guide a man, so far as I know, through the jungle of propaganda and fads that has overgrown Xtn [Christian] theology' (*SL* 293, 327). Pound may have first been introduced to Confucian thought through Allan Upward, author of *Divine Mystery*, which Pound reviewed in November 1913. Among Upward's many exploits, which ranged from living in Nigeria to becoming a politician in Wales, he co-published a series entitled Wisdom of the East. In 1904, the *Sayings of Confucius* appeared. Upward's impact on Pound was profound and he included a work by Upward in his Imagist anthology.

In *The Exile* of 1928, Pound displayed further allegiance to Confucius, alleging that not only moral but even economic problems could usually be solved by 'ref. to the *Ta Hio*;' earlier, in the autumn of 1927, he had actually spent several weeks translating the Confucian text (*Exile* 4: 109).

And when requested by a professor to offer a literary autobiography for a series published by the University of Washington, Pound sent, instead, a translation of the *Ta Hio, The Great Learning*. It appeared in 1928 as a chapbook.[1] Interestingly, as was so often his habit, Pound translated not from the Chinese but from a secondary source: J.P.G. Pauthier's 1858 French version, Pound providing an almost literal version of Pauthier.

Confucian thought, at first glance, seems antithetical to Pound in its stress on moderation and the realization of motivation before action. But it was the very enigma of Confucian writing and thought that intrigued him, the idea that the surface does not contain the meaning. It, furthermore, avoids the personal, psychological or individual in favor of correctness. Personal confusions are hidden. Its aesthetic was almost classical: *'To call people and things by their names, that is by the correct denominations, to see that the terminology was exact'* is precisely the expression that for Pound would unite Imagism with morality. It is found in his translation of Confucius' 'Digest of the Analects' (*GK* 16). Pound would also be pulled to the Confucian idea of order, needed within before it can be extended outward to society or government. Canto XIII states this succinctly: 'If a man have not order within him/ He can not spread order about him' (XIII/59)

Pound's absorption with Confucius and China began early. *Cathay* and the works of Fenollosa were an introduction, his essay 'The Chinese Written Character' a pivotal work for Pound's aesthetic. So effective were his translations in *Cathay* that in 1928 Eliot famously declared that 'Chinese poetry, as we know it to-day, is something invented by Ezra Pound' (*SPP* xvii). But Pound had to counter the view that Confucius was only a politician, telling Margaret Anderson that 'Confucianism is not propagandist' (*SL* 107). In 1928, he wrote in French to René Taupin that he wanted to give a new version of the *'Ta Hio* de Confucius:

> parce que j'y trouve des formulations d'idées qui me paraissent utile pour civilizer l'Amérique (tentatif). Je révère plutôt le bon sens que l'originalité (soit de Rémy de G., soit de Confucius).
>
> (*SL* 217)

The result is the 1928 edition published as a chapbook with a remarkable subtitle: *Ta Hio, the Great Learning Newly Rendered into The American Language*. In the thirties, Pound also turned to Italian publishers to secure the appearance of his Confucius translating his text into Italian, a language he was still learning.

Pound's embrace of the East and Confucius should not be surprising: the geography of his career has largely been eastward from America to Italy. After Venice (1908) and an interlude in England (1908–21), he moved to France (1921) and then Italy (1924) where he remained until his death in 1972 , except for an enforced stay in America from 1945–58. China and Confucian thought was an extension of his eastward journey. Pound, however, circled the globe through the incorporation of literatures diverse as Provençal and Chinese in his work. As Eliot noted, Pound is often most original 'when he is most "archaeological,"' discovering verse forms and sources from the foreign past (*SPP* xii, xi).

Chinese and Italian mixed in the late thirties when an Italian edition of *Confucius: Digest of the Analects* appeared in 1937 published by Giovanni Scheiwiller who would become Pound's favored Italian publisher. An Italian edition of Confucius' *Ta S'Eu*, translated by Pound, but assisted by Alberto Luchini, appeared in 1942 published in Rapallo with the translations appearing beneath the Chinese originals. It was followed in 1944 by *Testamento di Confucio* by Pound and Luchini, the first separate edition of Pound's Italian translation of Confucius but without the Chinese texts. The very year of Pound's arrest, *Chiung Iung, L'Asse che non Vacilla* by Confucius, Pound's Italian translation of *The Unwobbling Pivot*, appeared, although the bulk of the edition was burned immediately after the Liberation because it was mistakenly thought to be propaganda (Gallup 60, 166, 71, 73). In Italian, 'Asse' means axis; the text was condemned because it was thought to favor the Berlin-Rome-Tokyo Axis.

Confucius first appears in *The Cantos* in Canto XIII, where Pound idealizes moral and political order. The so-called Chinese Cantos (LII–LXI), published in 1940 and perhaps the most annotated section of the entire poem, present the Confucian view of Chinese imperial history from the Book of Rites through the Manchu period. It shows that empires flourish only when Confucian ethics rule, a principle Pound would try to apply to his assessment of the history. Confucius also confirms the importance of a strong leader, and how that individual sets the tone for the age, whether it be Malatesta or Mussolini. And it is in this series, the Chinese Cantos, that ideograms begin to appear in the poem, applying the Chinese visual alphabet as a hieroglyphic form of reading his poem, although Pound's attempt at writing ideograms alternated between frustration and pleasure (see *SL* 292.).

Confucius, who provided Pound with an entire system of ethics, is also present in the radio broadcasts Pound made for Radio Rome between 1941 and 1943, beginning before the U.S. entered the war. Pound cites him in his second and fifth broadcasts when he celebrates the simplicity of the Confucian system because 'if you start right, and then go on, start at the root and move upward, the pattern often is simple' (*EPS* 20). 'Coloring,' one of the late broadcasts, is almost entirely devoted to Confucius. *The Pisan Cantos* (LXXIV–LXXXIV), written under the stress of the Disciplinary Training Center at Pisa, is replete with Confucian ideas and references.

When arrested by Italian partisans on 3 May 1945, Pound slipped his text of Confucius' *Ta Hio: The Great Digest* into his pocket along with a Chinese dictionary and they stayed with him throughout his time in Pisa. The Confucian ideal sustained him in his despair and in the D.T.C. he alternated between composing *The Pisan Cantos* on the medical dispensary's typewriter and translating Confucius. The translation would appear in 1947 as *Confucius, The Unwobbling Pivot & The Great Digest*, the title suggested by one of two ideograms in the original title which depicted a rectangle balanced on an upright meant to suggest the immovable center of a swirling universe. Pound's copy of the Confucian *I King*, a book of divinations edited and with commentary by Confucius, contains this poignant inscription: 'full of wisdom, found too late' (*VL* 73). At one time Pound thought to conclude *The Cantos* with four Chinese characters showing the basic Confucian virtues. The half-title page of the completed edition of *The Cantos*, however, does display the Chinese ideogram for 'sincerity.'

From St Elizabeths hospital in 1946, Pound wrote to Charles Olson that 'if I had only read Confucius earlier, I would not be in this mess' (*VL* 73). During his confinement at St Elizabeths, Pound worked on a translation of the 300 poems that constitute *The Confucian Odes* begun in 1949. He completed the text in 1950, but it was not published until four years later because Pound insisted that the original Chinese texts be printed across from the translations. The publisher objected, although the collection finally appeared as *The Classic Anthology defined by Confucius*.

Important for Pound was his realization that the Confucian stress on inner order and harmony would balance the dynamic and eroticized force of creation in his other preoccupation at this time, the Eleusinian Mysteries. These were the ideas of the cult followers of Eleusis, Greek worshipers of earthly fertility who every four years decadently celebrated in honour of Demeter and Persephone. Homer preserved the Eleusinian myth in 'Hymn to Demeter' which narrates the abduction of Persephone, Demeter's daughter by Hades. References to the mysteries appear in Cantos XLV and LII, with allusions throughout the entire poem.[2] The Gnostic tradition of the Eleusinian Mysteries of Demeter provided Pound with a link to the deities of the underworld, including a descent into Hades and a set of mystic visions incorporated into *The Cantos*. Indeed, the idea of a hidden, or secret, mystery tradition is endemic to Pound's *Paideuma*. When he writes 'Between KUNG and ELEUSIS,' in Canto LII/258, Pound is declaring the basic opposition of the ethical system of Kung (Confucius) and that of the sacred mysteries represented by Eleusis. Between these two poles, one disciplined and orderly, the other anarchic and unrelenting, a human value system must be established. However, the presence of usury in Eleusis, cited in XLV/230, destroys the sacredness of the city.

Pound struggled between these two positions, seeking on one hand to return to the psychic fountain of religion identified with Eleusis (as he shows in an essay from 1931, 'Terra Italica') and on the other, attracted to the order and structure offered by Confucius. For him, religion could not be institutionalized into the dogma of the restoration of the temples, a theme in the essay which becomes a theme as well in his late cantos. To establish a pagan revival, one must follow the principles of a 'celestial tradition.' The *gnosis* of this 'celestial tradition' is 'a light from Eleusis [which] persisted throughout the middle ages and set beauty in the song of Provence and of Italy' (*SP* 53). The polytheism Pound evokes through the Eleusinian Mysteries and their esoteric rituals is rooted in the senses. Sex and pagan ceremonies were part of this activity which he made clear in 'Religio' (1939).

While Confucius and the Eleusinian mysteries dominated Pound's poetic thinking, he also maintained a steady stream of literary and cultural criticism, largely through the bi-monthly literary paper published in Genoa, *L'Indice*. His contributions between 1930 and 1931 promoted his image as a literary propagandist, repeating the role he played in London and Paris. The names of Joyce, Antheil, Lewis and Eliot began to appear with regularity. Soon, Basil Bunting, as well as Louis Zukofsky, began to appear in the journal. In late February, in a two-part series, Pound's 'How to Read' appeared. Not only was Pound perceived as a *pezzo grosso* ('big shot'), but his ideas on modern writing were being accepted in Italy. Encouraging work he felt important, getting work for his friends, having his own work promoted were the qualities that marked Pound's editorial as well as literary influence on *L'Indice* where he was trying to establish a new 'vortex.' Importantly, his own contributions were literary – he did not begin his Italian political and economic polemics until 1937 – and audacious, since Pound had decided he had to teach the Italians how to write in their own language. Pound believed that Italian literature had to become more international in its ambitions. On matters of style and translation, Pound encouraged Italians to be laconic: 'Every translation must be more concise than the original' he implored his readers in his October 1930 article, 'Lettera al Traduttore' (*EPCP* V: 238). But while celebrating the glories of the Italian literary and cultural past, he would also condemn its language:

> 93% of the printed matter in Italy is completely unreadable because it is all written in a dead cadence, but DEEEAAAD, dead in the tradition. Even brave and clever futurists fall back into this grey mud from time to time.
>
> (Pound in Redman 83)

Pound was now appearing regularly in a variety of Italian papers, ranging from *Il Mare* to *Il Meridiano di Roma* and *Marina Repubblicana*, and becoming as widely known as a journalist as a poet, with music, as well as politics, economics and, later, the war his preferred subjects. Throughout 1938, he assumed the role of music critic for *Il Mare*, reporting regularly on the concert season, although an article on Frobenius, followed by one on the *Divine Comedy* and another titled 'Orientamenti' appeared in three issues of *Broletto* published in Como, while 'Il problema del critico' was published in *Meridiano di Roma*. By 1944, his journalism appeared regularly in *Il Popolo di Alessandria* one of the new fascist papers emanating from the Republic of Salò, established by Mussolini and his supporters in the north. Over forty articles or letters by Pound would appear in that year.

Rapallo became Pound's literary transmitter constantly beaming signals on varying frequencies. Throughout the nineteen thirties, he 'broadcast' manifestos, theories, ideas and new cantos on its cultural airwaves. So stimulated was he by new possibilities that he even tried to write a mystery story with Olga. Concert promotion was another venture. Between 1933 and 1939, Pound and Olga organized a series of unique concerts in Rapallo believing that first-rate music could be performed in a small town. Olga and Gerhart Münch (pianist) were the two primary musicians, occasionally aided by a violinist who also conducted the local orchestra and a cellist from nearby Chiavari. Pound considered such concerts a 'laboratory' for music not performed in the major centers.

Interpretation was minimized to focus on a study of the music. Two programs from early concerts appear in *ABC of Reading*. Blocks of music would be performed, such as a set of string quartets or violin sonatas by different composers while the range was vast: from. medieval music to Chopin, from Mozart to Bartók. As he wrote to Tibor Serly, music old and new would be presented 'in manner that would lead to more *exact* estimation of the value of the compositions' (*SL* 344).

No form of expression at this time embodied Pound's diverse energies more clearly than his letter writing and its erratic, unconventional style which at first looked like the simulation of direct speech, although not quite direct speech. In fact, speech and writing actually played off each other in Pound's correspondence. Visual games take place on the page via layout, neologisms or play of sound, creating what Marjorie Perloff calls 'Poundspeak,' an associative rhythm mixing an American twang with the inflated voice of an aesthete (Perloff *Dance* 78). The stationery itself was a semiotic sign, its Gaudier-Brzeska profile at the top a bold, clear, decisive expression of the author's identity. No signature was necessary: the image, supported by an opinionated, radical, direct voice, was indisputable. Yet Pound's letters are also the source of some of his clearest ideas and poetic statements: they are essential reading. For Pound, the question of genre was subordinate to finding a voice and recording the essential details. Pound collapsed boundaries and, like his letter writing, his cantos at this period (notably the Adams set [LXII–LXXI]) were a patchwork of documents and interpolations.

Pound began to attract disciples to Rapallo and three of the most important were Basil Bunting, Louis Zukofsky and James Laughlin. Bunting first met Pound at a Paris café in 1923. The young Englishman from Newcastle, who had spent time in a British jail as a conscientious objector in 1918, had gone to Paris to work and experience its vibrant artistic life after a short time at the London School of Economics. Having little money, he worked as a laborer but in his free time he hung around the cafes on the Boulevard Montparnasse. Bunting had read and admired Pound's work and when he fell into conversation with him at a boulevard café, a literary apprenticeship soon formed. The 38-year-old Pound – Bunting was 15 years younger – was unafraid to offer his unorthodox literary views and when he realized the awe of his young acquaintance, his normally truculent manner evaporated. Meeting the American poet in his green jacket with blue buttons and mass of golden reddish hair impressed the young Englishman who wanted to be a poet and found reading Pound's 'Propertius' a transformative experience: 'Indeed, it was the one that gave me the notion that poetry wasn't altogether impossible in the XX century. . . . It was Ezra who discovered me' (*VL* 53). Pound soon introduced Bunting to Ford who employed him as a sub-editor at the *transatlantic review*. Just before he started, Pound got Bunting a job as a bartender at the Jockey Club in Montparnasse, its Wild West decor an unusual Parisian attraction. Man Ray, Tristan Tzara, Jean Cocteau and Pound were among the backers. In early 1924, Bunting accepted Pound's invitation to visit Rapallo, the two spending much time together through the beginning of 1925. In 1928–29, Bunting returned, joining Antheil and then Yeats who had arrived. Bunting, who had something of a musical background – for a short time he was a music critic in London – participated in various musical events organized by Pound and Olga. He also aided Antheil who was composing musical settings for Yeats' plays.

Bunting went to America in 1929–30 to rejoin Marian Culver whom he first met in Venice; they were married in July 1930. Four days after his wedding, Bunting sent a card to the young poet Louis Zukofsky which read 'Ezra Pound says I ought to look you up. May I?' (Alldritt 67). The 26-year-old poet, who had corresponded with Pound, enthusiastically replied and a long friendship began. By the end of 1930, Bunting returned to Rapallo and thought of settling there; he in fact remained until 1933, while publishing his first volume of poetry, *Redimiculum Matellarum* (Milan, 1930), aided by Pound who also edited his *Villon*, Bunting's first published long poem. Soon, Bunting appeared in three important anthologies: *Profile*, edited by Pound in 1932, *An Objectivists' Anthology*, edited by Zukofsky in 1932 and in *Active Anthology*, edited again by Pound, in 1933.

Bunting soon began to acclaim Pound in print, his article 'Mr Ezra Pound' in *The New English Weekly* of May 1932 praising Pound's technical virtuosity in verse. The following year, Bunting contributed to *The Cantos of Ezra Pound: Some Testimonies*, an important document offering testimonials from writers diverse as Joyce, Hemingway, Eliot, Ford and Williams on the value of Pound's long poem. This twenty-two page pamphlet, published in New York in 1933, was to introduce Pound's *A Draft of XXX Cantos*, published in the US for the first time, to a wider audience through the *imprimatur* of the leading writers of the day. After Bunting moved to the Canary Islands, where he lived from 1933 to 1938, he continued to correspond with Pound, challenging his ideas and supporting his work. In 1938, Bunting was one of two dedicatees, along with Zukofsky, of *Guide to Kulchur*.

Pound also mentions Bunting in Cantos LXXIV, LXXVII, LXXXI and CX.

Bunting's poem 'On the fly-leaf of Pound's Cantos,' written in 1949 during Pound's imprisonment at St Elizabeths, further honors Pound's work. It begins with 'There are the Alps. What is there to say about them?/ They don't make sense . . .' (Bunting 110). In a 1953 letter to Zukofsky, Bunting stated that 'Ez and Spenser, great galleries of technical accomplishment,' expressing his admiration for both (*VL* 54). Conversely, in his 1964 anthology *Confucius to Cummings*, Pound praises Bunting because his poetry faces contemporary problems directly and includes two of his poems (*CtoC* 313–16).

Zukofsky befriended Pound when he sent him 'Poem beginning "The"' and a work on Antheil. He had earlier been published in *Poetry* and in a few small magazines in New York. Pound accepted both works, the first appearing in the Spring 1928 issue of *The Exile* (No. 3), along with Yeats' 'Sailing to Byzantium' and a portion of Pound's 'Canto XXIII.' An editorial section at the back of the issue contains 19 points of advice from Pound including the declaration that 'Our intellectuals are lacking in savagery' (*Exile* 104). The next section opens with 'Quite simply, I want a new civilization,' a civilization at least as good 'as the best that has been' (*Exile* 108). The first line of an advertisement for Pound's new work, *Antheil*, tellingly begins with 'Ezra Pound answers the jeers and laughter of the mob' (*Exile* 111).

Pound thought Zukofsky's 'The' the 'first cheering mss. I have recd. in weeks, or months, or something or other' (*P/Z* 3). He would publish 'Critique of Antheil,' a poem, in *The Exile* 4. Zukofsky's 1929 essay entitled 'Ezra Pound: The Cantos' was one of the first on the work and earned Pound's praise and publication in Eliot's *Criterion*. To Zukofsky, he wrote that it was the first piece to credit him 'with an occasional gleam of intelligence or to postulate the bounds or possibility of an underlying coherence' (in Stanley 80). Zukofsky interestingly divided his essay into what he thought were the central pre-occupations of Pound's work: 'Ta Hio,' 'Translation,' 'Cantos 1–27.' A sentence from the 1929 essay pinpoints the double identity of Pound described as 'both the isolated creator and the worldly pamphleteer' (Zukofsky 69).

Correspondence between Zukofsky and Pound flourished and would continue throughout their lives; they met, however, only on three occasions: Rapallo in 1933, New York in 1939 and St Elizabeths in 1954. Yet Pound's importance for Zukofsky cannot be overstated, not only for his editorial acumen in revising Zukofsky's work but in sensing the young poet's own editorial ability. Pound's confidence in Zukofsky's talents led to his suggesting to Harriet Monroe that Zukofsky be put in charge of an issue of *Poetry*; the result was the important 'Objectivists' issue of February 1931, about which Pound sent Zukofsky numerous directives. Zukofsky's homage to Pound partly took the form of citing him on page four of his *magnum opus*, 'A', referring to a section from Pound's book on Antheil.

Believing in Zukofsky's talent as an editor, in February 1933 Pound asked Zukofsky to select American contributors for his *Active Anthology*. Before the two met in 1933, they exchanged 272 letters. Zukofsky believed Pound to be the most authoritative poet then writing; his dedication of *An 'Objectivists' Anthology* to Pound makes that clear. The full dedication states that despite Pound's erratic accomplishments in *The Cantos* and use of 'musical self-criticism' in Canto V, he remains 'for the poets of our time/ the/ most important' (*P/Z* 100). Pound's reply to Zukofsky begins 'Deerly beloved son' (*P/Z* 101).

Pound and Tibor Serly, Hungarian violinist/composer and a friend of Pound's, decided that Zukofsky should tour Europe in the summer of 1933. Reluctantly (because of the cost), Zukofsky agreed, making plans to arrive in Rapallo about August first. Two weeks before, Zukofsky was in Paris explaining to Pound that he did not come over to write about the French 'but to see you & discuss what can be done for "Murka." The important job is *there*' (*P/Z* 151). He also tried to set the time for his visit and departure 'depending on how persuasive & dictatorial you ken be' (*P/Z* 151). He needed to know because his funds were limited and he had to budget his hotel expenses. He also admitted that he could hardly see all those Pound had listed as important contacts in Paris which included Léger, Brancusi, Natalie Barney, Caresse Crosby, Cocteau, Aragon, Breton, Salvador Dali and Max Ernst.

Bunting greeted Zukofsky in Genoa when he arrived and escorted him to the apartment of Homer and Isabel Pound in Rapallo where he stayed during his visit. Zukofsky had met them in Philadelphia at Pound's urging before they made their own journey to Rapallo and decided to remain. Zukofsky's visit was instructive, although the young poet found Pound more overbearing in person than in his letters. Pound's enthusiasm for Zukofsky may have also lessened, especially when Zukofsky declined Pound's suggestion that he stay on in Europe and possibly establish a *salon* of some sort. For Zukofsky, Manhattan was world enough. In a note to the *Activist Anthology*, Pound unexpectedly criticizes 'Mr Zukofsky's Objectivists' for losing 'contact with language as language' (*AA* 253). Pound further objected to what he believed to be Zukofsky's obscurity of style; after receiving a prose manuscript from Zukofsky, Pound furiously wrote that Zukofsky needed to study the 'technique of FLOW' (*P/Z* 137). He also objected to a film treatment of *Ulysses* Zukofsky and his friend Jerry Reisman prepared and sent to Pound for his endorsement, accusing Zukofsky of being stuck in 1927. America is always fifteen years later than Europe he announced (*P/Z* 162).

But Zukofsky also learned several important principles from Pound, one the most valuable the precise and prescriptive code stated in the *ABC of Reading* attributed to Bunting and elaborated by Pound: '*Dichten = Condensare*': poetry equals condensation to the maximum degree. Great literature is the condensation of energy, 'language charged with meaning to the utmost possible degree' (*ABC* 92; *LE* 23). The goal was for an economy of language which Pound achieved and Zukofsky desired. But Zukofsky and Pound also disagreed, most notably about cummings: Pound praised him, Zukofsky did not. Pound celebrated Mussolini and his economic policies; Zukofsky found the man and his views dangerous.

Social Credit was equally contentious, Zukofsky rejecting Pound's argument, as he rejected Pound's claims, about the value of fascism and indictment of America. In 1935, for example, Pound dismissively wrote in the *New English Weekly* that 'the howls about 'Fascist danger' in America are mostly nothing but hypocrisy' (*EPCP* VI: 274). Zukofsky disagreed, proposing Communism as the answer, Lenin every bit the equal of Mussolini (*P/Z* 182–5). Asperity characterizes Pound's later exchanges with Zukofsky, although they somehow always managed to stay in touch, even though Zukofsky found Pound's anti-Semitism repugnant (although his own Jewish identity was complex and some-times unclear), while Pound found Zukofsky's seeming indifference to social action inexplicable. But during the 1950s when Pound was in St Elizabeths, Zukofsky visited and repeatedly sent him packages of books and food.

Another soon-to-be acolyte to visit Pound in Rapallo in August 1933 was the eighteen- year-old Harvard student, James Laughlin, a member of the Laughlin steel family of Pittsburgh. Laughlin, a member of the Harvard *Advocate* editorial board, was encouraged by Dudley Fitts, mas-ter of the Choate School, who had been corresponding with Pound, to write to the poet to ask for a meeting. Laughlin was hesitant but wrote in August 1933 during a European trip asking for help in understanding 'basic phrases of the CANTOS' and offering, in turn, to help attack American literary conservatism through his role at the Harvard *Advocate* and *Harkness Hoot* which he could do more effectively 'with your help'

(*EP/JL* 3). Pound replied, 'VISIBILITY HIGH' and Laughlin dropped in. On his return to Harvard, Laughlin began to get Pound in print, first in the *Advocate* where Canto XXXVIII appeared in February 1934. By the summer of 1934, Laughlin returned to Europe, staying for a while with Gertrude Stein and Alice B. Toklas in Haute-Savoie where he wrote press releases for their upcoming tour of America. In November, he returned to Rapallo for a two month stay at the 'Ezuversity':

> Where there was no tuition, the best beanery since Bologna,
> And the classes were held at meals in the dining room of what
> you called the Albuggero Rapallo,
> Where Gaudier's head of you sat in the corner, an astonishment
> to the tourists.
> Because it was too heavy to tote up to the fifth floor of Via
> Marsala 12/V
> And might have burst through the floor.
> And you showed me with some relish that if one looked at the
> back of the cranium it was quite clearly a scrotum.
> Literature (pronounced literchoor), you said, is news that stays
> news...
> Your conversation was the wittiest show in town,
> Whatever you'd heard or read was in your head as fresh
> as when it first came there.
> The books you loaned me were filled with caustic
> marginalia...
> (Laughlin, 'Collage' 154)

Class at this university began at lunch with Pound first offering commentary on his mail and the issues and people it presented. He would then move on to history and literature and the way he wanted it understood, all delivered in a colloquial style. Petrarch, for example, would be called 'Fat-faced Frankie.' He also employed one of at least five accents, according to Laughlin, whose favorite was the 'Oirrish' of Yeats. Every class was a performance and 'his hamming was part of his pedagogy' (Laughlin, *PWuz* 4–5). Reading the marginalia of the books Pound loaned Laughlin was another source of education. And after literature, Chinese and economic reform, music was Pound's great passion. The only time the didacticism halted was on the tennis court.

At work, Pound needed two typewriters because his vigorous typing meant that one was always being repaired. And in the fury of his composing *The Cantos*, observed by Laughlin, Pound seemed to work entirely from memory – 'more aural than visual memory' he adds. Pound also created the unusual format and irregular margin of the poem because he would not take the time to slap the typewriter carriage all the way back to the left. Wherever it stopped determined the indent (Laughlin, *PWuz* 8,7). When not attending 'classes,' Laughlin joined Pound swimming, playing tennis and attending the cinema, where Pound, in a cowboy hat, would sit in the gallery and roar with laughter at the screen.

Believing he might be a poet, Laughlin got an unexpected and stern directive from Pound as he was about to leave: 'No Jaz, it's hopeless. You're never gonna make a writer ... do something useful. ... Go back and be a publisher,' although the practical Pound made it clear that Laughlin had first to return to Harvard and finish his studies so that his family would finance the new venture (Laughlin, *PWuz* 7). He then told Laughlin to get in touch with Williams and Zukofsky and arranged for him to edit a literary page for the Social Credit magazine, *New Democracy*. This was in November 1935. The name chosen for the literary page was 'New Directions,' which Laughlin adopted for his publishing venture backed by his father and aunt who had an unused stable on her country estate in Norfolk, Connecticut, for the first office. In 1936, Laughlin published *New Directions in Prose and Poetry*, an anthology of experimental writing featuring Pound, Williams, cummings, Stevens, Moore and others. Laughlin financed the press with money his father gave him when he graduated Harvard in 1939. He used it to invest in a ski lodge in Alta, Utah, bringing him an annual return of $7–8000 a year for the press. And despite uneven sales, over the years Laughlin would keep all of Pound in print.

Yeats, who had joined Pound and Dorothy in Sicily in early 1925, shared their admiration of Mussolini, partly because he believed Mussolini illustrated the truth of his System outlined in *A Vision*. Mussolini represented the return of autocratic government (Maddox 224–5). In February 1928, an ill Yeats visited Rapallo with his wife, reporting to Olivia Shakespear that Pound and Dorothy seemed pleased with their Italian way of life. Yeats stayed through the spring of 1928 and returned again in the autumn when he and his wife took a nine room flat on the fourth floor of a new building near the port. Pound recalled Yeats's pleasure with Rapallo in Canto LXXVII. He saw Pound every day, although he disagreed with him about everything. Nevertheless, Yeats began to socialize with the literary set as defined by Pound: Hauptmann, Beerbohm, Aldington, Brigit Patmore, Bunting and George Antheil. Pound at this time was working on his translation of Cavalcanti and incessantly talking to Yeats about the Italian poet whom he proposed to Eliot at Faber to publish in an edition which would include a new commentary and facsimiles of the manuscripts. At first, Faber agreed but then found his requirements for facsimiles too costly; Aquila Press then agreed to do the work in 1929 but went bankrupt. Finally, Pound had the Italian texts and scholarly apparatus printed in Genoa with facsimile plates printed in Germany. All was bound at his expense in January 1932 in a somewhat chaotically edited version that had several texts appearing twice.

Yeats, newly revitalized during his stay in Rapallo, began to write about Pound, notably 'A Packet for Ezra Pound' (1929) which would open his revised edition of *A Vision* (1937). The short work begins with a paean to Rapallo and Pound, followed by a confessional section on automatic writing and the origin of his System. It ends with additional comments on Pound. The second section of the opening details Yeats' relationship with Pound, famously reporting that their opposite views are the very source of their lively engagement, Yeats calling him 'a man with whom I should quarrel more than with anyone else if we were not united by affection' (Yeats 3). He then summarizes Pound's remarks on the structure of *The Cantos* and how the work will be disjointed and fragmented, although it will exhibit two themes: descent and metamorphosis mixed with medieval and modern historical figures.

According to Yeats, characters and events in *The Cantos* are to appear without edges or contours: they will merge with one another. Yeats then outlines a lettered structure for the poem suggested by Pound (Yeats 4–5). In the 'To Ezra Pound' section, written in the form of a letter, Yeats offers political advice, telling Pound not to get elected to the Senate, followed by some comments on 'a new divinity' Yeats proposed, although he admits that 'you will hate these generalities, Ezra' (Yeats 27, 29). Pound, in turn, thought Yeats' ideas, 'very very very bughouse.' Opposite the inside rear cover of a 1966 reprint of *A Vision*, Pound wrote 'W.B.Y. Trying to make new pack of Tarot cards' (*SCh* 462; *VL* 77.)

Yeats' second winter in Rapallo began in November 1929 but was less triumphant. He again arrived ill and grew worse – so much so that on Christmas Eve he drafted his will and summoned Pound and Bunting as witnesses (Maddox 245). Yeats took six weeks to recover, his wife George burdened with nursing; Dorothy Pound did her shopping for her, while the hypochondriacal Pound stayed away, fearful of becoming infected. Only in May was Yeats fully restored and in July 1930 he and his wife returned to Dublin. But Rapallo released much in Yeats's imagination including 'Byzantium,' first sketched in the hills above the city in the spring of 1930 and completed in September that year. Nonetheless, Yeats constantly found Pound an enigma, an 'antithetical self' who 'produces the most distinguished work and yet in his behavior is the least distinguished of men' (Aldington, *Life* 105).

In Pound's literary as well as social world, politics vied with economics, the former overtaken by the latter when he began his primer, the *ABC of Economics* in February 1933 partly undertaken in response to meeting Mussolini the month before. An invitation to give ten lectures on economics in Milan at Bocconi University confirmed for Pound the perspicacity of the Italians and the correctness of his ideas which his 127 page booklet clarified. The tone is characteristically sharp and over-confident, filled with assertions that mix declaration with moral denunciation: 'an economic system in which it is more profitable to make guns...than to grow grain or make useful machinery, is an outrage, and its supporters are enemies of the race' is but one example (*SP* 233). The immediate problem is the distribution of wealth which must be corrected. His aim in the work is to make the fundamentals of economics simple and accessible to all, although what followed was a detailed account of wages, credit and productivity.

Major Douglas, Confucius, Van Buren, Jefferson and Marx are among Pound's sources, suggesting the range of figures he cites. Throughout the work, he claims to be 'a Jeffersonian republican' but 'the damning reign of the infamous Woodrow' lost these principles (*SP* 213). Authenticating Pound's claim as to the benefit of less work per day is his expertise: 'I have lived nearly all my life, at any rate all my adult life, among the unemployed. All the arts have been unemployed in my time' (*SP* 214). Economists, however, dismissed Pound's efforts to correct the manufacturing process, distribution of wealth and the creation of market value.

Mussolini had welcomed Pound on 30 January 1933 at the ornate Palazzo Venezia in Rome (*SCh* 490–91). The scale of the building was overwhelming: Mussolini's office was in the Renaissance Sala del Mappamondo, built for the Popes in the 15th century, and measuring 18 metres by 15 metres with 12 metre ceilings. Pound's admiration for the dictator stemmed from Mussolini's cultural awareness and effectiveness as a political leader which he saw akin to Jefferson. A recent biography of Il Duce, in fact, opens with this question: 'Which European politician of the first half of the twentieth century could be relied on to read the philosophical and literary works of his co-nationals and send their authors notes of criticism and congratulations?' And who but Mussolini kept copies of Socrates and Plato, annotated in his hand, on his desk

(Bosworth1)? News of Pound's forthcoming audience with Mussolini made the front page of the Rapallo newspaper, *Il Mare*, increasing his status in the town and for years he kept the official invitation pinned to his study wall.

The meeting had a decisive impact on Pound who was overcome by Il Duce's insights as Canto XLI records. There, Pound repeats Mussolini's perceptiveness concerning *The Cantos*:

> 'MA QVESTO,'
> said the Boss, 'è divertente.'
> catching the point before the aesthetes had got
> there;
>
> (XLI 202)

Mussolini quickly grasped the import of the poem, which Pound had likely sent ahead in advance of their meeting and which Mussolini was apparently looking at when Pound entered. He looked up and uttered the fateful words, 'But this is amusing.' The reported remark may mean the poem as a whole is amusing, the literal translation of the phrase, or that (as Pound explained to a visitor at St Elizabeths) when he entered, Mussolini, who was studying English, was examining a passage where one of Pound's characters was speaking in dialect. When Pound explained what it was about, Mussolini laughed, calling it *'divertente'* (Redman 96).

In *Jefferson and/or Mussolini*, Pound expands on their meeting in which he tried to explain his ideas on economics to the leader. And when Mussolini reportedly asked Pound, 'why put your ideas in order?' 'For my poem' was his response, Pound praising the ability of Mussolini to center immediately on the crucial issue of *The Cantos*: their structure (*J/M* 66). Pound then celebrates Il Duce as heir to a great line of American Presidents:

> The heritage of Jefferson, Quincy Adams, old John Adams, Jackson, Van Buren is HERE, NOW *in the Italian peninsula* at the beginning of [the] fascist second decennio, not in Massachusetts or Delaware.
>
> (*J/M* 12).

Much of Mussolini's appeal lay in what Pound understood as his progressive monetary policies. His political instincts made him a modern Jefferson, his economic intuitions an authentic Social Credit practioner who believed in the theory of the Just Price. Pound favored Mussolini's plans for corporative assemblies, land reclamation and the re-evaluation of currency. He also believed that Italian fascism was committed to breaking the stranglehold of international banking which he held responsible for the creation of wars. Pound was uncritical of the figure he called 'the Boss,' a figure of charisma and immense charm, and up to Italy's entry in the Second World War, of overwhelming popularity in Italy.

'A nation is great when it translates the force of its spirit into reality.' Pound or Mussolini? Mussolini on the eve of his 1922 march on Rome, although his rhetoric and Pound's are often difficult to separate, especially in Pound's radio broadcasts (in Adamson 261). Indeed, Mussolini's rhetoric of fascism and Pound's prose in the thirties and forties rhetorically share a great deal, beginning with their common theme of cultural renewal and spiritual revolution. But Mussolini, unlike Italian modernists who sought a similar program, was prepared to engage in the political action necessary to translate ideals into reality. Mussolini's attraction to risk was another captivating feature to Pound. To his troops in the first World War, Mussolini would often exhort them with articles entitled 'Audacity!' and 'Dare!', concepts that would deeply appeal to Pound. Break from a static mentality Mussolini urged as he provided the rhetoric of cultural renewal with a directness not unlike Pound's assertions to act, to 'make it new.' il Duce also required an internal discipline to make these new principles work, another ideal of Pound's. And Mussolini's support of order, duty, work and hierarchy were similar to the goals Pound identified in Confucius. By 1922, a spiritual revolution to restore public life became Mussolini's 'single most important rhetorical appeal' (Adamson 260). In the thirties and forties, Pound's exhortations on behalf of a cultural and political renaissance were not very different.

The impact of meeting Mussolini for Pound meant that he was heard by a head of state, one that was far-sighted and who understood the importance of artists in society. By contrast, when he visited the United States in 1939, Pound was denied a meeting with President Roosevelt and saw, instead, the Secretary of Agriculture, Henry Wallace, and the Idaho Senator, William Borah. But in Italy, he could advise Il Duce, although further attempts to meet with the leader were unsuccessful. Ironically, in May 1943, only months before his fall, Mussolini showed some interest in pursuing some of Pound's ideas on economics. An invitation for Pound to meet with him was sent to his hotel in Rome but after he had left for Rapallo.

Another reason for Pound's esteem of Mussolini, clear in *Jefferson and/or Mussolini*, is his belief that above all Mussolini was an artist,

an 'artifex' with 'a passion for construction' with 'STRONG ITALY...
the only possible foundation or anchor... for the good life in Europe'
(J/M 34–5). Mussolini had become the idealized figure Pound long
sought in history: the artist, politician, leader and reader of texts as well
as culture. He could also see through the fog of rhetoric and confusion:
'The DUCE sits in Rome calling five hundred bluffs (or thereabouts)
every morning' (J/M 35). He joins the pantheon of Malatesta, Confucius
and Jefferson, all men of idea and action.

But Mussolini and fascism were inseparable, the cult of the man
incorporating a belief in the ideas and correctness of fascist thinking.
Mussolini's authority comes '"from right reason" and from the general
fascist conviction that he is more likely to be right than anyone else is'
writes Pound (J/M 110). Such faith found expression through Pound's
adoption of the Fascist calendar introduced by il Duce. Beginning in
June 1932, Pound dated his own letters in this fashion, which started
Year 1 on 28 October 1922 when Mussolini and his followers arrived in
Rome. For a short period (1935–37), Pound included both the Christian
Year and the Fascist but starting in 1938, he used the Fascist calendar
exclusively.

Usury and the conspiracy of bankers began to obsess Pound in the
1930s. Canto XLV, for example (perhaps the shortest canto in the entire
work), devotes itself exclusively to condemning usury. 'With usura hath
no man a house of good stone/ each block cut smooth and well fitting/
that design might cover their face' he asserts (XLV/229). 'The Eunited
States ov/ America' was, along with the European powers, the prime agent
in the banking conspiracy (XLVI/235). Unquestionably, if somewhat
irrationally, Pound believed that economics and literature were inseparable: as he explained to one correspondent, 'economics always *has
been* in the best large poetry' (SL 294). To educate Britain and the
United States, and document the dangers of usury and banking, he
advocated a relatively new medium – radio, telling an Italian journalist
in 1934 that he wished 'to croon it over the air to the six million little
pink toes American bolsheviki, and the back woods heckers who take the
American Muck/ ury etc./' (LC 2). But it took six years and repeated
requests before he was allowed to go to Rome to make shortwave overseas
transmissions which would famously begin with 'Europe callin', Pound
speakin'. Ezry Pound speakin' (EPS 20).

Pound was thinking about radio in connection with *The Cantos* as
early as 1924 and in Canto XXXVIII includes a reference to Marconi. The
connection between Italy and the invention of wireless telegraphy did
not go unnoticed by Pound in Rapallo where the first radio transmission

was received in 1925, ironically from the BBC (Fisher 40). To his father, Pound wrote that the 'simplest parallel I can give [for *The Cantos*] is radio where you tell who is talking by the noise they make' (Fisher 40). It is reasonable to think of a radio poetic as much as any other for the entire poem, the transmission of ideas occurring without the interference of a narrator or limiting structure: 'Am leaving the reader, in most cases to infer what he is getting' he stated (Fisher 41).[3]

At times, however, such noise leaves the reader confused. In Canto LXXII, for example, Pound contrasts the unity of the past ('Caesar didn't split himself to fragments' [LXXII 436]) with the disunity of the present expressed through radio:

> Confusion of voices as from several transmitters, broken
>   phrases,
> And many birds singing in counterpoint/ In the summer
> morning
> > (LXXII/436 – the simile is more extended in the
> > Italian version, LXXII/430)

The juxtaposition of voices in radio required listeners to identify the speakers, precisely the technique Pound requests of readers of *The Cantos*. The poem itself is a radio dial that has continuous and sometimes contradictory sounds.[4] Mussolini's use of the radio to broadcast his fascist platforms was established by the time Pound settled in Rapallo, although Marinetti's manifesto uniting Futurism and radio would not be published until 1933, after his dramatic, on-the-spot coverage of the arrival near Rome of a celebrated pilot and former commander of the fascist militia, Italo Balbo. But the political, as well as artistic, importance of radio was immediately understood by Marinetti *and* Pound; Mussolini had perceived this earlier but Pound had been employing his radio poetic for nearly a decade. Theoretically, Rudolf Arnheim's study, *Radio* (1936), analysed the capacity to perceive sound without visual stimulus and offered an approach that Pound himself outlined to some of his readers. Arnheim: 'In the work of art, the sound of the word, because it is more elemental, should be of more importance than the meaning." Pound: "Skip anything you don't understand and go on till you pick it up again' (Fisher 72; *SL* 250).

The thirties was clearly a decade of prose for Pound, beginning with *How to Read*, his critical assessment of the teaching of literature in American universities. Characteristically irascible and self-assured, Pound had his own plan to halt a culture on the edge of spiritual collapse: establish a focused curriculum concentrating only on those writers he believed made genuine discoveries. An anthology might do the trick and he recounts his effort to edit a new, 12 volume collection in which each poem would be selected not because it was 'nice' but because 'it contained an invention, a definite contribution to the art of verbal expression' (*HR* 10). No British publisher, however, would touch it. Nevertheless, he outlines a method of organization based on the procedures of biology and physics: 'we proceed by a study of discoveries.' He then defends the function of literature in the state, explaining that 'it has to do with the clarity and vigor of "any and every" thought and opinion,' analysed with the care and precision of language (*HR* 12, 17).

But when language goes 'slushy and inexact, or excessive...the whole machinery of social and of individual thought and order goes to pot' Pound writes. Literature keeps words clean and 'great literature is simply language charged with meaning to the utmost possible degree' (*HR* 18, 21). Pound then proposes a list of core authors, writers he favors, starting with Confucius, Homer, Ovid, a provençal songbook, Dante and Villon, ending with Voltaire. Stendhal, Flaubert, Gautier, Coribere and Rimbaud, with Cavalcanti and Arnaut Daniel, if there is time. And 'after this inoculation he [the student] could be "with safety exposed" to modernity or anything else in literature.' A dependable 'axes of reference' has been established (*HR* 50–51)

But language is now in the keeping of the Irish (Yeats and Joyce) he argues and since the death of Hardy, 'poetry is being written by Americans.' All developments in English verse since 1910 'are due almost wholly to Americans. In fact, there is no longer any reason to call it English verse' (*HR* 43). His remedy, in a section headed 'Vaccine,' is to throw out all critics who 'use vague general terms.' The first demand of every critic is to know what he believes is valid writing and why. To study literature one must break it up 'into crumbs quickly dryable' (*HR* 49, 50). Optimistically, Pound ends by stating that the readings should not overburden a third or fourth-year student.

Other prose works of the thirties include *Make it New*, a collection of literary essays, and *Polite Essays*, polemical writings counterbalanced by the title. To educate by provocation was laudatory wrote one reviewer of *Make It New*, Samuel Beckett. *Guide to Kulchur* (1938) is a *summa* of Pound's thinking about a variety of subjects, beginning with Confucius and his *Digest of the Analects* and proceeding to discussions of the vortex, music, Italy, novels, *The Cantos*, economics, physiognomy and culture. Thought itself is not beyond Pound's scope (re *GK* 77) and the entire work is an attack on cultural philistinism. The epigram to

Jefferson and/or Mussolini, 'Nothing is without efficient cause,' might be more appropriate for *Guide to Kulchur*, a work that attempts to summarize all that Pound understood and wanted others to learn. Greek, Chinese, French and musical notes are some of the graphic elements used to transmit that knowledge which typically comes in pieces. But for Pound, this is the modern method: 'real knowledge goes into natural man in titbits. A scrap here, a scrap there; always pertinent' (*GK* 99). Also included in *Guide to Kulchur* is his 'Introductory Text Book,' a work composed of four short chapters, each a passage from Adams, Jefferson, Lincoln and Washington.

Pound turns to prose during this period as an effective way of expressing his ideas, an important adjunct to his poetry. And Mussolini may have again been the model: as a prolific journalist, Mussolini reached people in a more effective and popular manner through the press than through literature. Pound, urgently sensing the need to get his ideas out, understood the appeal of the press, although he used a variety of other forms as well: essays, lectures, anthologies, radio broadcasts and opera as he sought to influence and educate. But he also continued with *The Cantos*, publishing three new volumes in the decade: *Eleven New Cantos XXXI–XLI* in 1934, *The Fifth Decad of Cantos* in 1937 and *Cantos LII–LXXI* in 1940. Characterizing all three works is a stronger and more pervasive sense of both American and Chinese history.

Throughout his new writing, Pound sustained his poetic principle of 'make it new,' telling the young writer Mary Barnard in August 1934 that '*I still* think the best *mechanism* for breaking up the stiffness and literary idiom *is* a different metre, the god damn iambic magnetizes certain verbal sequences' (*SL* 260). As the poet Roy Fuller would write, 'it was Pound's rhythms, not his diction, which inaugurated the revolution' (*CH* 432). His use of the spondee and dactyl, at first creating discord, develop their own strength Fuller explained. Pound's new work demonstrates this practice, *Eleven New Cantos XXXI–XLI* beginning with a passage from Jefferson energetically signaling the focus of the first four cantos: America's earliest Presidents, with much of the material quoted from original sources. Jefferson is the Renaissance man who successfully creates his Nuevo Mundo. His letters and those of his correspondents in Cantos XXXI–XXXIV record the effort to establish good government in America and scorn for Europe: 'whether in a stye, a stable or in a stateroom . . . . / Louis Sixteenth was a fool. . . . The cannibals of Europe are eating one another again/ quando si posa' (XXXII/159). Contrasting the documentary method are inserted reflections by the aged Adams and Jefferson on such popular, contemporary politicians of the day as Clay, Calhoun and Webster. Contrast becomes the method of arrangement in the volume. In Cantos XXXV–XXXVI, it is between Vienna and Cavalcanti, Canto XXXV beginning without transition with 'So this is (may we take it) Mitteleuropa' (XXXV/172). But by the next set, beginning with Canto XXXVII, we are with Martin Van Buren, concluding the series with several cantos on war profiteers, swindlers against Hanno and, finally, in Canto XLI, Jefferson and Mussolini, the opening the well-publicized account of Mussolini's reaction to *The Cantos*. The end switches back to America in the 18th century and Jefferson. Importantly, the sequence would establish the eleven canto block, what Pound would call a decad, as the basic unit in which new Cantos would appear. The structure would generally pivot around the middle canto, in this case Canto XXXVI which differs from the five before and the five after. Instead of America's early leaders, Canto XXXVI begins with a comment on love and it soon becomes apparent that the work is a translation of a poem Pound had been working on since his youth: Cavalcanti's *canzone*, 'Donna mi Priegha.'

How love imprints itself on the memory is the subject of Cavalcanti's work, radically shifting from the documentary style and concerns of Cantos XXXI–XXXV to something more subtle and psychological. But the pause is temporary and the work quickly returns to the financiers, politicians and others corrupting America before Pound adapts Odysseus's sojourn with Circe in Canto XXXIX. But it is a modern Odysseus who speaks in a slangy, cosmopolitan manner:

> Fat panther lay by me
> Girls talked there of fucking, beasts talked there of eating,
> All heavy with sleep, fucked girls and fat leopards
>
> (XXXIX/193)

But if Pound's Homer is more amusing – in a very late Canto he has Leucothea offer Odysseus a peculiar trade: 'my bikini is worth your raft' (XCI/636) – his devotion to pagan ideals becomes more intense, echoing ideas he outlined in 'Credo' of 1930. Simplified, *The Cantos* reconstructs history in pagan terms. But as he continued with his epic, Pound rediscovered the ideogram first encountered in Fenollosa in 1914–16. It would provide a new instruction in thinking, allowing the representation of a signifying whole derived from the heap of concrete particulars he amassed as he sought a language 'full of detail/ Words that half mimic action' (*J/M* 22; XXXVIII/189).

The Fifth Decad of Cantos appeared in 1937, continuing the Latin tag
that appeared at the end of the previous volume: *'ad interim* 1933' ('in
the meantime'; XLI/206). This suggests the provisional and improvisa-
tional aspect of his work, the volume and its companion, *Cantos LII–LXXI*
(1940), constructing a cultural map for readers that has as its highlights
the founding of a bank in 16th century Siena, 18th century reforms
instigated in Tuscany, the history of China based on Confucian principles
and the career of John Adams. Collectively, these cantos diagnose
corruption in Western civilization through usury and seek alternative
solutions via new systems of exchange. Confucian thought and the
ideals of the early American Republic are the keys.

The Fifth Decad is various in its structure, as if Pound had still not
satisfactorily found a reliable order for his thought and presentation.
Beginning with the history of the Monti dei Paschi bank, Pound offers a
playful sense of Monti as 'A mount, a bank, a fund a bottom an/ institution
of credit' (XLII/209). Small caps spelling MOUNTAIN accompanied by
a pictograph add solidity to the term. (XLII/214). Indeed, more visual
elements begin to appear in the text of *The Cantos* with this volume and
following, as if Pound is simultaneously graphing his poem as he writes
it. This occurs with his use of dramatic typography as well as ideograms.
Law, nature and money unite through the success of the bank because
it has been able to 'keep bridle on usury' (XLIV/228), a statement
preparatory for the well known 'Usury' Canto, number XLV.

In this canto, Pound's declamatory voice catalogues the negative
effects of usury in western culture, continued in modern times in the
following canto that links usury with war. Banks have become non-
productive, making money out of nothing (XLVI/233). Orage, Marx, John
Adams, Jefferson, Napoleon, Rothschild and Roosevelt are among the
personalities playing a role in Pound's historical staging as he repeats
his claim that 'Usury rusts the man and his chisel/ It destroys the crafts-
man, destroying craft. . . . Usury is against Nature's increase.' 'Under
usury no stone is cut smooth' (LI/ 250). Ending the series are two dramatic
ideograms, Ching and Ming, the 'right name' which will reoccur near
the end of the Chinese Cantos (LX/333) and throughout the Adams
Cantos (re LXVI/382 or LXVIII/400). The first of the Chinese Cantos
in the following volume repeats the crucial lesson, 'call things by the
names' (LII/261).

In the midst of the cultural work accomplished by economics and
history in these cantos is the 'Seven Lakes Canto,' Canto XLIX, based
on a series of paintings and poems of river scenes in a Japansese manuscript book owned by Pound's parents. Foregrounding the seasons and

work, instead of myth and eroticism as seen in the surrounding cantos, the poem elaborates in delicate images and tone the inter-connectedness of time and work. The shift in tone is dramatic, the imagery precise, almost as if Pound, in the midst of his historical indictment, had to catch his breath:

> For the seven lakes, and by no man these verses:
> Rain; empty river; a voyage,
> Fire from frozen cloud, heavy rain in the twilight.
>
> (XLIX/244)

Cantos LII–LXXI begin retrospectively, recalling again the examples of Leopoldine reforms and the Monte dei Paschi bank where the true foundation of credit is 'the abundance of nature/ with the whole folk behind it' (LII/257). However, the first page of Canto LII contained an anti-Semitic attack on the Rothschilds and others, and originally had black lines marking these omitted passages: neither Eliot at Faber & Faber nor Laughlin, publishing the work in the States, thought them worthy of inclusion (they reappeared only in1986). To unify Confucian management and Greek fertility rites at Eleusis is the central task, expressed in the opening canto in the lines 'Between KUNG and ELEU-SIS' (LII/258). *Cantos LII–LXXI* place these ideas in action through a Confucian reading of Chinese history and pursuit of John Adam's ideals in a revolutionary America. Idealism and pragmatism join together. The archival texts cited in the Sienese cantos, those dealing with the bank, are also works that transmit authority and law. Textuality through documents validates history for Pound. Law becomes that of 'the just middle, the pivot' (LIII/269). Adams's claim that he is 'for balance,' followed by the ideogram Chung, 'the Unwobbling Pivot,' defines the ideal of law and Confucian reverence for documentation Pound venerates (LXX/413).

The bipartite structure of *Cantos LII–LXXI* (the first half, Cantos LII–LXI devoted to China, the second half, Cantos LXII–LXXI to Adams) is united by the identification of 'the Unwobbling Pivot' in western history. Identifying a dynastic element, whether via Confucius or Adams, is crucial because it is necessary in the conception of law as an authority which motivates the middle Cantos. Pound also moves away from the singular hero – Jefferson in the preceding volume, or Odysseus or Malatesta – in favor of Adams and the dynastic family which, among other things, edited and published the works of John Adams. The edition, edited by his grandson, included an account of him by his son.

Ancestry and lineage, Confucian attributes, replace that of the solitary man. Accompanying the publication of the first five hundred copies of *Cantos LII–LXXI* in America in September 1940 was a pamphlet entitled *Notes on Ezra Pound's Cantos* consisting of two essays: 'Notes on the Cantos' by one H.H., actually James Laughlin, and 'Notes on the Versification of the Cantos,' by an S.D., the young American poet, Delmore Schwartz. Pound was so pleased with the volume and its ending which linked John Adams, an enlightened thinker, with a Greek hymn to the sun and then the philosopher of light, Confucius, that he sent the edition to Mussolini. Pre-occupied with political developments, however, il Duce did not reply.

In April 1939, just before he published *Cantos LII–LXXI*, Pound revisited the United States, sailing on the *Rex* from Genoa. It was his first return since 1910 made possible by a small inheritance from Olivia Shakespear's estate; she had died in London in 1938. Pound believed that if he could see Mussolini in Italy, he could certainly see President Roosevelt in Washington. The goal was to drum some sense into America about the situation in Europe and urge them to stay out of any conflict which he was convinced would not spill over west of Poland. Another purpose was to lobby US Congressmen on the economic catastrophe enveloping the US and why Italy and America should be friends (*Dis* 118–19). Feeling intensely American, and eager to protect the country from economic and political ruin, he orchestrated his return. 'Am I American? Yes, and buggar the present state of the country, the utter betrayal of the American Constitution...' he proudly wrote in a letter just months before his journey (*SL* 322). Arriving in New York, he immediately gave a press conference while stretched out in a deck chair before going off to e.e. cummings' apartment. He arrived on Hitler's birthday (20 April).

In Washington, he tried to see H.L. Mencken, succeeded in seeing Archibald MacLeish (soon to be Librarian of Congress), and, unexpectedly, William Carlos Williams. Among politicians, he saw George Tinkham, Congressman from Massachusetts with whom he had corresponded and US Senator William Borah of Idaho; Borah's aide, Charles Corker, provides a vivid account of the poet in the corridors of power: Pound, he wrote, was 'a flamboyant character actor constantly and obviously playing (or overplaying) Ezra Pound....He translated everything he said into at least three languages, to make his point clear, although he knew that I was a farm boy from Idaho who spoke only English. The talk was of economics and world politics... as a performer he carried it off well. He did indeed speak poetry rather than prose' (*EPWB* 81). Pound spent about 20 minutes with Borah who was staunchly anti-fascist and a leader of the fight for the neutrality of the US in the European war. Ironically, Pound's letters to Borah, sent to him over the previous year, were likely never seen by him, as Corker makes clear. Nevertheless, Borah appears twice in *The Cantos*.

Unsuccessful in his political lobbying, Pound returned to New York, spent some brief time with Williams (who told Laughlin that 'the man is sunk...unless he can shake the fog of fascism out of his brain' [Wilhelm 2: 150]), met Zukofsky again at the studio of Pound's old friend Tibor Serly, and, for the first time after long correspondences, met Mencken, Mary Barnard and Marianne Moore. He also visited an ailing Ford Madox Ford, then in New York. In May he stopped at Harvard to give a reading, actually a recording of him 'bellowing his cantos into a microphone for a grammy-phone record' (Wilhelm 2: 153). He also saw Laughlin, then in his final year of university, and the poet Theodore Spencer. Yale and Fordham were also brief stops before his return to Hamilton in June to receive an honorary degree. The inscription partly read 'you have found that you could work more happily in Europe than in America...but your writings are known wherever English is read' (Wilhelm 2: 155). The event rated an editorial in *The New York Times* under the headline, 'Dr Ezra Pound,' declaring that 'he would have been a professor himself if he hadn't majored as a prophet' (*NTY* 13 June 1939: 22). Four days later, he sailed for Italy.

6
'Nothin' Undecided': Rome, Pisa, Washington, 1940–58

I trust there is nothin' Undecided about my position.

(Pound, April 1942)

When Pound returned to Italy in late June 1939, the war had begun. Germany had annexed Bohemia and Moravia, and Italy had invaded Albania. Distressed by the failure of his visit to America and fearing that Roosevelt would push America into the looming conflict to get itself out of the Depression, Pound oddly remained aloof from events around him. But gradually, he realized the severity of his situation after Germany invaded Poland in September 1939. At that point, Pound considered leaving Rapallo, telling Congressman Tinkham that he was ready to play politics in Boston, adding 'I can at moments be a serious character' (Wilhelm 2: 161). The Congressman did not take up the idea. Pound then turned away from the war, promoting musical events with Olga, holding a successful Vivaldi Week in Siena during Christmas 1939 and spending more time in Venice at Olga's 'Hidden Nest' – her small house at 252 calle Querini. Like Sant'Ambrogio, it became a welcomed refuge. He also began to spend time with the philosopher George Santayana who had recently retired to Italy from Harvard.

Pound was entering a transitional time: the war was beginning to limit his travel and correspondence, especially overseas; it also began to intrude in his thinking, diverting him from his poetry. Furthermore, mentors like Ford were dying, but new ones like Santayana were emerging. Pound was eager to learn from the philosopher whose concepts of naturalism lent a foundation to a portion of Pound's aesthetic. Santayana's idea of art as 'that organic or external rearrangement of matter by which a *monument* or a *maxim* is established in the world and an element of traditional form is added to culture' particularly echoed several of

Pound's own ideas of art and accomplishment (Santayana *Phil* II: 501). The philosopher also explained logic in terms that Pound understood: it was no more than a 'refined form of grammar' (Santayana *Realms* 439). Immersed in the ideogramic method, having just competed *Cantos LII–LXXI*, Pound welcomed the sharpness of logic and philosophic thought aimed at the idea of paradise (*SL* 331). Santayana at first considered Pound to be no more than a 'spasmodic rebel ... full of scraps of culture but lost, lost, lost in the intellectual world' (Wilhelm 2: 161). However, his correspondence with Pound continued through the St Elizabeths years and Pound found Santayana's ideas useful in what became a polemic against metaphysics. In the 1940's Pound was apparently preparing a notebook in Italian for Santayana on pragmatic aesthetics. But having finished his short pamphlet *What is Money For?* published in 1939, Pound was now ready to tackle elements of his long poem again now armed with Brooks Adam's *Law of Civilization and Decay*, introduced to him by Santayana. This work demonstrated an inextricable link between economics and art. Santayana's appeal, as noted in Canto LXXXI, was one of intellectual friendship encouraged by their shared admiration for the accomplishments of Mussolini (*Dis* 127–8).

By mid-1940, Pound had sketched what the remaining third of *The Cantos* might look like: a version of an earthly paradise and he told Eliot that he thought the 9th century Irish philosopher John Scotus Erigena would play a major role. Scotus authored the statement that 'authority comes from right reason,' a dangerous position in the face of Church authority. His remark that 'all things that are are lights' appears in Canto LXXXIII/548. Coupled with his continuing interest in Cavalcanti and Dante, Pound was preparing to move forward with his epic, understood as 'a poem including history' (*SL* 334; *ABCR* 46). The war, of course, would intervene and change not only Pound's life but the direction of his poem, radically shifting the nature of the paradise he would construct.

Pound began to lobby the Ministry of Popular Culture for support in his attempt to popularize fascism, first in the form of a dual language publication. An evaluation of Pound by an Italian bureaucrat, however, ended the plan; Pound, wrote the functionary, 'is a man of intelligence and culture ... but is a bungler' and has fantastic ideas about economic and financial questions. In the US he is appreciated as a poet but 'as a political and economic writer, he is not seriously considered' (Wilhelm 2: 170). Undiscouraged by his rejection, Pound pursued the possibility of playing some role in the Ministry of Popular Culture which coincided with his realization of the importance of radio as a propaganda tool, partly the result of his listening, and then writing, to the propagandist Lord Haw-Haw (William Joyce) beamed from Germany (*Sch* 592).

Pound spent the fall of 1940 in Siena with Olga as she continued her revival of Vivaldi and assisted Count Chigi, supporter of the Academia Musicale Chigiana. Mary visited, at one point traveling with Pound to Rome where he attempted to sort out her citizenship with the possible idea of repatriation to America. It did not happen; instead, with Olga, the three went to Venice. But Italy was soon embroiled in the war, attacking British forces in North Africa, invading Greece and suffering the defeat of their fleet at Taranto. But in the midst of this turmoil, Pound found his voice and a new identity. The source was radio.

Economic education not propaganda was Pound's initial aim when he started to write for the radio in late 1940, the first scripts read on Radio Rome by English speaking announcers. His effective use of radio partly resulted from the 1931 BBC broadcast of *The Testament of Francois Villon*. This was a technical and theoretical breakthrough for radio opera and in preparation the producer, E.A.F. Harding, tutored Pound on the potential and importance of the medium. The two met in Paris in May 1931 and the crash course in radio technique and production stuck with Pound as Harding reported on the 'highly charged, production-intensive atmosphere [at the BBC] where technological and artistic discoveries were daily events' (Fisher 3). This coincided with Pound's thinking about technology and machinery expressed in his essay 'Machine Art' (1927–30) in which he focuses on the aesthetic value of function because it is a mechanism of producing a work. Art becomes *technê* or construction rather than imitation, in Aristotle's terms 'the skill of making' (*GK* 327). Pound's essay 'Pragmatic Aesthetics' (ca. 1940–43) summarizes these ideas as he reiterates the specific: 'Art is the particular declaration that *implies* the general' (*PAesth.* 158). The experience of preparing the BBC broadcast thoroughly absorbed Pound and prepared him for the effective use and understanding of radio which *The Cantos* anticipated. In November 1934, he was asked to speak to the United States by the Foreign Ministry and on 11 January 1935, Pound gave his first short-wave address entitled 'come il Duce resolve il problema della distribuzione.' The next speaker on the program was Enrico Fermi on radioactivity.

Although he was at first upset at the gift of a radio from Natalie Barney in March 1940, Pound soon realized that 'what drammer or teeyater *wuz*, radio is. Possibly the loathing of it may stop diffuse writing' (*SL* 342). He told Ronald Duncan, however, that he anticipated radio in the 'first third of Cantos' yet 'was able to do 52/71 because I was the last survivin' monolith who did not have a bloody radio in the 'ome.' But, he admitted, one had to adjust to the presence of radio and learn the skill of 'picking the fake in the voices' (*SL* 343). By early 1941, Pound was making records of his talks to be broadcast, on average, twice a week on the *American Hour* program. He would often record batches of ten or twenty speeches at a time on visits to Rome, writing the scripts in Rapallo. He ended his talks when the Fascist government fell in July 1943, although he offered more scripts and ideas to Mussolini's government in exile in Salò.

More specifically, between January 1941 and 1943, Pound began to broadcast over 120 speeches on shortwave radio broadcasts from Rome to the US. The death of Joyce occurred in the first month of these activities, an event Pound marked with a broadcast entitled 'James Joyce: To His Memory,' containing this characteristic note: 'There is so much that the United States does not know. This war is proof of such vast incomprehensions, such tangled ignorance, so many strains of unknowing...' (*P/J* 273).[1] Some talks were pre-recorded onto discs so that Pound could control their content. All were written on his typewriters in Rapallo and first read to Olga who even suggested topics for him to discuss. When Pound got permission to read his own scripts on air, he also requested that specific music be played at the beginning and end of his talks (Fisher 199). Pound favored speaking in dialect as the only appropriate language to address the American listener who was not receptive, he asserted, to solemn or formal pronouncements.

Preceding and following Pound's broadcasts were selections from Italian opera or American dance music. His voice would follow a female announcer's and he would speak in a staged Yankee or weird brogue, rolling his r's as he did when reading his poetry out-loud. Pound quickly understood the potential impact of his audio lectures and the importance of persistence: 'I suppose if I go on talking to you kids LONG enough I will get something into your heads' he began on 8 June 1942 (*EPS* 162). A little insult would also catch the listener's ear he thought: 'If there is anyone capable of serious thought anywhere in range of this broadcast, let him at least try to think what I mean by the following statements' (*EPS* 150). But his method was always shorthand: 'My notes for Rome radio and my thoughts are telegraphic... agenda or agendum, more use than discussion,' while he understood that 'nothing solemn or formal will hold the American auditor' (in de Rachewiltz, 'Fragments' 164). Radio also possessed for him something of a Dantesque '*radiare*' to radiate outward.

Pound also used the occasion of his talks to promote his Cantos, prefacing his presentation of Canto XLVI with 'the footnotes... in case there is any possible word that might not be easily comprehended' (*EPS* 34). After his prose introduction, he read the entire Canto. In explaining recent fascist history, useful to grasp his canto, he would cite British examples from his past: in describing the decennio exposition in Rome, held to mark the first decade of Mussolini's reign, he notes that the Italians set up the old 'Popolo d'Italia, very like what had been the New Age Office in London. Except that Orage's office contained a couple of drawings by Max Beerbohm which have never been published' (*EPS* 34). Pound also provides a gloss on Roman history and Latin phrases, plus parallels, especially between Troy as 'the common grave' and the way 'gold [is] the common sepulchre.' Citing Greek in the canto, he translates it as '[usury, destroyer of] men and cities and governments' showing that 'HELARXE,' is 'more or less twisted from a line of Aeschylus; about Helen of Troy destroyer of men, and cities' (*EPS* 34). Pound believed the airwaves would be an effective means for his poetry to be heard. Although the broadcasts would become anti-Semitic, anti-Black and anti-American, they nevertheless provide important autobiographical and historical statements in a style free from 'static,' summarizing Pound's thought on numerous issues that preoccupied him over the previous twenty-five years. At one point he planned to collect some 300 radio speeches in Italian for free distribution in the schools (de Rachewiltz, 'Fragments' 170).

The persistent theme of the broadcasts was that America should not go to war and that the falsifications of history must be challenged. The testy, impatient tone of the talks with their undercurrent of wry humor were linked to, and likely influenced by, the method of *The Cantos*. When he writes in Canto LXXII/436, 'Confusion of voices as from several transmitters, broken phrases/ And many birds singing in counterpoint' he may in fact be alluding to the multiple sounds of radio *and* his experiences as a studio broadcaster. Another paradigm for Pound's critical view of America was the skeptical tradition of American expatriate writers: Henry James in his biography of Hawthorne or *The American Scene*; Edith Wharton in passages from *Custom of the Country*; Henry Adams in sections from his *Education*; or Gertrude Stein in her prose all presented critiques. America, to these writers, did not measure up to the cultural life of Europe.

Pound insisted that his broadcasts were not propagandist, at least not in favor of the Italian government which gave him assurances that he would not be sending out *their* propaganda. Such a disclaimer, he thought, would absolve him of the crime of aid and comfort to the enemy. The talks were examples of free speech and his defence of the US Constitution which enshrines the freedom of the press and speech. 'Free speech without free radio speech is as zero' he wrote in Canto LXXIV/446. He believed he was fulfilling the mandate of 'the natural patriot,' a phrase Hemingway used to identify him in 1931 (de Rachewiltz, 'Fragments' 158). The manner of Pound's writing throughout the war was that of a 'Puritan didact' in the tradition of the American Jeremiad. (Kenner in Laughlin, *P as wuz* xii). Pound's castigating, moralizing voice, focused on identifying error to hasten change in political, economic and social spheres. 'I don't so much write as roar' he told James Laughlin in 1941 (*EP/JL* 132). His moral earnestness, but without the wit or playfulness of his earlier prose, had its origin in the American Puritan tradition and in the American roots of his family and their strenuous moralism, including his parents' church activities and missionary work. Pound's constant reminder to his readers of how far they had fallen from the ideals of the Founding Fathers is clearly in this tradition. The monitory role of Jefferson and Adams must be re-constituted if America is to achieve a mercantile-free future. Over and over, Pound conveys a sense of mission which the radio broadcasts, in particular, capture.

Pound zealously sought an ideal but the more he pursued this goal, the more he seemed to be speaking only to himself. The disparity between possibility and fact caused Pound to admonish, lecture, reproach, scold and rebuke his reader/listeners, the result of his desire to direct, list, program and instruct his many 'students.' Among some sympathizers, this led to a kind of bewilderment, as Marianne Moore told T.S. Eliot, 'I cannot see why Ezra Pound exhausts himself trying to engender intelligence in the whole world.' Pound himself soulfully admitted his disappointment late in *The Cantos*: 'That I lost my center/ fighting the world' (Moore 318; CXVII/ 822).

Yet Pound's passionate need to denounce American corruption was, ironically, the catalyst for his continued writing during the war, whether through radio broadcasts, journalism or poetry. With the war surrounding him in Rapallo, he still regularly journeyed to Rome (on a special government rail pass) to record, developing a new circle of friends which included the daughter of William Michael Rossetti, Olivia Rossetti Agresti, and the beautiful American, Amélie Rives, who also praised Mussolini on the airwaves. Oscar Wilde introduced this striking woman to her future husband, an Italian prince, at a London garden party.

Because of the war, Mary joined Olga in Sant'Ambrogio in August 1941, a period of semi-seclusion, with Pound occasionally visiting as he traversed the steep trail of the *salita*, often bringing food. Olga told villagers Mary (who had no idea of Dorothy) was a cousin to avoid raising suspicion over her identity as a foreigner (*SCh* 601). Pound's US passport was extended for six months in the summer of 1941 and at first he announced that he would go back to the states, but then reversed his decision. Refusal to acknowledge Mary's US citizenship by the US Embassy, preventing her travel, may have contributed to his decision to stay. Homer Pound's injury from a fall and difficult recovery (he was 83) in November 1941 may have also prompted him to give up any plans of returning. It was also frightfully expensive to get six (Homer, Isabel, Dorothy, Olga, Mary and Pound) to Lisbon and then by 'flying clipper' to New York, the only safe route out of the country. On 7 December 1941, Pound was in Rome having dinner with Reynolds Packard, an American journalist, who immediately told him to get out of Italy when they heard the news of Pearl Harbor; Pound refused, although he stopped broadcasting for six weeks (Packard 66). Two days after Pearl Harbor, however, he wrote to Adriano Ungaro, an official at the Ministry of Popular Culture, that he wanted to continue broadcasting, believing that his talks were not in any way harmful to his status as a US Citizen. But while continuing with his broadcasts, Pound translated a novel by Enrico Pea (who described him as a figure both 'cultivated and barbaric' [Pea 443]) and worked on a translation of an economic text by Odon Por; when he finished this, he began to retranslate Confucius's *Ta Hio*.

A question emerges, however: why did Pound support the fascist cause so vehemently and unreasonably? Reynolds Packard records Pound's reply to the question: I believe in it, he answered and 'want to defend it. I don't see why Fascism is contrary to the American philosophy. I am only against Roosevelt and the Jews who influence him' (Packard 67). Another answer might be the acclaim he received in Italy and neglect he felt in America. Hemingway had a similar explanation for Pound's embrace of fascism. To Nancy Cunard, he explained that Pound turned bitter against America because he never had the recognition he deserved; the English also rejected him, while the French ignored him. Only Italy considered him important (Cunard 128). Laughlin even shared this view, although it is simplistic because it overlooks Pound's long admiration of men of authority who morally, as well as politically, could transform a country. Confucius, Malatesta, Jefferson and Mussolini are the prime examples and another source of his belief in the fascist movement. But Pound's obdurate support of Mussolini, pursuit of monetary crime and attachment to 'men of power' in the fascist government would lead to his downfall.

The Federal Communications Commission in Washington began to monitor and tape Pound's broadcasts starting on 2 October 1941. They did not intend to prosecute Pound but were merely recording all broadcasts transmitted to North America from Rome Radio – and since Italy and the US were not yet at war, no one paid much attention to the impassioned, vitriolic and often irrational remarks of the poet. After Pearl Harbor, however, a new concern emerged. Warned by several that further broadcasts could lead to trouble because the US was now directly involved in the war, Pound, nevertheless, decided to continue, beginning again on 29 January 1942. This time the talks were even more hysterical. Compounding the situation for Pound, recently notified by the Italians that he could live under the Italian Supreme Command for the duration of the war, was the death of his father in February 1942. The loss was grievous and may have reinforced his decision to stay, although there is some evidence that he half-heartedly tried to get tickets for the last repatriation train for Americans from Italy (Wilhelm 2:191). In May 1942, he actually attempted to board the final train for journalists leaving the country but was stopped by the American *Chargé d'Affaires* in Rome. Pound could then only hope for an Italian victory, but by now even his sponsors in America were turning against him.

One of his staunchest supporters was now one of his strongest opponents: *Poetry* magazine. In an April 1942 editorial headed 'The End of Ezra Pound,' Eunice Tietjens declared that Pound's broadcasts were 'deliberate attempts to undermine the country of his birth through enemy propaganda.' She then castigated Pound as 'the perpetual adolescent of American poetry' who is likely committing treason by continuing to broadcast and expressed hope that his behavior would now mean 'the end of Ezra Pound' (Tietjens 39, 40). Another who conveyed reservations over his talks was his wife, Dorothy: Pound promptly excluded her from his private readings, now directed only to Olga and Mary. Reflecting the ambiguity of the times, even some fascists questioned his sincerity. The President of the Fascist Institute of Culture, Camillo Pellizzi, suspected that Pound was a spy, believing that his incomprehensibility on air expressed a code understandable only by American listeners.

By 1943 serious cracks appeared in the Axis war effort with setbacks on the Russian and North African fronts. But after a hiatus in February 1943, Pound resumed his talks and regularly traveled again from Rapallo to Rome. In July, however, the Allies invaded Sicily and bombs began to fall on Italian cities with Rome a target on 19 July; by 25 July Mussolini was deposed and arrested. Sent to an isolated ski resort, he was rescued by German commandos in September and taken north where he tried to remake his government at Salò. The next day, Pound was indicted for treason in Washington, the recorded broadcasts key evidence. A more detailed, second indictment would be issued two years later. The principal charge in the first indictment was that Pound had asserted that 'citizens of the United States should not support the United States in the conduct of the said war' (Wilhelm 2: 197). In a formal letter to the U.S. Attorney General on 4 August 1943, Pound sought to refute the charges, claiming in clear prose that 'I have not spoken with regard to [this] war but in protest against a system which creates one war after another.' 'I have not spoken to the troops' he insisted, adding that 'free speech under modern conditions becomes a mockery if it do not include the right of free speech over the radio' (*LC* 367, 369). The poet Lawrence Ferlinghetti pithly summed up Pound's argument when he recently proclaimed 'dissent is not unAmerican.'[2]

Pound continued to broadcast, at least until early September, when he decided another trip to Rome was necessary to find out what was happening, He witnessed terrific upheaval, however, because the Germans had seized control of the Fascist city to prevent capitulation to the Allies. After two days, he knew he had to return north and on 10 September, five days after American troops landed in southern Italy and two days after Italy capitulated to the Allies, he departed, leaving a small attache case, his walking stick and wide brimmed Borsalino hat with the staff at the Albergo Italia, his favorite Rome hotel. He expected to be back; the fifty-eight year old poet then set out on foot for Gais in the Tyrol to see his daughter.

Pound's harrowing trip of some 450 miles with only a knapsack was frightening. Canto LXXVIII provides one account of the journey, partly in terms of myth. Peasants, working people and others assisted as he traveled north to Bologna which a cancelled passage from Canto LXXXIV further narrates:

> One night under the stars
> >   one on a bench in Rieti
> > one on Bologna platform
> > > after food at the cab-driver's friend's trattoria
> > ...understood why Hem had written,
> > that is, his values.

(CPost 206)

The reference to Hemingway is to his idea of life as an adventure which Pound was now experiencing through his difficult journey that took him by foot to Fara in Sabina northeast of Rome and on to Rieti, fifty miles north of the capital. He then continued on a train with members of a disintegrating Italian army, although the train did not quite make it to Bologna. However, Pound did, soon finding another train to Verona. There, he halted for a day to decide whether or not to go north to Bruneck and on to Gais, or to the coast toward Rapallo. He chose Gais and hitched another train ride, arriving at the foster family caring for Mary in an unrecognizable state (*Dis* 184–5; LXXVIII/498). The title of a cancelled passage, however, written in Pisa related to this journey is 'INCIPIT VITA NUOVA:' ('here begins the new life' [*CPost* 204]). But in retelling the tale of Pound's trip in *Discretions*, Mary sensed rejuvenation and victory in his arrival (*Dis* 190–5).

Triumph at completing the fearful journey meant he could at last unburden himself of guilt over his personal past. Witnessing the horror of war and the danger so many, including himself, faced, he knew he must tell Mary the truth: that he had a wife, Dorothy, who had a son of her own living in England (*Dis* 186–7). He even revealed that Olga had wanted a son, not a daughter. But as the war came closer closer, he had little time to stay. The local police suggested he would be safer in Germany, an offer he declined. He had to return to Olga and Dorothy in Rapallo and he and Mary soon went to Bolzano where he obtained papers to travel south. Boarding a train with only a single passenger car – the rest were flatcars loaded with cannons – he muttered to his daughter, 'always preceded by something' (*Dis* 195). At Salò, he stopped briefly to meet the new Minister of Popular Culture, hoping to resume his broadcasting from Milan, the new center of Mussolini's government of the north. He then continued on to Rapallo.

Nineteen forty-four and forty-five were difficult for Pound as the Allies overcame Italy. Living conditions deteriorated rapidly and food became scarce. Olga worried that an Allied victory might mean that Pound's broadcasts would be used as evidence against him (*O/E* 151). Bombings of Rapallo and Genoa became intense, while some foreigners, like the Anglican priest Father Desmond Chute, who had tutored Mary, were deported as enemy aliens to work in war hospitals (*Dis* 147–8). Numerous alerts and bombings in Zoagli, a village on the other side of Sant'Ambrogio, occurred with more frequency, as Pound alternated between his apartment in the harbor and Olga's flat up the *salita*. Mary, now eighteen, took a job, first, in the Municipal Hall of Gais and then in a convalescent hospital for Germans above Cortina in the Dolomites.

By May 1944, however, the situation in Rapallo became tense. The Germans ordered an evacuation of everyone with seafront apartments: Pound and Dorothy had twenty-four hours to leave. Olga invited them to join her up the hill in Sant' Ambrogio. Pound first removed most of his papers and books to the Casa del Fascio, a municipal building which had a large but unused room set aside for a library. The remainder of his materials went up to Casa 60, six large rooms with two Ezra-made arm-chairs, several small tables, books and files but without electricity, a phone or running water, although it had a stunning view of the sea (*O/E* 129, 154). Isabel Pound remained at her apartment on the other side of Rapallo.

Dorothy moved into Mary's room at Casa 60 with its furniture from Yeats. It was a difficult time, Olga deciding that she should have little to do with Dorothy, spending the first night in her own room playing a Mozart Concerto which Dorothy found surprising. '*I* couldn't have done that' she told Pound the next morning who reported the comment to Olga who did not play again. Most evenings, Pound and Dorothy sat in the dark listening to BBC broadcasts on a battery operated radio (*O/E* 154). They tried to act civilly to one another, Olga contributing her meager salary from teaching English at a technical school in Rapallo to the cost of food. Only afterwards did Olga admit that she felt used by Dorothy, cooking, cleaning, finding food 'which I only undertook owing to her [Dorothy's] incapacity, so that E. should not suffer' (*O/E* 155). Mary's sense of the situation in *Discretions* appropriately identifies the tension and dislike that lasted for nearly a year (258). On 4 June 1944, Pound read that bombs had severely damaged the Tempio Malatestiano in Rimini, his touchstone for Renaissance culture (the report was an exaggeration it turned out: Redman 261). On the 5 June, Rome was liberated, followed by the Allied invasion of France on the 6th. His world, externally and internally, was being attacked, surviving only in fragments.

In the spring of 1945, Italian partisans in Rapallo rose up against the Germans who fled. Americans soon arrived and on 29 April Mussolini, captured by partisans, was executed. On 2 May Pound went down the hill to the new American headquarters at the Hotel Europa to explain his reasons for the Rome Radio broadcasts, asking to be taken to Wash-ington to give information to the State Department. No one understood what he wanted or who he was. He returned to Casa 60. On 3 May other Americans had returned and on that day Dorothy went down to make her weekly visit to Isabel Pound, while Olga went to meet the American commanding officer. He had no time for her but when she wearily climbed back to her home to report to Pound, she found the door locked and him gone. He had been arrested by two Italian partisans of the Zoagli Group eager to turn him in for a ransom. He was working at his typewriter on the Legge bi-lingual edition of Mencius, one of the four classics of Confucius when they pounded on his door with a rifle butt and ordered him to go with them. He slipped a small Chinese dictionary in his pocket and the Confucius as he was roughly escorted away, stooping to pick up an eucalyptus pip from the *salita* (mentioned in Canto LXXX 520). To the woman who lived on the ground floor, he made a gesture with his hand that mimicked a noose as he departed. Another harrowing journey was to begin.

Questioned first by the partisans, Pound asked to be taken to the American command in nearby Chiavari. With Olga, who had located him and brought food, he was driven to the town but left at a partisan prison because the driver could not find the US headquarters. The officer in charge recognized '*il poeta, amico d'Italia*' and refused to take him in. They soon went by jeep, however, to Lavagna and a US headquarters, Pound believing that once he told his story, charges against him would be dropped. A Colonel Webber greeted Pound, whom he had heard of, but had no idea what to do with. He offered Pound and Olga some food and then sent them on to Genoa and the Counter Intelligence Corps headquarters where they sat in a dark hall unguarded all night. Pound was not questioned until 4.30pm the next day. Following another night at the center, Pound was then interviewed by Major Frank L. Amprin, sent from Rome. Pound did not know that Amprin was an undercover FBI agent from the Department of Justice and not an Army officer. Assisting Amprin was Ramon Arrizabalaga, the commanding officer of the CIC. In intimate conversations in-between the interrogations, Pound and Olga shared their experience, Pound later telling Mary that Olga 'saved me from stupidities' making him see that he 'should not babble and joke about being "the American Lord Haw-Haw"' (*O/E* 161). Nevertheless, the first of a series of official re-tellings of his life story had begun which would find poetic resolution in *The Pisan Cantos*.

In the midst of his questioning, Pound asked Amprin to help him send a telegram to President Truman explaining that he, Pound, was capable of settling a Confucian peace with the Japanese that would be acceptable to China as well. He also drafted a final radio broadcast he titled 'Ashes of Europe Calling,' a grim parody of his usual 'Europe Calling'opening. Reading a paper while Pound was again questioned, Olga unexpectedly learned that Pound was condemned as a traitor by the US government. Meanwhile, with assistance from Pound, Amprin and Arrizabalga established a six page 'Sworn Statement' by Pound on his activities and motives between 1940 and 1945 (Document 6, *LC*). Unsatisfied with the final document, however, Pound prepared two addenda, one entitled 'Outline of Economic Basis of Historic Process' (Document 7, *LC*) in which he argues that Mussolini went wrong when he failed to receive Pound's translation of Confucius in time to reform his government.

On 7 May, Amprin drove Olga back to Casa 60, produced a letter from Pound allowing him to examine the poet's papers, and left for Genoa with books, letters and radio scripts. Dorothy, who had returned to learn that Pound had been taken way on the 3rd, waited two days and then went to stay with Isabel Pound at Villa Raggio. When Amprin returned a week later, he left with Pound's Everest portable typewriter with it's broken *t* and told Olga that no one, not even next of kin, could communicate with Pound (*PC* XII). But the three weeks Pound would spend at Genoa were productive: he was instructing his captors, refining his ideas and working on his English translations of Confucius. A well-known photograph of the poet typing while at the Counter Intelligence Corps in Genoa in May 1945 records his concentration on the translation project and indifference to his surroundings. He felt so comfortable with his interlocutors that on several occasions he gave the fascist salute when they entered the room and rationalized that it was the fall of Mussolini's regime that allowed him to get to the center of Confucius' meaning (*LC* 9,113).The headline over a photo of Pound in *Stars and Stripes*, the U.S. military paper, for 22 May 1945, read 'Italians Bag a Yank Fascist.'

On 24 May, Pound managed to write a note to Olga suggesting that he was going to Rome but on that very day, Pound was handcuffed to a black prisoner and loaded into a jeep to be driven to the Disciplinary Training Center at Pisa and placed in an exposed, reinforced steel cage inside several barriers of barbed wire located near the perimeter fence with a view of a military road beyond the stockade. The guards called these cells 'the bird cages.' The purpose of the camp was for court-marshaled soldiers to work out their sentences by undergoing one year of strenuous re-training which, if satisfactorily completed, meant they could rejoin their units. Some prisoners, however, who committed capital offences, were awaiting transfer to Federal prisons in the US. Two were sent to be hanged. Pound, the only civilian imprisoned at the DTC was forbidden to have any conversation with other prisoners in his area. He was given food once a day; at night he slept on the damp concrete floor when not kept wake by powerful floodlights that were on throughout the darkness.

After several days of scorching sun, Pound was allowed a pup tent inside his steel cage which reminded him of the gorilla pen at the Rome zoo. Hours were spent watching an ant colony or wasps build a nest; he exercised by playing imaginary tennis and shadow boxing but dizziness and claustrophobia caused two camp psychiatrists to suggest that the sixty-year old might experience a mental breakdown if such conditions continued; they recommended his move to the medical compound. After approximately three weeks in the steel cage, Pound was shifted and he soon began to work again, writing with a pencil in longhand on cheap writing pads on a packing crate desk; these holograph manuscripts, numbering more than 300 pages, form the first text of *The Pisan Cantos* (Bush, '"Quiet"' 188; *PC* XXIII). Eventually, given permission to use the typewriter in the dispensary in the evenings, he began feverishly to revise, correct and add to his original drafts. When not typing, accompanied by his characteristic high-pitched humming, Pound often lectured anyone who came by on economics, usury or the necessary steps required to reform the world (*LC* 15–16; *PC* XV). He would then return to his work: *The Pisan Cantos* and a new translation of Confucius to appear as *The Unwobbling Pivot & Great Digest*.

Allowed to type, Pound nevertheless soon found that supplies were often limited. His typing became unorthodox: words were incomplete, while lines broke at unusual places as he rushed to return the typewriter carriage. Parts of Canto LXXIV, for example, had to be written on sheets of toilet paper, while cross-outs, cancellations and erratic additions made the typescripts almost unreadable even to himself (Bush, '"Quiet"' 173ff). He then initiated a complicated process to create a fair copy: he first mailed the new cantos to Dorothy. She would then take them to the Caffé Jolanda in Rapallo for Olga to pick up for retyping by Mary who had by now re-joined her mother at Casa 60.[3] Only via this circuitous route were clean copies of *The Pisan Cantos* prepared.

Throughout that summer, Olga and Dorothy also exchanged polite notes at the Caffé about Pound's situation. Olga would often go to Genoa to send messages to Pound from both of them, although Dorothy protested that Olga might be supplanting her role as wife. Olga, however, reminded her that her difficult task was essential: 'it is of vital importance to safeguard E's reputation in every way . . . that cannot be done by bickering among our selves or showing anything but a united front to strangers' (*O/E* 164). They soon settled their disagreement as Mary sent down some food and books, and Dorothy some money she claimed Pound left. Only two months after Pound's arrest did Dorothy officially learn where Pound had been kept: Pisa, less than an hour from Rapallo.

In late September, Dorothy received three letters from Pound, filled with instructions and requests. In a ninth letter, dated 23 September

1945, he included a typed copy of Canto LXXXI, perhaps the best known of *The Pisan Cantos* for its account of his vision – 'there came new subtlety of eyes into my tent' – and his declaration of poetic freedom: 'To break the pentameter, that was the first heave.' An affirmative expression reinforced a renewed spirit: 'What thou lovest well remains/ the rest is dross' (LXXXI/540, 538, 540–1). Dorothy quickly realized that this and the later cantos are 'your self, the memories that make up yr. person' (*LC* 131).

Pound's 'Note to [the] Base Censor,' copied in a letter to Dorothy of 4 November 1945, explains *The Pisan Cantos* as a jagged recollection of memory and reflection combining the past with events in the camp and observations of the natural world around him. He furthermore insists that the work contains 'nothing in the nature of cypher or intended obscurity,' although it requires some awareness of the preceding seventy-one cantos and possesses, 'an extreme condensation in the quotations.' Importantly, he writes that:

> the form of the poem and main progress is conditioned by its own inner shape, but the life of the D.T.C. passing OUTSIDE the scheme cannot but impinge, or break into the main flow. The proper names given are mostly those of men on sick call seen passing my tent.
>
> (*LC* 177)

Serenity and indignation define the work as a whole as he alternates uneasily between lyricism and didacticism.

On 3 October 1945, Dorothy visited Pound for the first time for one hour; she reported to Olga that he looked healthy and was working on Confucius and more cantos. He can receive letters from anyone but can write only to her (Dorothy). Olga used the opportunity to write often, among other things, offering news of mutual friends in Paris who died during the war years, a prompt, perhaps, for Pound's recall of these figures in the cantos he was writing. In one note, she remarked that 'I felt it the best thing they could have done for the *Cantos*, to shut you up for awhile. She [Olga] is glad he has begun to sing again' (his mother, however, was less pleased, telling Dorothy that she was disappointed in them: 'after five months undisturbed I expected something more valua-ble' [O/E 166; *LC* 133]).

In 1945, Dorothy made a second journey to see Pound, a prelude to the time she would spend in Washington to be near him during his years at St Elizabeths. Her letters to him during 1945–46 also dealt with news of the outside which he craved and possessed a 'compassionate practicality' in contrast to his own scattered thoughts and directives found in his replies (*LC* 19). Her calm resolve matched Pound's passionate intensity. Indeed, since he believed that only an attorney who had 'written a life of J. Adams and translated Confucius' could defend him, 'otherwise, how CAN he know what it is about?,' he felt that *he* was the only one who could represent himself (*LC* 159). Dorothy, Laughlin and others prevailed, however, and at the appropriate time he had proper representation.

By the middle of October, Pound's restlessness and impatience were becoming more acute. He told Dorothy that she must write to Congressman Tinkham; to the commander of the DTC, he suggested he be released on parole to Rapallo. Convinced he could be of immediate political use, he told the commander that in view of the situation in China and Japan, the 'bottling of my knowledge now amounts to suppression of military information.' Accompanying the letter on its right margin was a set of ideograms (*LC* 171). Distracting him from his anxiety over his future was a visit from Olga and Mary on 17 October.

Almost one month later, Pound's waiting would end. On 16 November 1945, two officers surprised Pound in the dispensary and told him he would be departing for Washington in an hour. After they left, Pound walked to the door, turned with a half smile and to the officer present put two hands to his neck and jerked upward. A letter he was typing to Dorothy two days earlier broke off with a sudden pencil scrawl: 'Leaving probably Rome. love E' (*LC* 189). At 8.30pm he was bundled in a jeep and driven for more than five hours to Ciampino airport near Rome. At 8.30am he was aboard his first flight, heading to Washington where he arrived, after a stop in Bermuda, on the evening of 18 November. Two US marshals met him at Bolling Field and promptly booked him in the District of Columbia jail, from which he would write 'this cell modernist with fine high mess hall below & four story windows, enormous high sala [hall] under the cliff dwellings' (*LC* 207). Arraigned the next day, the Judge, appropriately named Laws, denied his request to defend himself. A young Quaker civil liberties lawyer, Julien Cornell, agreed to defend him and on 20 November, Cornell reported to Laughlin that Pound seemed 'very wobbly in his mind,' flitting from one idea to another, unable to concentrate on answering a single question. He also suggested the possibility of pleading insanity, Pound apparently unstable from his long internment in Pisa (*LC* 22). Pound's legal saga had begun, underscored by a fresh indictment of nineteen acts of treason issued on 26 November 1945.

A transfer to Gallinger Hospital for a psychiatric exam followed and four psychiatrists concurred: he was insane and recommended he not stand trial. Judge Laws ordered him transferred to St Elizabeths Hospital for the Insane, a federal institution, pending a full hearing. He was admitted as case number 58, 102 on 21 December as a determined Dorothy prepared to leave Rapallo and Pound's mother and travel to be with him in Washington. He was first installed in Howard Hall, which housed its patients in small cells: Pound would call it the 'hell hole.' Locked in a solitary cell, his fear of claustrophobia returned and he constantly protested his incarceration. When asked by the admitting psychiatrist to explain his extreme fatigue, Pound 'replied in rage and exasperation, "all of Europe is on my shoulders"' (*LC* 25). The doctors felt he was psychotic; Pound felt he was a lost Odysseus or a modern Villon condemned to the gallows. As the poet Charles Olson would write, 'suddenly he [Pound] is in history, along with John Adams and Martin Van Buren' (Olson 21).

His letters to Dorothy at this time conveyed his anxiety and concern about *not* knowing what was happening on the outside. But soon, visitors began to appear from Olson to his old friend, Ida Maple. Olga now desperately wanted to come but Pound dissuaded her, telling her that he discouraged Dorothy as well, although she was taking that step on her own. Olson, visiting in early January 1946, noted how restored creatively Pound seemed as he regained his vigor, despite 'all the corruption of his body politic' (*LC* 26). Olson had been at Pound's late November 1945 arraignment where he had seemed frightened, unsure of himself and strangely mute. In 1946 at St Elizabeths, Pound was strong and energetic, his eyes 'no longer hooded with hate' (Olson 36). But his clarity sometimes wavered as his despair re-surfaced. Unlike the DTC where after a while he was well-treated with nature as solace and writing a possibility, at Howard Hall, he had nothing, telling Cornell of:

> a world lost
> grey mist barrier impassible
> ignorance absolute
>   anonyme
> futility of might have been
> coherent areas
>   constantly
>   invaded,
> aiuto [help]
>
> (*LC* 251)

On 13 February 1946, Pound's hearing took place before Judge Laws and the jury returned a verdict of 'unsound mind.' He was ordered back to St Elizabeths and when Olson revisited him the next day, an excited Pound greeted him by waving newly typed copies of Cantos LXXIV–LXXXIV delivered to him that morning by Laughlin (Olson 72). Pound was also now reading fiction, enjoying *Parade's End* by Ford and several novels by Arnold Bennett. He also continued with his work on the Confucian odes which restored a sense of personae for him which *The Pisan Cantos* had dropped in favor of personal recollection. He also resumed his role as tutor to the world, telling Omar Pound, for example, to read only the essential writers: Confucius, Homer, Frobenius. Pound insisted to Laughlin that he publish a 'nucleus of civilization, more organic than a Five foot shelf' (*LC* 30). The energetic, voluble Pound had returned as a doctor's report of 13 March 1946 confirmed: in discussion, Pound suddenly became 'quite animated in his conversation, bangs the desk, jumps up, raises his voice, becomes flushed and displays evidence of energy... [and] often punctuates his vituperations with picturesque profanity' (*LC* 30). Doubly exiled, in an alien America and in a locked cell, Pound once doodled that his nationality was 'paradiso perduto' (*LC* 32). By 10 July, however, Dorothy was with him and by January 1947, he was moved to the more amenable Cedar and then Chestnut Wing of the Central Building where he would remain for the next eleven years; routine and regularity, necessary for his creative life, had been restored.

No part of Pound's life has received such scrutiny as his arrest, time at Pisa and imprisonment at St Elizabeths because in this Dantesque drama of imprisonment and separation from family, friends and books he composed *The Pisan Cantos* (LXXIV–LXXXIV), eleven cantos that form the celebrated apex of his long poem.[4] Originally, ten cantos made up the Pisan series but after learning of the death of a young English journalist/ poet he was translating into Italian, (J.P. Angold), plus the impending deaths of several fascist collaborators, Pound recalled his many friends killed in World War I and began Canto LXXXIV in which he also inserted several phrases from Dorothy's letters (*LC* 117). In the isolation and harsh surroundings of the DTC, and while undergoing the intense review of his life through the on-going interrogation by FBI and military security agents, Pound's past emerged again. Indeed, the very process of daily engaging his past through the interrogations resulted in the merging of personal and literary memories combined with feelings of self-criticism and ethical responsibility that became the catalyst for *The Pisan Cantos*. Anticipating the process was the arduous journey from Rome to Gais, resulting in his need to confess his personal story to Mary. The retrospective and meditative *Pisan Cantos* erupted on the typewriter of the DTC's dispensary, Pound typing furiously as if he sensed that he might not have time to finish.

The Pisan Cantos is Pound's memory book decoding and recoding his past in a kind of quest for internal harmony in the face of destruction. He seeks to redeem light and reason and throughout the poem the imagery of eyes and sight transform the work from a record of images to a process of healing. Following a dark night of the soul in Canto LXXXII, for example, eyes reappear as forms of compassion and peace. Recasting several of his draft Italian verses written while composing Cantos LXXII and LXXIII, Pound draws from nature in a series of symbolic passages such as that on ants at LXXX/533. The powers of natural observation and discovery of the paradisical energies in nature contribute to the purification of the poet's will: to discover that 'the ant's a centaur in his dragon world' is to gather 'from the air a live tradition' (LXXXI/541, 542). Importantly, all is grounded in the everyday: 'When the mind swings by a grass-blade/ an ant's forefoot shall save you' (LXXXIII/553). But the structure of the poem altered as Pound mixed autobiographical memory with interruptions from camp life and history.

In *The Pisan Cantos*, visionary poetry mixes with diary and reminiscence. His model for this form is the lyric and episodic *Testament* of Villon with Dante as a backdrop. The very first lines he wrote at Pisa, memorializing the hanging of the prisoner Louis Till, evoke Villon's gallows. A loose, lyrical progression alternates with a narrative of memory expanded by the activity and action of nature. Identifying with Villon, rather than Dante or Confucius, links the poem with the vision of the outcast rather than the governor, an irony given his earlier veneration of strong figures such as Adams, Jefferson or Confucius. The late addition of Canto LXXXIV, a farewell to a series of figures that were important to him – Mussolini, Pierre Laval and Quisling – meant re-framing the entire sequence which caused him to shift ten angry lines to the beginning of Canto LXXIV forming a new and urgent opening to the sequence (see LXXIV/445). The drama of *The Pisan Cantos* was, then, an afterthought and resulted from an editorial change, the new opening announcing a more political poem.

Opposing the political, however, and suggesting the complex contradictions that characterize the *The Pisan Cantos*, a work that both resists and employs the lyrical, is the visionary, introduced in the line, 'To build the city of Dioce whose terraces are the colour of stars.' This immediately follows the hostile opening of Canto LXXIV (LXXIV/445). This second theme of redemption confronts the horrors of war and death but, simultaneously, the need to reclaim the past. Balancing a concern with terror and natural beauty ('Arachne mi porta fortuna, LXXIV/466), compassion becomes a lyrical search for an unknown but imagined future reshaped and redefined:

> Le Paradis n'est pas artificiel
> but spezzato apparently
> it exists only in fragments unexpected excellent sausage,
> the smell of mint, for example
>
> (LXXIV/458)

Current criticism of *The Pisan Cantos* challenges the thematic contradictions within the poem focusing on whether the work is one of repentance or not: to what degree do the eleven cantos continue Pound's subtle support of fascism? Are they a lament for the passing of the fascist and Nazi collaborators, or are they a reluctant recantation of past crimes? There is no clear answer partly because throughout the sequence, Pound's aesthetic and ideology contrast.[5] Technically brilliant, the poems also demonstrate a new, confessional mode emerging from the poet's dark night of the soul, a cry that:

> nothing matters but the quality
> of the affection –
> in the end – that has carved the trace in the mind
> dova sta memoria
>
> (LXXVI/477)

With the Malatesta and, perhaps, the Chinese Cantos, *The Pisan Cantos* are one of the most successful and sustained sequences in the entire poem. Pound sensed this in Pisa when he told Dorothy in October 1945 that 'the new Cantos are simpler in parts [and] there is a certain amount of new technique' (*LC* 137). In the poems there is no distinction between past and present events as the cantos defy paradigms and fulfill his mandate, borrowed from Confucius, 'Make it New' (Perloff, *Dance* 19–20).

Published in July 1948 – also the year the first complete one volume edition of *The Cantos* appeared – *The Pisan Cantos* won the first Bollingen Prize, offered by the Library of Congress in 1949. This created an instant furor. Competing against Book Two of William Carlos Williams' *Paterson*, two ballots were required, the first inconclusive. The committee, composed of Conrad Aiken, W.H. Auden, T.S. Eliot, Robert Lowell, Katherine Anne Porter, Karl Shapiro, Allen Tate and Robert Penn Warren, among others, attempted to prepare the public for its decision by explaining in an official press release that to consider elements other than poetic achievement 'would destroy the significance of the award' and in principle deny the 'validity of that objective perception of value on which civilized society must rest' (*Case* 45). The public did not agree: to award a Congressional prize to a fascist sympathizer accused of treason but declared insane and currently in a federal hospital for the mentally ill was unacceptable. Newspapers, magazines, radio commentaries, editorials and letters to the editor expressed outrage. Debates, forums and public exchanges occurred, *The Partisan Review*, for example, running commentaries from three of the jurors in response to an editorial, while *The Case Against the Saturday Review*, published as a pamphlet, took on the conservative views of the magazine, extended by a poetic dialogue further attacking the journal by the former Librarian of Congress, Archibald MacLeish. The debate takes place between Mr Saturday and Mr Bollingen. Some asserted in the press, however, that Pound was not even mad, while others, like Congressman Jacob Javits, demanded a congressional inquiry into the circumstances surrounding the award.

No book of twentieth century American poetry likely created such controversy as *The Pisan Cantos*. But receiving what immediately became the most controversial poetry prize ever given in the US seemed appropriate for Pound, although the approach known as New Criticism – the analysis of only the verbal surface of the text, not its context or origin – was being tested. How valid was such a method? Was it right to exclude the author and his politics from an evaluation of the poetry? Ironically, *The Cantos* as a whole largely rejected the New Critical approach, demonstrating the value of context, history and biography for understanding cultural practice.

The 'poem including history' had itself become history, a front-page headline in *The New York Times* exposing the prejudice that surrounded the award: 'Pound in Mental Clinic, Wins Prize/ For Poetry Penned in Treason Cell' (20 February 1949). This was misleading, of course, in that virtually the entire poem was written before Pound arrived in Washington. Some evidence, however, suggests that Pound's friends proposed a strategy that would lead to his winning the prize in order to embarrass the US Government into releasing him. Receipt of the prize would dramatize Pound's situation to the world and step-up the push to have him freed (MacLeish 120). But the $1000 prize for the best volume of poetry published in America by an American, sponsored by the Bollingen Foundation, subsidized by the Mellon family of Pittsburgh and awarded by the Library of Congress, was much needed by Pound. The strategy of release, however, backfired as anger against Pound re-ignited.

One consequence was that control of the award would be removed from the Library of Congress and go to Yale. And the same year of Pound's controversial win, another noted poet was honored: T.S. Eliot won the Nobel Prize for Literature. During his nearly thirteen years at St Elizabeths, Pound, in a remarkable way, flourished. His limited freedom actually enhanced his work by forcing concentration and completion. He had access to books (notably from the Library of Congress), food and intellectual stimulation once visitors were allowed. Having long advocated that America should support its artists, he now found that support while institutionalized. After his move from Howard Hall to the Chestnut Ward in 1947 and with the granting of privileges to sit and walk outside, his situation improved. He also never once sought to escape. Indeed, he did not want to escape, something even his physicians noted. Imprisonment helped him concentrate and gave him an identity; some supporters even thought that Dorothy did not want him released, because she knew that if he returned to Italy, it would be to Olga (Cornell 46; Wilhelm 2: 271). Confinement actually aided his cause – to write and promote his ideas on economic reform; his imprisonment lent him an authority which his release could not. His voice and presence remained noticeable precisely because he was imprisoned, while strangely contributing to his overall mental well-being. America, not St Elizabeths, was the problem; or, as he would declare on his return to Italy in 1958, 'all America is an insane asylum' (SCh 848).

When visitors did arrive, Pound held court: poets, editors, students, friends, cranks, admirers and disciples joined him to learn more about economic history, governmental abuse, monetary crimes and poetry. Not only did Charles Olson, Robert Lowell, e.e. cummings, Alan Tate, Louis Zukofsky, Marianne Moore, Marshall McLuhan, Hugh Kenner, Archibald MacLeish, W.S. Merwin, and Randall Jarrell appear, but Thornton Wilder, Alice Roosevelt Longworth, Stephen Spender, Elizabeth Bishop, Katherine Anne Porter, Langston Hughes, Ronald Duncan, H.L. Mencken, William Carlos Williams and Robert Creeley visited. Of course, Laughlin, T.S. Eliot, and even Henry Crowder, Nancy Cunard's black lover who was then living in Washington, came.

Dorothy Pound selflessly visited every day, making Pound her sole preoccupation and often acting as his spokesperson and manager of his business affairs. A young Chinese woman aided him with his Confucian translation, while a professor of Greek came regularly for nine years to assist with the language; the Greek scholar Edith Hamilton visited occasionally. Moral and financial support also emerged, sometimes from unlikely sources. Marianne Moore wrote in 1946 that 'misfortune does not alter friendship' and sent him ten dollars, despite her disagreement with his anti-Semitic views. 'Don't be embittered. Embitterment is a sin...' she added (*MMSL* 461). Pound continued to edit her work, especially her La Fontaine translations adding comments in the margins. At one point, she acknowledged that 'the pernicious relative clause had done me a world of harm. I can get the straight order of words and try for active verbs and forego "hard bestead" and "ceaseless" etc.' 'A sentence does not have to have a verb so far as I am concerned' she told him; 'writing, to me, is entrapped conversation' (*SLMM* 473, 476).

Other events far from Washington occurred during these years: in 1946, his daughter Mary married an Italian-Russian prince without a fortune (Boris Beratti, later de Rachewiltz); in 1948, his mother died. In 1952 and 1955, Olga visited. Mary came in 1953.[6] But if Pound seemed more relaxed during this period, often photographed lounging in a lawn chair in casual dress, he never forgot that he remained a 'caged Panther' (LXXXIII/550), restrained and watched. But he also began to write.

The first important poetic work Pound undertook was his translation of the Confucian Odes, an anthology of poetry Confucius originally edited. The work appeared in 1954 as *The Classic Anthology Defined by Confucius* and it again revealed his sensitivity to language as a sensuous medium. This had been preceded in 1949 by his *Selected Poems* and in 1953, *The Translations of Ezra Pound* edited by Hugh Kenner which confirmed Pound's versatility as a reader of foreign languages.

Prose also began to emerge designed partly to keep his name in the public's eye: *Patria Mia* (1950), a collection of articles that originally appeared in Orage's *New Age*; *The Letters of Ezra Pound*, edited by D.D. Paige (1950); and then *The Literary Essays of Ezra Pound*, edited by T.S.Eliot (1954), one of Pound's most influential books. The collection stressed the aesthetic rather than the political Pound. Another motive for the constant publication of Pound's work during this period was to establish his *bona fide* literary credentials for a public and government that continued to kept him a prisoner and deny his literary importance.

Not all of his friends agreed with his ideas, however, and several criticized him, especially about his anti-Semitism: Marianne Moore and Laughlin were among the most vocal. In 1952 Moore referred to him as the 'fearsomely resilient Ezra' but added 'profanity and the Jews are other quaky quicksands against which may I warn you? You have seen turtles or armadillos, possibly when annoyed and I sometimes have to be one of them' (*SLMM* 502). Five years later, she berated him again: 'Ezra, you are intolerable, to defy me, about the Jews who are not mine alone but everybody's benefactor; and foolish' (*SLMM* 539). But she also sent him funds to ease his comfort: 'Decent money is hard to get – even near the Bureau of Printing and Engraving – so I enclose a few *pour boires* for Dorothy to administer? or for a taxi' (*SLMM* 540). Laughlin was similarly critical of Pound's anti-Semitism and reluctantly published controversial passages in *The Cantos*, although he never approved of them.[7] During this time Pound began to associate with individuals linked to segregationist and white supremacist groups. John Kasper and Eustace Mullins, both young disciples, quickly became spokespersons for racist organizations. At one point, Kasper opened a Greenwich Village bookstore called Make It New with Nazi literature in the window. Soon, Kasper and David Horton, another admirer of Pound, began to publish the 'Square $' series of booklets with contributions by Pound. Kasper's anti-Semitism and racial slurs increased, however, at one point calling himself 'Segregation Chief' of The Seaboard White Citizens Council headquartered in Washington. Kasper, encouraged (or at least not dissuaded) by Pound, began to espouse his views more publically, as did Eustace Mullins. A Virginian, Mullins called himself Director of the Aryan League of America; he would later publish a biography of the poet in 1961 (*SCh* 800–1). Pound's susceptibility to young admirers with racist views and appearance in small magazines with pro-fascist, anti-Semitic leanings may have delayed his release from St Elizabeths. In *Discretions*, Mary de Rachewiltz expresses her dismay at these connections of her father's (*Dis* 293–4).

But efforts to free Pound continued. To encourage his release, T.S. Eliot and others organized an evening devoted to Pound's work at the Institute of Contemporary Art in London in the spring of 1953. Eliot chaired the session which included talks by Herbert Read and J. Isaacs and readings of Pound's poetry by Peter Russell and Donald Hall. R.P. Blackmur, the critic, was in the front row, as was Eliot's friend John Hayward. But when J. Isaacs mildly praised F.R. Leavis for his support of *Mauberley*, a ruckus broke out. First, there shouts of 'shame,' and then pushing and shoving in the back of the room. As the violence grew, two audience members had to be ejected: Dylan Thomas' friend, John Davenport, and Graham Greene (*RP* 92–3).

The constant publication of new work by Pound in the fifties generated a new debate: how could one so competent in literary terms still be deemed unstable? Why hadn't Pound gone to trial? Dr Overholser, director of St Elizabeths, came to Pound's defense: there is no essential change in his condition and he remains 'extremely bombastic and opinioned, highly disorganized in his train of thought' he wrote to the Justice Department (Wilhelm 2: 280). The publication of the Confucian Odes exacerbated the situation: they were recognized as marvelous but how could one be mentally capable of translating and publishing but not be brought to trial, asked the Assistant Attorney General, Alexander M. Campbell. Dr Overholser again defended, explaining that Pound still suffered from many paranoid delusions and that there is no evidence that he did 'any productive literary work during his stay in the Hospital.' Most of the translating was done before he arrived (Wilhelm 2: 284). This was not entirely true, of course; in 1951, for example, Pound translated and published Sophocles' *Elektra* and *The Women of Trachis*.

Dorothy Pound increasingly played a decisive role, writing the English lawyer, A.V. Moore, for example, that there must be clemency. Pound is

not insane: but so shaken that he could not possibly stand trial. The least little thing fusses him. He won't have the word pardon used – saying he has committed nothing v. the constitution. He also uses the phrase 'the Treason was in the White House, not in Rapallo.'

(DP, 9 April 1953)

Earlier, in a series of letters to Gladys Bing in England, Dorothy defended Pound, telling her that Pound had no interest in Italian fascism '*save* in so far conducive to Social Credit.' Dorothy also expressed dislike of America and eagerly wished for a return to Europe (DP, 19 June 1947). A month later, she writes that she is 'trying to keep him focused on to his Chinese – when his wits are strong enough . . . he can be more useful in Poetry-world than the Economic' (DP, 9 July 1947). 'Once more I take my pen-in-hand for Ez' she begins a letter of 29 August 1947, identifying her role as amanuensis, spokesperson and defender.[8]

In 1955 Pound published the next portion of *The Cantos: Section: Rock-Drill* which appeared first with his Italian publisher Vanni Scheiwiller in Milan and then New Directions in New York a year later. The volume would seemingly contradict Dr Overholser's claims about Pound's condition. However, a postscript to a 1954 letter to the Assistant Attorney General, rationalizes the work: 'we have many patients in this Hospital who have, while unquestionably psychotic, written poetry, some of it of a high standing' (Wilhelm 2: 285). *Rock-Drill*, with its toughness and certainty, rises to that level. The pugnacious title alludes to Jacob Epstein's *avant garde* sculpture of 1913 of a grim, robotic figure astride an industrial drill but also refers to Wyndham Lewis' 1951 review of Pound's *Selected Letters* entitled 'The Rock Drill.'

Rock-Drill reverts to a pre-Pisan form, the first part replacing the first-person voice of *The Pisan Cantos* with a more imperial, Confucian persona: 'Our dynasty came in because of a great sensibility' reads the first line of the first poem (XXXV/563), referring back to the Chinese and American Cantos. The second part of the volume looks forward to a possible *paradiso*.

Pound outlined the careful plan of *Rock-Drill* in 1954 to Scheiwiller explaining that there are '3 chinese/ 2 american/ 6 paradise' with America and China the historical poles of the *Cantos* connected by Europe and Italy (Bacigalupo 232). The emphasis on Chinese characters, with occasional Latin glosses and brief English quotations, makes for at best difficult poetry in *Rock-Drill*, at worse, unreadability (Cantos XCVIII and XCIX more effectively merge Chinese characters and blocks of thought).

Civic virtue and courage, as well as pagan mysteries and neo-Platonism in medieval thought, drive the sequence thematically. Cultural progress, the section argues, results from individuals who courageously resist decadence and manage to renew a national honour. John Randolph of Roanoke, Virginia, a subject of a biography by Henry Adams, and an opponent of slavery, is Pound's example (Canto LXXXVIII–LXXXIX); incidents in Randolph's life, notably a duel with Henry Clay whom Randolph charged with forging a letter, although he had decided *not* to fire on Clay, demonstrate the possibilities of reclaiming principle using the visual signs of a deck of cards in the text to draw parallels between a deck and the days of a man's life (LXXXVIII/609).

Cantos XC to XCV are the center of *Rock-Drill*, cantos which describe the rites of an initiate into mystical love. Beginning with Scotus Erigena's belief that '*Ubi amor, ibi oculus*' ('where there is love there is sight,' XC/626), Pound begins to incorporate various languages to confirm the interwoven elements of love, the center of which is 'La Luna Regina' (XCII/639). These calculated ceremonies dominate the final cantos of the set, with Pound turning at last to holy wanderers and, finally, Odysseus as imagined by a neo-Platonist: the shipwrecked figure of *Odyssey V*.

To convey the multiplicity of experiences in *Rock-Drill* (and some suggest its confusions), Pound relies on musical notation, ideograms, Egyptian hieroglyphics, Greek, Latin, Italian and English. Time in the series compresses and we move without transition from Randolph in America to Caesar in Rome, KATI in Egypt and D'Annunzio in Italy. The goal is 'the luminous eye' (XCIII/649) and realization that 'Le Paradis n'est pas artificiel/ but is jagged' (XCII/640). At one point, he prints the aces of four suits of playing cards but with the spade printed upside down, although this was a printer's error Pound let stand (LXXXVIII/609).

But in his search for 'the crystal wave' which should 'mount to flood surge,' Pound presents pages of ideograms, lines of Greek, and broken or fragmented English (XCV/664). The constant allusions in the midst of developing other thought distract the reader who finds the absence of an argument distressing.

Yet the theme of love and light emerges to draw together the whole which a passage from Richard of St Victor summarizes: 'UBI AMOR IBI OCULUS EST' ('where there is love, there is the eye,' XC/629), echoing a similar statement by Scotus (XC/626). When Pound could order his own stationery in 1946, printed as a crescent at the top was this statement: 'J'AYME DONC JE SUIS' ('I love; therefore I am'). The litany of ascent that is Canto XC sets the tone for the recovery *The Cantos* has now begun, ever so slowly, to enact. Shadows still exist but the possibility of paradise has returned.

Simultaneous with the appearance of *Rock-Drill* were new efforts to release Pound, notably in Italy with the formation of 'Amici di Ezra Pound.' A petition requesting his release and signed by Eugenio Montale, Alberto Moravia and Salvatore Quasimodo, plus others, was given to the US Ambassador to Italy, Clare Booth Luce. Another petition was presented to Mrs Luce in 1956 with the names of Ignazio Silone, Mario Praz, Giuseppe Ungaretti and other prominent Italian writers. *Time* magazine, edited by her husband, Henry Luce, ran an editorial on 6 February 1956 asking that charges against Pound be dropped. *The New Republic* and *The Nation* offered similar editorial opinions. That same year Archibald MacLeish visited Pound, a generous move since Pound had earlier castigated MacLeish who replied with equal vigor. Yet MacLeish had influence in Washington and once he saw Pound's appalling conditions, he decided to act. His review of *Rock-Drill* in *The New York Times* of 16 November 1956 ended with a description of St Elizabeths and Pound's untenable physical and mental situation. A letter drafted by MacLeish but signed by Frost, Eliot and Hemingway made its way to the Attorney General on 14 January 1957, pointing out that Pound had been held for eleven years for a crime for which he had not been tried. Action for his release was underway, although it would take more than six months to achieve his freedom.

Frost led the cause at MacLeish's behest, holding two meetings with the US Deputy Attorney General, William P. Rogers. Soon, the Under Secretary for State asked to meet with Dr Overholser to discuss 'this difficult individual,' Ezra Pound. Rogers, newly elevated to Attorney General, wrote to MacLeish to say that he was inclined to think that a way out might be found. Dorothy Pound then wrote on 1 February 1958 to assure the government that Pound would immediately return to Europe if released. Further negotiations between Frost and the government ensued, with Sherman Adams, White House Chief of Staff, playing an important role in convincing President Eisenhower that Pound's condition would not improve and that he, therefore, would never stand trial. American public opinion by this time had become indifferent to his actions and the threat of Communism seemed much greater than fascism. On the 18 April 1958, the treason charges were dropped and Pound was freed, although in the custody of his wife as 'Committee for Ezra Pound' with certain terms and conditions Pound must acknowledge. This also meant that Dorothy would have formal control over all his business matters. Olga found this distressing because it meant Pound was not truly free. Nevertheless, his release was greeted with worldwide applause, a Paris headline proclaiming 'Ezra Pound, le Mallarmé U.S. ne mourra pas chez les fous' (End 35). Pound left St Elizabeths on 7 May.

Among the many admirers, hangers on and visitors to the Chestnut Ward at St Elizabeths during Pound's stay was Marcella Spann, a serious young woman with a reserved manner from Texas who appeared in April 1957. Her conservative demeanor contrasted with the artist Sheri Martinelli who had been flamboyantly directing the group of young Pound disciples with more enthusiasm than understanding. A student of American poetry, Spann was unsure about her new job as an English instructor at a junior college in the Washington area. Pound invited her to visit him to get literature direct, not from textbooks, and tried to provide her with self-confidence by 'assigning' her an anthology which would eventually appear in 1964 as Confucius to Cummings edited by Pound and Spann. She would detail the process of attending the Ezuversity on the lawn of St Elizabeths in two later articles but her growing involvement with Pound quickly made her part of his retinue.[9] When he was released in 1958, she, in fact, joined Dorothy as part of the party returning to Italy. But by then she was acting as Pound's secretary and aide, Dorothy becoming too frail to conduct his day-to-day affairs, Mary too preoccupied with her young family in Italy. However, the presence of Marcella in Pound's life, while bringing a youthful and attractive feminine presence, also brought tension. Mary was surprised by her arrival but Olga was shaken, Dorothy, perhaps, grateful.

Pound and Dorothy spent two months after his release arranging passports and passage back to Italy, although finances remained a problem. At one point, Hemingway sent a $1000 check to Pound who was too proud to cash it. Instead, he had it framed in plexiglass and used it for a paperweight. Before heading to New York for their departure on

30 June, Pound visited his childhood home in Wyncote, PA. now owned by a Carl Gatter. He was warmly welcomed but in the middle of the night, after a long chat with the new owner, Pound wandered down the street to the Calvary Presbyterian Church which his father helped to found and searched for a tree he had planted with a friend. He could not find it in the dark and didn't want to trespass. He returned to the home at 166 Fernbrook Avenue to rest. A night in Hopewell, New Jersey at the home of Alan C. Collins, president of the Curtis Brown literary agency, preceded a stop to see William Carlos Williams in Rutherford, New Jersey. It was 29 June 1958, his last night in America (*SCh* 846– 8). The next day, the only outsider permitted to visit arrived: the photographer Richard Avedon, a friend of Laughlin's who photographed the two poets together, Pound, shirt unbuttoned, chest exposed, standing with both hands on the shoulders of the seated Williams and, in another powerful image, Pound grimacing with eyes shut at the camera, Lear-like in his pain. This would be Pound's visual legacy to America.

On the 30 June, Pound arrived at the *Cristoforo Colombo* for the voyage to Genoa stopping first at Naples. Joining Pound and Dorothy in the small cabin with three bunks was Marcella Spann. Present for the departure was Omar, as well as Norman Holmes Pearson from Yale, representing H.D. 'Don't look so sad,' Pound told Pearson as he was leaving (*End* 62). When they arrived in Italy on 9 July – Mary's birthday – newspapermen surrounded him on board and he offered his usual mix of opinion, declaration and bombast. Asked to name America's greatest poet, he named himself and when asked for a photograph he grandly stood and raised his right arm. The image of Pound offering the fascist salute raced around the world. Escaped from America, Pound wasted no time broadcasting his return to Italy and controversy.

7

'The European Mind Stops': Drafts, Fragments and Silences, 1958–72

> When one's friends hate each other
> how can there be peace in the world?
> Their asperities diverted me in my green time.
>
> (CXV/814)

Pound found his return to Italy more difficult, in some ways, than his departure. At seventy-three, his arrival at Brunnenburg brought problems not peace. Appearing with Dorothy and Marcella raised immediate difficulties for Mary whose marriage in 1946 against her mother's wishes created a rift between the two and contributed to the estrangement between Olga and Pound. Olga was also jealous at having to share Pound with yet another (and much younger) woman whom he constantly wanted near him; this new and unclear grouping naturally complicated life at the castle.

A veneer of goodwill first existed, Pound willingly participating in the celebration of Mary's birthday in the village and seemingly content with the Dorothy/Marcella arrangement. But tensions soon emerged, not only because of the unusual living situation but because of his isolation in a remote mountain castle far above the town of Merano. After twelve-and-a-half years at the center of controversy, debate and American poetic life, Pound was now removed from the scene. The loss resulted in alternations of energy and fatigue as tensions swirled around him; he also found the altitude difficult and the castle uncomfortable. Even the scenery was not enough to satisfy him.

During the early months of his return, Pound was reminded again of his American past. In 1958, H.D. completed her memoir, *End to Torment* which she wrote during the year of his release from St Elizabeths, sending a copy to Pound at Brunnenburg. He responded with a few suggestions and a note: 'there is a great deal of beauty in it.' A few days later he added, 'Torment title excellent but optimistic' suggesting something of his own sense of his current situation (*End* xi).[1] In several of her last letters to Pound, HD signed them 'Dryad,' the name he had given her when they were young in Pennsylvania. As she recalls their youth together, she links Pound's political isolation and imprisonment after World War II to the shock and rejection he felt in Philadelphia on his return from Wabash College following his resignation after a minor scandal.

In its form, the memoir parallels the late Cantos. The structure is somewhat like a journal mixing memories with circumstances of recollection as resonances rather than logic connect the past and present. A persistent theme is their intertwined lives, not only in their early attempts at poetry but in her following him to Europe after his 'shocking' departure of 1908 and their decisions to remain there. Ironically, it was in Europe that she recalled her American life with Pound, writing *End to Torment* while recovering from a fall in Kilsnacht, Switzerland. It opens in 1905 and closes in 1958 with an account of the Pounds' departure to Italy, provided to her by Norman Holmes Pearson. The expansive character of Pound dominates the crowded cabin, lecturing Pearson on college entrance exams, while Marcella sat on the bunk where the shirtless Pound lay, and Dorothy smiled, holding a yellow rose, H.D. had instructed Pearson to give her. Omar acted as guardsman against the press. 'Your rose was with them,' Holmes wrote to H.D., his final words, the final words of H.D.'s memoir, ' "It is for the *Paradiso*," I said at the end' (*End* 62).

Unaccustomed to life in an unusual and mixed foreign setting, Marcella found Brunnenburg difficult. She could not relate to Mary who did not hide her displeasure with her presence. By March 1959, Pound, himself, had had enough of the tensions and left with Dorothy and Marcella for Rapallo, taking rooms at the Albergo Grande Italia. Reports from visitors there suggested that Marcella was secretary-nurse to Pound, each individual with their own bedrooms. Dorothy spent most of her time in her room reading, although Marcella's intrusive presence created a frosty atmosphere (*SCh* 857). In a curious fashion, Pound had duplicated his situation with Dorothy and Olga in 1944–45 when they shared the small Casa 60 amid enormous strain.

After a brief return to Brunnenburg to allow D.G. Bridson to make a film about him for the BBC, Pound took Dorothy and Marcella on a short tour of Italy in May. One of the first stops was the spot where the D existed, north of Pisa. No camp but a rose nursery stood where the steel cage once reigned. At Sirmione on the shore of Lago di Garda, their next stop, Pound, whose behavior swung radically from depression to elation, asked Marcella to marry him, her youth rekindling his own ideas of sensuality. Dorothy, of course, would not hear of it and by the early fall, Marcella had departed for America.

Laughlin, visiting Pound at this time, reported to Williams in October 1959 that Pound seemed in a 'terrible depression and collapse of physical energy. He talks a lot about dying and just lies around and broods.' Marcella, who hated Italy, had left and Dorothy had lost a good deal of her energy, he continued. The entire situation is 'hopeless' because 'Ez, miserable as he is, is still so damn stubborn, he just won't listen to sense' (*WCW/JL* 229–30). Olga had also heard a rumor that Marcella was Pound's new lover; upset, she sought details from Laughlin who corrected this mistake, or what he believed to be a mistake (*O/E* 217). Olga was, nevertheless, disturbed at not hearing from Pound.

By the early sixties, however, Pound's life gestured toward stability as he gravitated more toward Olga rather than Dorothy or Brunnenburg. This was significant because Pound and Olga had had little contact between 1955 and February 1959: she had broken off correspondence after her 1955 visit to St Elizabeths and the discovery of Sheri Martinelli, followed by Marcella Spann's accompanying Pound to Italy. She had also become estranged from Mary once Pound returned and shortly after told him that she wanted all his papers and possessions, which included the Gaudier-Brzeska bust, removed from Casa 60; the ostensible reason was the possible sale of the house.

In 1960, Olga had let calle Querini in Venice to an American admirer of Pound who had visited him at St Elizabeths, the same year Casa 60 was sold. She had little choice but to move to another cottage further up the hill. There was even a strained relationship with Mary who had been in much contact with her since Pound returned.

In January Pound reported to Olga from Brunnenburg of a terrible Christmas: 'Crazier when I got out of bughouse than when in' (*O/E* 221). At Mary's urging, he left Brunnenburg for Rome and the apartment of Ugo Dadone, a retired military attache, former fascist and friend of his son-in-law. It was there he would meet the American poet Donald Hall in February and March 1960 for three days of interviews, telling him when he arrived that 'you – find me – in fragments.' Alternating between energy and exhaustion, Pound struggled to make the interview clear. To Daniel Cory he had admitted 'one day I talk like a parrot and the next I can find nothing to say' (*RP* 114; *SCh* 863). The edited interview would appear in *The Paris Review* 28 (Autumn 1962). By May 1960, however, Pound was ill and Mary had to come and put him in a Rome clinic.

Almost every weekend, Olga visited from Siena where she was still working at the music academy; she found Pound suffering, refusing to eat, given to long silences and fearful. He made little progress and Olga, with Mary's consent, decided to move him back to Brunnenburg, although rather than reside in the castle, he took up residence at another clinic nearby in Martinsbrunn. By the fall, Pound improved, although Olga's commitments in Siena to performing and programing limited her visits. She was also writing a scholarly introduction to a set of Vivaldi letters. At his recovery from what was essentially a urinary illness, Pound returned to Olga and Sant' Ambrogio in April 1962. The reunion at the new Casa 131 was dramatic and genuine: Olga quit her job at the Accademia and began to care for Pound full time.

Remarkably, despite Pound's age and growing fragility, accelerated by the confusing and at times combative personal situation, his artistic power and sense of imagery did not diminish. A late passage summarizes his condition:

> A blown husk that is finished
>   but the light sings eternal
> a pale flare over marshes
>   where the salt hay whispers to tide's change
>
> (CXV/ 814)

A stay in another clinic, this time in Rapallo, followed, Pound slowly recovering, spending most days rereading *The Cantos* and making notes and corrections. By June 1962, however, he needed an operation to prevent uremic poisoning. The operation was a success and his fits of depression and refusal to eat abated. On the day he was released and returned to Sant'Ambrogio, Dorothy Pound left Rapallo for Brunnenburg with Omar. She did, however, send a letter with a check to cover his expenses.

By September, Olga moved Pound to 252 calle Querini in Venice. They had returned to the 'Hidden Nest,' and he was strong enough to attend a dinner hosted by the Society of Venetian Writers to mark his receipt of an award from the Academy of American Poets. But it was a melancholy, transitional time with the news of the death of William Carlos Williams and a second prostate operation in the Rapallo clinic. Recovering, however, he was able to join Olga in Siena. Alternating between Sant'Ambrogio and Venice, Pound's life at last seemed to reach some stability, although he was beginning to fall into the silence that would characterize much of his last years.

An incident in 1964, however, displayed the alternating fits of speech and silence that Pound experienced as he battled the loss of energy and poetic inspiration. His self-criticism and concern for others, particularly Olga, emerged in an encounter with James Laughlin who had published Pound since 1938 but rarely with any legal agreements. Pound would just tell Laughlin to go ahead with a book and he would do it. But as Pound's health faltered in the sixties and his mood shifted, Laughlin had difficulty obtaining editorial direction from Pound: 'I hear from him in spurts and splashes' he told the Boston lawyer who administered the decisions of the court-appointed 'Committee,' Dorothy Pound (Nadel 61).

Decisions had to be made concerning the republication of Pound's work as numerous textual, copyright and even testamentary questions emerged. Laughlin needed answers and so in August 1964 he and his wife Ann journeyed to see Pound and Olga in Sant'Ambrogio, as well as Mary and Dorothy in Brunnenburg. At a lunch in Portofino on 19 August 1964, Pound at one point leaned over and said to Laughlin 'couldn't have done worse. . . should have had sense enough to hold out on something. . . .I don't need to be as crazy as this' (Nadel 62). Retrospection, regret and self criticism were evident. In two letters from Italy to the Boston lawyer, Herbert P. Gleason, Laughlin expands on Pound's condition and attitude, emphasizing that Pound, despite his age, is still energetic and has a strong appetite. But he also suffers from a 'deep and profound melancholy, terrible remorse and horrible anxieties' (Nadel 62). For distraction he reads Sartres' *Les Mots* out-loud in French to Olga, who, in turn, manages to get Pound to read *The Cantos* out-loud which she tapes. But in company, Pound hardly speaks, yet in working over *Cantos* corrections with Olga, Laughlin would be surprised by Pound's short, often self-deprecatory or remorseful interjections over the situation he had put Olga in.

Pound's major source of worry was money and whether or not Olga would have enough to live on after his death. He distrusted the royalty statements he was shown and pleaded with Laughlin to provide some financial security for Olga. At one point, Pound went to his room and typed out a page detailing all that Olga had done and stuffed it into Laughlin's pocket. The $300 dollars a month they received from Dorothy was enough, however, for their expenses, Olga told Laughlin, although repairs were needed to their sparsely furnished apartment which contained an early Léger, a Max Ernst and photos of the Schifanoia frescoes that bear on *The Cantos*. Laughlin in his letter notes how dependent Pound is on Olga and how anxious he becomes when she is not near him.

Nevertheless, Olga was cheerful and confident that she could care for Pound. The one literary matter Laughlin did accomplish was Pound's reluctant approval to reissue his first book, *A Lume Spento*, for which he wrote a brief preface; he also approved a paperback selection of *The Cantos*.

A second letter details Laughlin's visit to Brunnenburg and his surprise at Dorothy's good health, although she had only formal interaction with Mary. Laughlin is struck by her failure to feel sorry for herself and marvelous dignity. She still seems to love Pound greatly despite the way he has treated her and 'much of her life centers around looking after his affairs' and cataloguing his material not in Mary's archive. She also expressed admiration for Olga's caring for Pound and did not once refer to any financial assistance she might have provided for Pound during their early years together in an effort to advance a claim for his royalties or payment for the possible sale of his archive (Nadel 65). A return visit by Laughlin to Pound found him in a weaker state but still obsessed with Olga. Asked to clarify certain obscure parts of the late cantos, Pound could do little more than stare at the page. His depression and silences were rarely dispelled, despite the help of certain medications. Concerned, Laughlin departed, although he repeatedly reassured Pound that Olga's future would be secure.

During this unsettling period, Pound continued sporatic work on *The Cantos*, publishing a new set in 1959: *Thrones de los Cantares (Cantos 96–109)* incorporating Spanish in the title to sustain the internationalism of the work and re-employing his use of *cantares* for the cantos which he had used in reference to the work in the fifties (Bacigalupo 231–2). In an interview, he explained the enigmatic title:

> The thrones in Dante's *Paradiso* are for the spirits of the people who have been responsible for good government. The thrones in the *Cantos* are an attempt to move out from egoism and to establish some definition of an order possible or at any rate conceivable on earth.... *Thrones* concerns the states of mind of people responsible for something more than their personal conduct.
>
> (*RP 242*)

In another comment, Pound refers to 'the domination of benevolence' and, following a remark on Dante, provides another site of meaning: consider 'the allegories of the virtues in the upper level of the frescoes in the Palazzo Schifanoia in Ferrara.... the poet has passed through "the casual" and "the recurrent" and comes to the values that endure like the sea. *Los cantares*. Compare Mallarmé's *"mots de la tribu"* – the tale of the tribe' (Bacigalupo 232n.1)

The thirteen cantos of *Thrones*, written at St Elizabeths but finalized at Brunnenburg and published first in Italy, extend the citational method of quotation and reference seen in *Rock-Drill* repeating some of Pound's favorite subjects: Confucian ethics, medieval thought and Dante. But several new topics also appear: Byzantium, the economic ideas of Alexander del Mar and the legal writings of Sir Edward Coke. Canto XCVI focuses on the organizational skill of the Lombards and how such concepts transferred to Byzantium; construction of the ideal city is finally realized. Alexander del Mar, author of a *History of Monetary Systems* is the focus of the next Canto, followed by two cantos on Confucius supplemented with ideograms as he seeks to display a 'constructive imagination' (XCVIII/708). Indeed, the act of building, whether a government, a structure or an idea, is the thrust of *Thrones*. Nature with its order complements Confucius with his ethics as Pound imagines an object where:

> Filiality and fraternity are the root,
> Talents to be considered as branches.
> Precise terminology is the first implement,
> > dish and container,
> After that, the 9 arts.
> AND study the classic books,
> > the straight history
> > > all of it candid.
> > > > (XCIX/ 730–1)

Yet the old themes remain: 'Monetary literacy, sans which a loss of freedom is consequent' battles the faults of history, American and European (CIII/752). But fragmentation and constant citation prevent an easy narrative or thematic unity as languages, as well as references, mix with greater intensity, the final lines of the last canto joining English, Greek, Italian and French (CIX/794). Yet the quest for coherence persists, Pound telling his Italian publisher in 1956, for example, that one cannot read the final cantos until one has read and understood the earlier.

The manner of citation, quotation and reference in *Thrones*, often to slightly obscure or forgotten historical figures such as Sir Edward Coke, Speaker of the House of Commons under Elizabeth I and author of the *Institutes of Law*, is similar to *Rock-Drill* but equally distracting. The palimpsest of legal codes from Justinian to the Lombards and even St Anselm requires study and attention. The lack of a clearly sustained image or subject – although Byzantium is always in the shadows – gave many the impression that Pound was bored with poetry at the same time he sought to imagine all of culture as a work of art. But the abbreviated material of *Thrones* constantly prevents clarity.

Begun as a continuation of *Rock-Drill*, *Thrones* veers off into its own multiple directions and may be the least successful section of *The Cantos*, although it possesses moments of individual brilliance. But the foregrounding of sources over the poetry results in writing which is uneven as Pound searches in the poem for a law giver and rebel in the figure of Sir Edward Coke or, perhaps, himself. By including the Coke cantos, however, Pound extends his normal eleven canto sequence, unbalancing the work as a whole. From 1934 (*Eleven New Cantos*) through the Pisan sequence and *Rock-Drill*, he maintained the eleven-canto structure. Nevertheless, Pound envisioned a final volume of Cantos, possibly reaching 120 in total (Dante had only 100), beginning with the story of a Wadsworth ancestor who saved the charter of the state of Connecticut from royal confiscation (CIX) and ending with the treatment of Na Khi culture and legends of highland China. When he finally turned to extending his work, however, it took a different, more personal direction.

Coinciding at this time with his thoughts on poetic closure for *The Cantos* were several prizes and recognition: in 1962 Pound received $500, *Poetry*'s Harriet Monroe Memorial Prize, the most distinguished prize the magazine ever awarded. Pound's reply was a mixture of gratitude and regret: 'if it gives me a chance to admit the multitude & depth & gravity of my errors, go ahead. If it claims that I did advertise the magazine, & encourage Harriet, that may be a justification.' He signed the letter, 'Ezra Pound,/ a minor satirist who/ at one time contributed to/ the general liveliness by scratching/ a few barnacles off the language' (*DE* 452). The following year he received the Academy of American Poets award.

But silence increasingly dominated his life, admitting to an Italian interviewer a few months after his 77th birthday, '"I have lost the ability to reach the core of my thought with words"' (*SCh* 881). To a French journalist in 1965, he said 'I did not enter into silence; silence captured me' (Kamm 38). Even dinner with Stephen Spender and Isaiah Berlin elicited no words from Pound except for one or two brief, almost inaudible phrases (*SCh* 883). Visitors who would politely ask short questions received long silences; when Olga asked him a question, he only nodded in response. But despite his aging and depression, Pound still enjoyed travel and in 1965 he went with Olga to London to attend the memorial service for T.S. Eliot in Westminster Abbey. After the service, he wrote his first piece of prose for publication since 1959, a brief *apologia* for

Eliot, beginning with 'his was the true Dantescan voice – not honoured enough, and deserving more than I ever gave him' (*SCh* 888). During that visit, he was encouraged to make corrections to *The Cantos* but showed no interest; however, a short time after the trip, Faber and Faber unexpectedly received a copy of the text with sections marked up for excerpts so that a *Selected Cantos* could be published. In a letter to Laughlin, he cited Olga's prodding as the key to its being done and in a letter of 1966 to Laughlin included the fragment on Olga dated 24 August 1966 which appears as the final passage in the long poem beginning with the 1987 Faber edition and post-1979 New Directions editions of *The Cantos* (Stoicheff 68).

Expecting to return to Italy after his London visit, Pound at the airport suddenly insisted to Olga that he wanted to go to Dublin to see Yeats' widow; they did. He continued to travel in the summer, in July 1965, attending several events at the Spoleto Festival where Gian-Carlo Menotti produced Pound's opera, *Le Testament de Villon*. While there, he gave a public reading of the poems of Robert Lowell and Marianne Moore but not his own. Outside the auditorium, however, he was persuaded to read from *The Cantos* before a large crowd and the tv cameras. In 1966 he returned to Spoleto, this time to read his works from the stage. To celebrate his 80th birthday in October 1965, he returned to Paris where Natalie Barney gave a party for him at her home on the rue Jacob. Here, he made his remark to reporters about silence capturing him. He attended a performance of Beckett's *Endgame* and muttered to Olga, as the characters spoke their lines from garbage cans, 'C'est moi dans la poubelle' (*SCh* 889). Pound wrote to Beckett to compliment him on the play; the next day, Beckett paid a visit. They met again in 1970, but apparently exchanged no words. After a period of time, Beckett, stood up, embraced Pound and left (*SCh* 890).

Other travels in this period included Greece and, in the winter of 1967, Zurich, where Pound visited Joyce's grave, a moment enigmatically captured in Horst Tappe's photograph of Pound standing in his top coat, scarf and hat staring at the figure of Joyce with leg crossed, book open and cigarette in hand turning his upper body toward Pound and quizzically looking in his direction. The image suggests something of the distance yet affinity between the two writers and it appears as if Pound is speaking and Joyce is attentively listening. Pound also returned to Paris that year to mark the French translations of three prose works: *ABC of Reading*, *How to Read* and *The Spirit of Romance*.

Pound's most unexpected trip occurred four years later: New York. He had been invited to attend an opening exhibition of *The Waste Land* manuscript which Valerie Eliot was preparing for a facsimile edition. Unannounced, Pound called the New York Public Library from the airport to speak to Mrs Eliot; he was having some difficulty entering the country. The matter was straightened out. Shortly after, Laughlin learned that Pound and Olga had arrived and were in a hotel on 45th Street better known for its temporary clientele than its comfort. Laughlin rescued them and removed them to his country home in Norfolk, Connecticut with Walter de Rachewiltz's, Pound's grandson then studying at Rutgers University, driving. Pound and Olga then accompanied Laughlin to Hamilton College where Laughlin was to be awarded an honorary degree. Pound received an ovation as he entered and sat on the stage in cap and gown; he did not speak. After returning to New York, they settled at Laughlin's Greenwich Village apartment. Olga then went to her birthplace of Youngstown, Ohio, while Pound stayed behind. They both went to see Marianne Moore in Brooklyn and also visited Philadelphia before flying back to Italy.

New work at this time formed slowly and only the appearance of a pirated, mimeographed version of unfinished poems, entitled *Cantos 110–116*, spurred Pound on to try and finish his long poem. Most of the composition of what became *Drafts & Fragments* occurred between 1958 and 1960, a period of frequent moves for Pound which, among other things, meant that various people typed and retyped passages for him. Arriving in Italy in 1958 with draft typescripts, Pound, when not dealing with domestic difficulties from which, of course, he had been protected during the 1945–58 period, began to reorganize his material and subject it to the emotions of possession, love, guilt, devotion and jealously. His interest in the Na Khi suicide ceremony and his translation of Sophocles' *Elektra* and *Trachiniae* in 1949 and 1950 reinforced the pain and consequence of conflict. However, a short trip to Venice with Marcella in the fall of 1958 led to the exuberant opening of Canto CX. One version of that opening took the form of an ode to love.

'Purification' is a concept that threads through this late volume, the result of the many personal conflicts he was encountering. Just as Pisa was the catalyst for remembering and reviewing his past, so, too, did the conflicts surrounding Pound, compounded by increasingly poor health, cause him to face the past as well as the present, and attempt to make, if not amends, at least a reconciliation with that past. But instead of re-acquainting Pound with his past, his occasional trips about Italy with Marcella and Dorothy led to disenchantment, intensifying a further sense of unhappiness with the present. His re-constituted but broken world replaced the economic and political paradise outlined in *Rock-Drill* and *Thrones*. Merging the natural, political and economic paradise envisioned earlier was not possible; such desire remains scattered in *Drafts & Fragments*.

More specifically, moving to Rapallo in March 1959 with Dorothy and Marcella meant repeated unrest, reflected in his difficulty in developing an opening sequence for this last section. When Marcella finally left in October, she took with her Pound's gift of a series that had been written up to that point, containing a provisional CX, a 'CXII' and 'CXIII,' plus four poems numbered in Arabic numerals, 114 to 117. Over the next few months, she retyped them and sent them back to Pound in August 1960. But again, Pound 'fiddled,' shifting, re-writing, redistributing material.[2] Pound was losing hope in attaining the Dantesque fusion of love with nature and unity of private/civil order he identified in Dante's *Paradiso*. A paradisal closure for the poem and perhaps his life seemed impossible.

The appearance of the pirated edition, the catalyst for Pound's final volume, is a complicated tale. When Donald Hall interviewed Pound in Rome in February/March 1960 for *The Paris Review*, he offered to pay Pound if the magazine could print some unpublished material. Pound reluctantly agreed, offering, first, a translation of a set of Horatian odes he had been working on, some letters to Basil Bunting and some lines left over from *Thrones*. None of this was right Hall thought and Pound finally offered him the reworked typescripts Marcella Spann had retyped in America and sent back to Pound, fragments of Cantos numbered 110–117. Reassembling the material quickly, Pound sent them to Hall for publication (*RP* 130, 154–6, 158–61, 176–7).

Pound actually sent two separately edited groups of cantos developed from the draft material. He wanted Hall to retype them again to establish fair copies. When Hall retyped the two sequences, he made two carbons of each page and shortly after lent a graduate student his own copy of the second set, from Canto CX to '116' without the appended '113' which were retyped by a friend of the student with a carbon, one set kept by the undergraduate. Several years later in 1967, after returning from four years at Cambridge, the student met Ed Sanders in New York, an underground publisher. In answer to the question, 'any manuscripts we can get into print?' he offered the copied version of the second set of Hall's typescripts. They were retyped yet again on Gestetner paper and mimeographed in Sander's apartment. Three hundred copies of *Cantos 110–116* by Ezra Pound by the Fuck You/Press then appeared in 1967, a work that is a *mélange* of untidy passages written in a fragmentary manner.

Laughlin saw the edition that fall and immediately met with Sanders, realizing that the pirated edition needed a quick response. He wrote to

Pound urging him to 'authorize' a proper selection of this late material for a New Directions volume and most importantly copyright. Exchanges took place, Laughlin receiving incomplete versions of Cantos CXI, CXII and CXV. Pound responded to Laughlin's queries about proofing and corrections with laconic statements that were more enigmatic than helpful. His ill health and poor vision made more detailed work impossible. It is likely that Pound worked from the set second set of retyped cantos, emending in his own hand and then having Olga retype them before sending them on to Laughlin. The volume known as *Drafts & Fragments* appeared in 1969, but it led to further debate, notably about the ending.

Editorial rather than poetic decisions determined the conclusion to *The Cantos* with Laughlin and Eva Hesse, Pound's German translator, formulating the final texts. The process began with the inclusion of 'CXX' which first appeared in the 1972 New Directions volume, but not in the 1976 Faber and Faber edition. To further complicate the matter, Pound showed Laughlin in 1966 what he thought would be the ultimate canto, a fragment which essentially dedicates the work to Olga and has become in post-1979 editions the ending of the complete *Cantos*. Pound never sent it to Laughlin for inclusion in *Drafts & Fragments*. Peter Stoicheff unravels the complicated revisions of *Drafts & Fragments* (which he notes has at least six different versions), plus the titling of such final cantos as 'Notes for CXVII et seq.' and Laughlin's role in the process in *The Hall of Mirrors* (61–73). But as he surmises, the disruptive history of the final manuscript poems attests to the indeterminate ending of the work, confirming Pound's own unwillingness or inability to offer a unifying resolution. None of the options for closure seemed to him complete. *Drafts & Fragments* remains the least authorially sanctioned portion of the poem; not even the title was Pound's choice.

But what of the poetry rather than compositional history of this final volume of *The Cantos?* Recalling Pound's own disenchantment with the text and the challenges in untangling its multiple options for closure – plus his loss of control over its final form – *Drafts & Fragments* still contains some of Pound's finest, if limited, writing. Unlike earlier sections, however, that display a unity of at least subject if not theme – the Adams Cantos, the Pisan sequence – *Drafts & Fragments* is the most fragmented portion of the entire work, a collection of shards rather than a single, solid rock. Consolidating his paradise was not possible as the impetus for publication came not from Pound but external forces. His anxiety over the poem's end matched the complicated process of its publication from which Pound largely withdrew. The interrogations of self that occur in passages from *Drafts & Fragments* duplicate the interrogation of the poem as a whole as it gestures, but never quite reaches, its end. Pound was not ready to end *The Cantos*; but the pirated publication of *Cantos 110–116*, forced his hand. The value of the poetry in *Drafts & Fragments* resides in its self-interrogative nature which remains admittedly incomplete but also strangely sustains the work after its publication. That is, the complexities of its formation insure a constant re-editing and review of the text, even after Pound's death. The dynamic of the text continues long after its appearance because of the textual conundrums and confusions that remain unresolved. Sections of *Drafts & Fragments* demonstrate Pound's own re-interpretation of the poetic and politics of his work, a sustained commentary on the text as a whole, or at least up to Canto CIX. And in *Drafts & Fragments*, Pound not only admits some misdirection but actually withdraws from some of the work's more strident declarations. Rather than resolve *The Cantos, Drafts & Fragments* is a re-consideration of a series of crucial ideological foundations for the poem, notably fascism, anti-Semitism and the idea of paradise. Beginning in CX, the re-evaluation culminates in 'From CXV,' CXVI and 'Notes for CXVII et seq.' Curiously, the final section of *The Cantos* re-edits and reshapes the poem, adding further currency to the work's unfinished nature.

The original opening image of 'the quiet house at Torcello' – a cathedral – becomes 'Thy quiet house' in final form, but both evoke the paradise Pound sought (CX/797). In this world where 'Foam and silk' are the fingers of Artemis, Pound hopes to locate a personal as well as cultural victory, but because 'love be the cause of hate,/ something is twisted,' he soon realizes that all he can muster 'From time's wreckage shored/ these fragments shored against ruin' (CX/798, 800, 801). The notes for the cantos that follow, or portions of cantos, quickly break down into pieces that do not unite, although they possess individual power. Canto CXIII is a stunning unity of light and reflection as Pound, if only for the moment, senses continuity and flow:

> and to know beauty and death and despair
> and to think that what has been shall be,
> flowing, ever unstill.

– followed by '3 lights in triangulation' as Dante will see three circles of light at the end of 'Paradiso.' But this is preceded by 'Pride, jealousy and possessivenessl' (CXIII/807). In these 'triangular spaces,' Pound has found both confirmation and threats to his paradise resulting in a self-consciousness that begins to control the final cantos of the poem (CXIV/811) as Dante did at the opening of 'Paradiso:'

> nearing its desired end,
> our intellect sinks into an abyss
> so deep that memory fails to follow it.
>
> (Dante 379)

But Dante and Pound sense a trembling, intermittent light (Dante 380, 521; CXVI/817 cf. LXXIV/449: 'all things that are are lights'). But Pound resists the writing of 'a genealogy of the demons,' preferring to believe 'ubi amor, ibi oculus,' although he knows that coherence will escape him (CXIV/813; CXVI/815), As the hoped for unity unravels – 'the European mind stops' – the verse takes on a more erratic appearance creating on the page what in a different context he calls 'a tangle of works unfinished' (CXV/814; CXVI/815), although he still hopes that 'to confess wrong without losing rightness' (CXVI/817) can be accomplished. In 'Notes for CXVII et seq.,' this become the plaintive cry:

> That I lost my center
> fighting the world.
> The dreams clash
> and are shattered –
> and that I tried to make a paradiso
> terrestre.
>
> (822)

Here, through language both direct and regretful, Pound acknowledges what he could *not* achieve, as Dante does in the final few lines of 'Paradiso' summarizing his failure to see how the 'human effigy/ suited the circle and found place in it' (Dante 541). Pound ends, however, optimistically with the line 'To be men not destroyers' (Notes/822, 823). Concluding the poem is the fragment dated 1966 praising Olga, lines 'for the/ ultimate CANTO' (Fragment/824):

> That her acts
> Olga's acts
> of beauty
> be remembered.
>
> (824)

Love and regret intertwine as Pound completes, but does not resolve, his epic, the harmonic pattern he sought for evaporating in a personal statement of love, analogous to Dante's end where desire and will unite 'by/ the Love that moves the sun and the other stars' (Dante 541). 'Affection,' Dante writes earlier in 'Paradiso', 'follows/ the act of knowledge' (Dante 521).

Love, however, was tested in 1971 when Pound's daughter Mary published her memoir, *Discretions*, the year Pound turned eighty-six. In the work, she suggested that growing up was not entirely idyllic as she resisted her mother's desire for discipline and sought her father's love. Visitors still called on Pound at this time and a few were allowed to meet him, although he alternated between long bouts of silence and bursts of energy. He and Olga attended only limited events such as the memorial service for Stravinsky at San Giorgio where Pound's 'Night Litany' was read by the Mayor of Venice. In February 1972, Marianne Moore died and Olga arranged a memorial service in Venice where Pound read Moore's 'What Are Years?' That same year, another controversy, this time over receiving the annual Emerson-Thoreau Medal of the American Academy of Arts and Sciences erupted. The Council of the Academy rejected the recommendation of the nomination committee; in response, five members of the Academy resigned and Katherine Anne Porter returned her medal (*RP* 189–90). His 87th birthday on 30 October 1972 was celebrated with a small party at calle Querini organized by Olga, with guests – two at a time – making their way up the narrow stairs to honor him. But within a few days, he had to be taken by ambulance boat to hospital, although he walked erectly from the 'Hidden Nest' to the waiting boat. Twenty-four hours later, however, at 8pm on 1 November 1972, he died with Olga holding his hand. The funeral took place two days later at the Church of San Giorgio Maggiore, the body then carried by gondola for burial on the island of San Michele in the lagoon, not far from the graves of Stravinsky and Diaghilev. Dorothy Pound died in England a year later in 1973. Olga, honored in Rome in 1985 with the Ristori Prize for her research on Vivaldi and 32 years as Executive Secretary of the Accademia Musicale Chigiani, lived until 1996, celebrating her one-hundredth birthday at Brunnenburg in 1995. After her death, she was buried next to Pound at San Michele. A commemorative plaque placed by the *Comune di Venezia* on 252 calle Querini, the house Olga's father bought her in 1929, celebrates the nearly fifty years Pound lived in the home, '*in un mai spento amore per Venezia,*' 'in his never extinguished love of Venice.'

An assessment of *The Cantos* is not easily achieved, Pound himself recalling Bunting's remark that 'the Cantos refer, but do not present'(*SCh* 898.). Part of the problem is their incomplete form deriving not only from compositional indeterminancy but from the way Pound treats time spatially, making the past the here and now. But there are no dates in myth. Pound sought coherence, not in terms of a Dantean unity following a map of Aquinas that would take one from hell to paradise, but in terms of a harmony achieved through clarity between spiritual order and its 'forméd trace,' Pound's 'paradiso/terrestre' (XXXVI/178; 'Notes for CXVII/822).

William Carlos Williams wrote in *Kora in Hell* that 'Ezra Pound is the best enemy United States verse has' (*SL* 156).[3] This contradictory statement, divided equally between praise and condemnation, suggests something of Pound in competition with himself which the closing sequence of *The Cantos* confirms. In his attempt to renew the cultural capital of his time, Pound committed errors of judgement and thought which he recognized at the end. His inability to provide authoritative closure for his poem, offering only a kind of fragmented dispersal, reflects his own sense that while he understood what was necessary to make his life and the poem cohere, it could not be fully transposed to either the page or his life. Yet he had hope: 'it coheres all right/ even if my notes do not cohere' he writes in CXVI/817. The paradise he conceived exists in the mind if not in actuality. And the fragment to Olga at the end is recognition of her strength and endurance, although he is aware of the distance that remains between self and language. But if the ending of *The Cantos* is ambiguous, so is a final evaluation of Pound's life.

Pound's accomplishments are clear but so are his faults. Not only did he promote writers like Eliot, Joyce, Frost and H.D. but he revitalized English poetry and established the internationalism of American writing. He also validated the presence of American writers and American writing in Europe, while his editing of journals and anthologies presented new voices and original forms, challenging the *status quo*. His own poetry set the pattern for innumerable younger writers from Charles Olson to Allen Ginsberg and Roy Fisher – as well as the earlier generation of Yeats, Eliot, H.D. Bunting and Zukofsky.[4] Robert Lowell celebrated him in a sonnet; J.M. Coetzee, South African writer and Nobel Prize winner, upheld Pound as an exemplar of the fortitude an artist needs to withstand 'exile, obscure labour and obloquy for his art' (Coetzee 20). In the evolution of his writerly identity, Coetzee makes Pound's centrality absolutely clear. Charles Bukowski, who idolized Pound for his energy, rebelliousness and directness, sharply summarized his importance for contemporary poets when he wrote, 'A POUND IS ONLY BORN EV 3 THOUSAND YRS.' 'A real poet,' he proclaims alluding to Pound, 'has one fist of steel and one fist of love' (Bukowski 76, 68).

If, as Pound claimed, 'artists are the antennae of the race,' he was their transmitter and broadcaster all in one, setting the dial for a modernism that radiated throughout the greater part of the last century (*ABCR* 73). Richard Aldington in *Life for Life's Sake* tried to explain the enigma, writing that Pound was 'the most generous of men. He is sensitive, highly strung, and irascible. All this throwing down of fire-irons and sputtering of four-letter words is merely Ezra's form of defense against a none too considerate world' (105).

But Pound's politics, from fascism to anti-Semitism, has made his acceptance difficult. Charles Olson hated Pound's views but could also admonish those who automatically rejected him: 'For christ's sake have the courage to admit that Pound faced up to the questions of our time' (Olson 15). Marianne Moore alternately rejected his politics yet valued his literary insight. Even Laughlin maintained admiration for the work, disdain for the politics and disgust over the racial slurs. Williams was similarly charitable at the beginning but then intense in his rejection of Pound's claims for Mussolini, anti-Semitism and racism. Donald Hall summed up the quandary: recalling his trepidation at interviewing Pound, he remarked that he was 'in awe of his poetry, aghast at his politics' (*RP* 113). Pound's own late defense of his anti-Semitism seems half-hearted and incomplete: 'Motto for *Agenda:*' he half-jokingly wrote to the editor William Cookson: 'How can anyone go antisemite in a world that contains Danny Kaye. E. Pound?'[5]

Pound's views repeatedly test the critical resolve of those who read *The Cantos* and early poetry with admiration. Here, Williams is again representative, becoming increasingly intolerant of Pound's ideas and behavior, at one point telling Laughlin in 1940 that Pound 'is more of an infant than I believed. . . . he's a misplaced romantic. . . . And he's batty in the head' but, and it's an important 'but,' 'in spite of it all he's a good poet.' The difficulty is that Pound 'hasn't the least idea where he hits true and where he falls flat' (*WCW/JL* 54). Williams objects to Pound's patronizing letters which are 'the mewings of an 8th grade teacher,' but he does possess 'a complex ear for metrical sequences, marvelous! And he has a naively just concept of the value of knowledge – in other words, he is a poet, a great one, but a musician – never!' (*WCW/JL* 59). Pound is constantly a challenge, a poet of extraordinary ability and importance but a figure of complex, contradictory ideas, sometimes impossible to tolerate but always teaching us the necessity to understand.[6]

In the end, Pound recognized an Emersonian state of incompleteness, Emerson writing in 1844 that 'I know better than to claim any

completeness. . . . I am a fragment and this is a fragment of me' ('Experience' 491). Pound realized this condition late in his life, not only in
terms of his failure to resolve *The Cantos* but in terms of the unsettled
elements of his life including the status and security of Olga, the ambiguous position of Dorothy (in the center *and* at the margin), the complex
situation of his children and the uncertain state of his reputation and
exile. Recognition of this fragmented condition was not so much a defeat
as an acknowledgment of a situation more existential than moral. Yet
his failure to resolve history – his own and that of the text – into a story
is the very story of his poem and his life. The collision between the
alphabetic writing of the West, with its tradition of orderly narratives
and the metaphorical East invoked by the Chinese ideograms in his text
'marks the limits of the Western *epos*' (Froula 154). But this may be the
point: two worlds in conflict. The juxtaposition of text and sign creates
fragments of meaning because no single form, such as the epic, or single
period of history, such as 20th century America, can any longer encom-
pass universal themes. This is what Pound harshly discovered. The open
form of *The Cantos* and Pound's life signal the end of coherent experience or a single belief. There cannot be a unifying narrative or conviction
to either the modern epic or one's personal history. Closure of a text and
even of a life is imaginary, completeness and coherence an illusion.

Nevertheless, Pound insistently believed that literature had a duty to
society. In *How to Read*, he asked if literature has a function in the state.
Of course, he answered: 'it has to do with the clarity and vigour of "any
and every" thought and opinion. It has to do with maintaining the very
cleanliness of the tools, the health of the very matter of thought itself'
(*LE* 21). This is the Pound who posted precepts on a wall in Rapallo for
the people to follow, one of them encouraging the population to live in
a way that 'your children and their descendants will be grateful to You'
and another of a more Confucian nature: 'When the archer misses the
bull's eye, the cause of the error is within himself' (*O/E* 218–19). Finding
it difficult to locate an audience for his pronouncements, however,
Pound would often rely on defiance or self-dramatization.

The fascination with Pound, however, has found its way into popular
literature, as well as the popular imagination: Richard Stern drew on
Pound's life and ideas in *Stitch* (1965) in which an aged American sculptor
(rather than poet), living in Venice with his long-time American
companion, expresses Poundian regret at his failure to recognize benevolence when it was offered, while announcing the end of a European
paideuma (Stern 62). *In Famous Last Words* (1981) Timothy Findley
made Pound and Hugh Selwyn Mauberly central characters in an

account of the end of World War II. Findley's play, *The Trials of Ezra Pound* (1994) narrates the tensions of Pound in Washington based on transcripts from Pound's preliminary hearings of 1945/46 to determine whether he was a traitor or unfit to stand trial. Pound's recorded broadcasts for Rome Radio form his speeches in the play. Bernard Kops has written *Ezra*, a play performed in 1981 focusing on Pound's interrogations with cameos by Mussolini, Vivaldi and Frank Amprin (FBI agent), as well as Dorothy and Olga. An unpublished play by Kenneth Arnold, *House of Bedlam* (1977), tells the story of a *menage à trois* with the 60 year old poet and his mistress and wife sharing a house with the poet's 18-year-old daughter. *Poundemonium* (1989) is an experimental novel by the Spanish writer Julián Ríos. It is the story of three Spanish bohemians who, when they learn of Pound's death, decide to honour him by revisiting sites in London associated with his life and work. C.K. Stead's novel, *Villa Vittoria* (1997) is set partially in Rapallo and deals with Pound, Dorothy and Olga, all renamed in the book.

Images of Pound, whether in painting or photography, represent an energetic figure of artistic creativity, often caught in the act of writing, talking or composing. The 1923 picture of him standing with Joyce, Ford and John Quinn attests to his authority and importance as a facilitator of modernism; the photo of him typing furiously in May 1945 at the Counter Intelligence Corps headquarters in Genoa records his determination and concentration on writing as a way out of, and into, his life. The photographs of him by Vittorugo Contino in old age in Venice display a poet still meditating between his life and art. Of course, from his earliest days Pound was aware of his image and its impact: his life is a record of portraits, busts and even profiles, the most important from that early period the Hieratic Head cut in marble by Gaudier-Brzeska in 1914.[7]

Further inscribing the importance of Pound is the appearance of three new texts ennobling his literary stature: the first, *Canti postumi* (2002), edited by Massimo Bacigalupo, is a comprehensive selection of deletions, rewrites and cancelled passages from *The Cantos*. This bilingual (English-Italian) edition, supplements the full edition edited by Mary de Rachewiltz, *I Cantos* published by Mondadori in 1985. *Poems and Translations* by Pound (2003), appearing in the Library of America series, is the largest one volume edition of his work to date. Edited by Richard Sieburth, the book, at 1363 pages, marks Pound's addition to a culturally significant enterprise: the republication in a uniform edition of key American writers. Pound now joins Whitman, Frost and Stevens, among many others, in a series he long-ago called for: reasonably, priced standarized editions of

192 Ezra Pound: A Literary Life

American 'classics' accessible to all. Sieburth has also edited and annotated
The Pisan Cantos (2003), making the text accessible to many first-time
readers. The publication of all three volumes marks the sudden rise of
Pound's cultural capital some thirty-one years after his death.
But from every engagement with Pound, two questions emerge: not
only the expected one about whether his politics interfere with the
reception of his work but another: is he a foundational figure of Modernism as well as the pre-cursor of postmodernism? The first will never
be satisfactorily answered and recent critical efforts to explain his fascism
and its contribution to his modernist writings are balanced by those
who find it impossible to separate the interference of politics from
poetry.[8] The second is equally puzzling and inadequately answered.
Pound's essentialist cast and logocentric fascination with the word
place him largely outside of the postmodern paradigm, but his reliance
on fragments and indeterminacy make the claim to his postmodern
caste valid. Fenollosa's essay 'On the Chinese Written Character' is
a crucial text in this argument since it marks Pound's shift from an
early poetics of 'freeplay' to one insisting on the 'right word;' or, as he
explains, 'the more concretely and vividly we express the interactions
of things the better the poetry. We need in poetry thousands of active
words...'(Fenollosa 28). Pound's practice of 'collage,' using different
textual elements without recourse to an overall unifying idea, supplementing his faith in finding the right word, is furthermore a modernist
practice often interpreted as a prelude to postmodernism.
    Translation also aids in positioning Pound. According to his principles,
translation is the 'modernist' domestication of the foreign through the
use of 'active words' in contrast to a postmodern technique which lets
the 'otherness'of the secondary author – the voice of the translator –
appear. For all of his *collagiste* innovations, Pound's version of history is
motivated by a desire to tirelessly reveal the mythical and historical
plots that have plagued us. As he notes in Canto XLVI, '19 years on this
case/ first case. I have set down part of/The Evidence. Part' (234). Pound
also pursued his *grands récits*, believing the epic still to be the form for
poetically expressing his age, although he admitted late in his life that
his error may have been to write a paradise when it should have been
an apocalypse (*RP* 241). He also defended an Arnoldian belief in culture:
'I am writing to resist the view that Europe and civilization is going to
Hell' (*RP* 242).
    Pound's essentialist quest expressed itself in his persistent commitment
to the 'totalitarian,' historically embodied in Malatesta, Confucius,
Jefferson and Mussolini, all encompassing what the fasces, a bundle of

reeds bound with an axe, represented: 'strength through unity and discipline.' Fascism for Pound was more than a political program: it was an orientation to life in which a perfected order is equally practical and theoretical, intellectual and moral (Doordan 233, 232). It asserted an ancient ideal realized by modern methods, the quintessential epistemology Pound sought to capture in his long poem. Finding the means to do so, however, remained elusive. Believing that Italian fascism was a renaissance and a revolution, he nonetheless realized that it had failed when he returned to Italy in 1958 and that he had been attempting to reclaim a past that had dissolved: 'somebody said that I am the last American living the tragedy of Europe' he famously stated at the end of his *Paris Review* interview (*RP* 244). But throughout the political obsessions, economic distractions and mental confusions, throughout exile and imprisonment, Pound always remained an 'impassioned moralist' (Levin in *RP* 190).

In his art and actions, Pound promoted resistance, resisting English conservatism, French neglect, American aggression and, finally, the destruction of Europe. The title of Chapter XXIII of *Jefferson and/or Mussolini* is, appropriately, 'Resistance.' Pound's life was an act of resistance against literary fads, political power, cultural authority and moral hegemony. But he also understood clearly the vital role of literature in changing society. Directness, misunderstood by some as simplicity, was part of this agenda, a means to bring one closer to accurate meaning which he articulated in the *ABC of Reading* when he argued that 'the perfectly simple verbal order is CHARGED with a much higher potential. ... If you are trying to show what a man feels you can only do it by clarity' (*ABC* 191). Simplicity *is* clarity for Pound.

Pound, wrote Robert Creeley, 'proposed the *power* of poetry,' but he frequently found society objecting to its authority. Hence, his repeated lecturing, hectoring and cajoling the public into accepting its importance. But their resistance meant a barrage of books, declarations, essays, editorials, letters and poems. Appropriately, Yeats originally placed him in Phase 12 of his Great Wheel in *A Vision*, 'The Forerunner,' along with Nietzsche.[9] Action and movement are at the core of Pound's work. Impatient with culture re-defining itself, with literature renewing itself and with life re-constituting itself, he sought to accelerate these changes himself. The title of a 1932 article clearly sums up his ethos: 'For Action.' This critique of editors and the need, especially in America, to register contemporary facts honestly is characteristic of his repeated call to arms. Although lines from the final cantos express resignation, the overriding portrait of Pound is one of purpose and accomplishment, although there is always more work to be done: 'the poet's job is to *define* and yet again define till the detail of surface is in accord with the root in justice' (SL 277). 'He blustered his way in, he blustered his way out,' H.D. said of Pound, but William Carlos Williams more accurately identified his impact. Pound's purpose, he declared, 'has been modern. His thrust has been into the Future' (H.D *End.* 49; *CST* 6).

Notes

Introduction

1. Dorothy Shakespear, 'Notebook, 19 March 1910,' *Ezra Pound and Dorothy Shakespear, Their Letter: 1909–1914*, eds Omar Pound and A. Walton Litz (New York: New Directions, 1984) 16. Hereafter, *EP/DS*.
2. Stella Bowen also reported that Pound developed a highly personal and very violent style with much 'springing up and down and much swaying from side to side' when he danced. Bowen, *Drawn from Life* (London: Virago, 1984) 49.

1 'Mastership at One Leap': 1885–1908

1. The newly refurbished Pound house is now headquarters of the Ezra Pound Association and the new home of the Hailey Cultural Center. At the entrance to the house is a plaque which identifies the building as the Pound birthplace and bears this quote: 'I have beaten out my exile.'
2. For a detailed description of the Wyncote home and a remarkable photograph of Pound in his 'den,' see Wilhelm, *Am Rt* 67–9.
3. *Hilda's Book*, given to H.D. in 1907 by Pound, was discovered among the personal papers of H.D.'s friend Frances Gregg following her death in 1941 in the bombing of Plymouth. It eventually came into the hands of Peter Russell who sold it to Harvard University. Several of the poems in *Hilda's Book* appeared in *A Lume Spento* (1908) and *Personae* (1926). H.D.'s *End to Torment* publishes *Hilda's Book*, pp. 67–84. The poems also form the first section of Ezra Pound, *Poems and Translations* [ed. Richard Sieburth] (NY: Library of America, 2003) 3–17.
4. On how he decided to be a poet at such a young age, see Donald Hall, *Remembering Poets* (NY: Harper & Row, 1978) 229. This interview originally appeared in the *Paris Review* 28 (1962): 22–51.
5. The volumes are at the Harry Ransom Humanities Research Center at the University of Texas at Austin, TX.
6. For a more sympathetic account of what happen, Pound sleeping in his clothes on the floor after giving the chorus girl tea and his bed, see the report of Viola Baylis in *Am Rt* 176.

2 'My Music is Your Disharmony': 1908–14

1. Proust visited Venice in May 1900, partly out of homage to Ruskin (who had recently died) and to his great *Stones of Venice*. The 'Sojourn in Venice' section of Proust's *The Captive*, Vol. 5 of *In Search of Lost Time*, narrates the adventure. Thomas Mann visited in 1911 and published *Death in Venice*

the following year. Hugo von Hofmannsthal's essay 'A Memory of Beautiful Days,' appeared in 1908, while Claude Monet spent from 1 October to 13 December 1908 in the city. Ruskin's phrase identifying the 'amphibious city,' followed by his remark that it is a 'sea-dog of towns,' appears in his essay 'St Mark's Rest.'

2. Concern over the physical appearance of *A Lume Spento* highlights Pound's early sense of the visual importance of a text and realization that how a poem looks effects its reading and understanding. Throughout his career, he would be alert to the nuances and value of layout, design, typography, paper and even jacket blurbs. Deluxe editions of his early cantos met rigorous design and production standards. Form as thought, shape as text, were fundamental ideas of Pound's from the publication of his first book to the last.

3. Mathews also arranged an invitation for Pound to dine at the newly established Poets' Club when both George Bernard Shaw and Hillaire Belloc were present. He also met that evening the novelist Maurice Hewlett. Hanging around Mathews' shop, he also encountered apprentice poets like himself, including Laurence Binyon, Keeper of Prints at the British Museum, and Selwyn Image, a member of the Rhymers' Club.

4. Tragically, Ione de Forest committed suicide at 19 at her home in Chelsea, the subject of Pound's 'Ione, Dead the Long Year,' written seven years after her death.

5. To his father Pound would write in 1909, 'no special furor during the last week' and then describe Sunday evenings with Victor Plarr of the Rhymers' Club followed by 'Yeats Monday evenings; a set from the Irish Lit. Soc. eats together on Wednesdays and a sort of new Rhymers gang on Thursdays.' Pound in Longenbach 12–13.

6. Lowell's six points included using 'the language of common speech, but to employ always the *exact* word;' 'to create new rhythms;' maintain complete freedom in choice of subject; 'to present an image' because 'we believe that poetry should render particulars exactly;' 'to produce poetry that is hard and clear, never blurred nor indefinite.' Finally, she wrote, 'most of us believe that concentration is of the very essence of poetry' (Lowell, 'Preface,' *Some Imagist Poets* [Boston: Houghton Mifflin Company, 1915] vi–vii).

7. For Pound's account of the journey, see Ezra Pound, *A Walking Tour in Southern France, Ezra Pound Among the Troubadours*, ed. Richard Sieburth (NY: New Directions, 1992). The importance of this journey for the development of *The Cantos* and as an antecedent of Imagism and Vorticism is only now being understood. See Sieburth's introduction and Peter Nicholls, 'Pound's Places,' *Locations of Literary Modernism*, eds Alex Davis and Lee M. Jenkins (Cambridge: Cambridge UP, 2000) 159–77.

8. Wyndham Lewis in Peter Brooker, *Bohemia in London* (Basingstoke: Palgrave Macmillan, 2004) 52. Canto XIV illustrates Pound's vehemence clearly:

> The slough of unamiable liars,
> 　　bog of stupidities,
> malevolent stupidities, and stupidities,
> the soil living pus, full of vermin,
> dead maggots begetting live maggots,

slum owners,
usurers squeezing crab-lice, pandars to authority

(XIV/63)

3 'The Noble Crested Screamer': 1914–20

1. Pound, 'Hudson: Poet Strayed into Science,' *Little Review* VII (May/June1920) 13–17; rpt. *SP* 399–402.
2. Pound's involvement had its own irony, however, sinceearlier that same year, his own stilted verse in *Lustra* was parodied in the *Egoist* by Richard Aldington. The series, called 'Penultimate Poetry,' included the following:

> The apparition   of these poems   in a crowd:
> White faces   in a black   dead faint.

Witemeyer reprints the set on pages 198–99.

A review of Wilde's *The Picture of Dorian Gray* in the *Daily Chronicle* of 30 June 1891 referred to the novel's 'flippant philosophisings' and 'trail of garish vulgarity which is over all Mr Wilde's elaborate Wardour Street aestheticism.' Wilde, *The Picture of Dorain Gray*, ed. Norman Page. (Peterborough, ON: Broadview, 1998) 273.

3. In 1959, Pound repeated that he 'learned' from Browning and that, more enigmatically, 'the whole of the novel in England after Browning is indebted to Browning. And then again there is a whole lot of Browning that has never been built on' (Bridson164).
4. Iris Barry, 'The Ezra Pound Period,' *The Bookman* (October 1931: 165) For another comic but slightly distorted view of Pound at this time see Ford Madox Ford, *Return to Yesterday* 373–5, 399–401.
5. For Pound on Frazer and *The Golden Bough* see *LE* 343. For Pound and the energy of the primitive see, first, Hulme's 1914 essay 'Modern Art and Its Philosophy' and then Pound's article, 'New Sculpture,' *Egoist* 1 (19 February 1914) 67–8. Another influence on 'Three Cantos' was Alan Upward, a lawyer who lived for a time in Nigeria and developed strong anthropological interests; he was part of Yeats' occult circle. His uniting suggestive etymology with a fluid, spiritual universe – see *The New Word* (1910) – affected Pound's thinking about the etymological origins of myth. Pound reviewed Upward's book in 1914 in *The New Age* (23 April 1914), as well as Upward's *The Divine Mystery* (1913) on the myths behind religion, in *The New Freewoman* (13 November 1913).
6. For a detailed consideration of the themes and form of the poem, see John Espey, *Pound's Mauberley* (1955; Berkeley: Univ of California Press, 1974).
7. Yeats in Tytell 131. In his autobiography, *Life for Life's Sake*, Richard Aldington offers a telling comparison between Pound and Eliot, the former starting out 'in a time of peace and prosperity with everything in his favour, and muffed his changes of becoming literary dictator of London – to which he undoubtedly aspired – by his own conceit, folly, and bad manners.' Eliot, by contrast, began 'in the enormous confusion of war and post-war England, handicapped in every way. Yet by merit, tact, prudence and pertinacity he succeeded in

doing what no other American has ever done – imposing his personality, taste and even many of his opinions on literary England' (Aldington 217).

4 'Bring Order to Your Surroundings': 1920–29

1. 'Pound's musical experiments were a byproduct of his studies in poetic versification' and for him, as one recent music critic has explained, 'the reason form was so important was that in it lay the "music" of all poetry, whether actually set to music or not.' Poetry for Pound resided in sound not semantics; hence, his view that poetry was not 'literature' but 'performance art.' Richard Taruskin, 'Ezra Pound, Musical Crackpot,' *The New York Times* 27 July 2003: Section 2: 24. While criticizing Pound's unorthodox ideas about notation and structure, Taruskin does admit that *Le Testament de Villon* constitutes 'Pound's slim sound claim to musical immortality' (*ibid.*).
2. See Massimo Bacigalupo, 'And Some Climbing' – Ezra Pound and Dante,' *Agenda* 34 (1996–97) 150. Also useful is Stephen Sicari, *Pound's Epic Ambition, Dante and The Modern World* (Albany: State University of New York Press, 1991).
3. Antheil, who would occasionally take a pistol with him to the concert stage to intimidate critics and hecklers, described the premiere of his Paris career in October 1923 in this fashion. After his piano was wheeled out in front of a 'huge Léger cubist curtain' and he began to play, rioting erupted: 'I remember Man Ray punching somebody in the nose in the front row. Marcel Duchamps was arguing loudly with somebody else in the second row. In a box nearby, Erik Satie was shouting, "What precision! What precision!" and applauding. . . . In the gallery the police came in and arrested the surrealists who, liking the music, were punching everybody who objected.' Antheil, *Bad Boy of Music* (Garden City, NY: Doubleday, 1945) 7–8.

5 'The Indifferent Never Make History': 1930–40

1. Pound offered later English versions of the *Ta Hio* in 'The Great Digest,' Confucius, *The Unwobbling Pivot & The Great Digest* (1947) and Confucius, *The Great Digest and The Unwobbling Pivot* in 1953. Italian versions appeared in 1942 and 1944.
2. For details on the Eleusinian Mysteries see Boris de Rachewiltz (Pound's son-in-law), 'Pagan and Magic Elements in Ezra Pound's Work,' *New Approaches to Ezra Pound*, ed. Eva Hesse (London: Faber and Faber, 1969) 174–97; Leon Surette, *A Light from Eleusis: A Study of Pound's Cantos* (Oxford: Clarendon Press, 1979); Demetres P. Tryphonopoulos, *The Celestial Tradition, A Study of Ezra Pound's The Cantos* (Waterloo, Ont.: Wilfrid Laurier University Press, 1992), especially ch.2.
3. Daniel Tiffany in *Radio Corpse, Imagism and the Cryptaesthetic of Ezra Pound* (Cambridge, MA: Harvard University Press, 1995) argues that Pound was theorizing the use of radio in his union of the Image with figures essential to the history of 'telephonic media (inscription, transmission, radiation and reanimation).' But Tiffany also recognizes Pound's sometimes contradictory view of radio which Pound suggests both fosters and inhibits expression (235–36).

4. For a detailed discussion of Pound and radio, and links between radio and Futurism, Dada and Surrealism, see Margaret Fisher, *Ezra Pound's Radio Operas: The BBC Experiments, 1931–1933* (Cambridge, MA: MIT Press, 2002), ch. 2.

6 'Nothin' Undecided': Rome, Pisa, Washington, 1940–58

1. The text originally appeared in *If This Be Treason* printed for Olga Rudge in Siena in 1948 and reprinted in *P/J* 269–73.

2. Lawrence Ferlinghetti, 20th International Ezra Pound Conference, Sun Valley, Idaho, 5 July 2003.

3. The Caffé Jolanda, in the center of Rapallo, was the location for another important event: the first meeting of Olga and Mary with Dorothy's son, Omar. The two women had gone to meet John Drummond, a young British soldier and friend of Pound's; a young US soldier happened to enter shortly after and Drummond called him over. It was Omar on leave and visiting his mother (*EP/OR* 166–7).

4. Pound began *The Pisan Cantos* with Canto LXXIV, Cantos LXXII and LXXIII, the so-called 'Italian Cantos,' written earlier in 1944 and appearing in the Italian newspaper *Marina Republicana* in 1945. Because of their offensive content, however, they remained excluded from the complete Cantos until 1985 when Mary de Rachewiltz included them in her dual language edition, *I Cantos*. They now appear in proper sequence, Canto LXXII followed by an English translation by Pound, Canto LXXIII remaining untranslated in English editions of *The Cantos*. For an annotated translation of the two cantos see Massimo Bacigalupo, 'Ezra Pound's Cantos 72 and 73: An Annotated Translation,' *Paideuma* 20 (1991): 11–41.

   Canto LXXII deals with the spirit of the recently deceased Futurist Marinetti trying to appropriate Pound's body in order to continue to fight in the war but he is preceded by Ezzelino da Roanno, a 13th century fighter in whose voice Pound calls for the damnation of the Italian peacemakers. Canto LXXIII represents Cavalcanti extolling the heroism of a young girl who leads a group of Canadian soldiers into a mine field after they raped her. Both Cantos incorporate Mussolini's call to arms, his '*riscossa*,' outlined in what was his final exhortation to Italy on 16 December 1944. Even before Cantos 72 and 73 were printed, however, Pound continued with Italian sequels, although he did not directly use the material in *The Pisan Cantos*. Reproductions of the aborted Italian Cantos 74 and 75, written in January and February 1945, appear in Ronald Bush, '"Quiet, Not Scornful?"' The Composition of *The Pisan Cantos*,' *A Poem Containing History: The Cantos of Ezra Pound*, ed. Lawrence Rainey (Ann Arbor: University of Michigan Press, 1996) 169–211. The unpublished cantos nevertheless contain visionary moments that Pound would rely on for portions of *The Pisan Cantos*. Also see Bush, 'Towards Pisa: More from the Archives about Pound's Italian Cantos,' *Agenda* 34 (1996/97) 89–124. Following the article are selected passages from the Italian drafts translated by William Cookson.

5. For an interpretation that confronts these challenges, see Ronald Bush, 'Modernism, Fascism, and the Composition of Ezra Pound's *Pisan Cantos*,' *Modernism/Modernity* 2 (1995): 69–87.

6. Olga's 1955 visit was tense because of Pound's close relationship with Sheri Martinelli, a painter who was with him daily at St Elizabeths. An argument between Olga and Pound resulted in a break in their union and, for a time, the cessation of all correspondence. (*O/E* 210–12).
7. See Laughlin, 'Ez as Wuz,' *Pound as Wuz* (St Paul, Minnesota: Graywolf, 1987) 13 and *EP/JL passim*.
8. Dorothy Pound correspondence, McFarlin Library, University of Tulsa, Tulsa, OK.
9. Marcella Spann Booth, 'Through the Smoke Hole: Ezra Pound's Last Year at St Elizabeths,' *Paideuma* 3 (1974): 329–34; 'Ezrology: The Class of '57,' *Paideuma* 13 (1984) 375–88. Also see David Rattray, 'Weekend with Ezra Pound,' *The Nation* (16 November 1957: 343–9) rpt. in *A Casebook on Ezra Pound*, 104–117. A further revealing account is Carroll F. Terrell, 'St Elizabeths,' *Paideuma* 3 (1974) 363–79.

7 'The European Mind Stops': Drafts, Fragments and Silences, 1958–72

1. The title actually originated in a letter from Professor Norman Holmes Pearson to H.D. announcing Pound's release: 'and now another canyon has been bridged by Ezra's end to torment' (*End* ix).
2. For a detailed discussion of the composition of *Drafts & Fragments*, see Peter Stoicheff, *The Hall of Mirrors: Drafts & Fragments and the End of Ezra Pound's Cantos* (Ann Arbor: University of Michigan Press, 1995).
3. Pound's energetic response to this charge appears in *SL* 156–61.
4. Others influenced by Pound include the language poet Jackson Mac Low, whose experimental *Words and Ends from Ez* (1989) uses unusual typography for his own representation of sections of Pound's *Cantos*, altered to his voice and vision. The opening section 'borrows' from Cantos I-XXX. One portion reads:

> saiD
> 'Erit,
> tZ meRe ss nArration,
> Peu mOisi,
> piUs rdiN.

5. Pound to Cookson in 1959 letter rpt. in *Agenda* 21st Anniversary issue, 1980. The issue contains forty-five letters from Pound to Cookson.
   Was Pound an Italian Fascist? Probably not, since he was not a nationalist nor a militarist. Pound did not see the state as an authoritarian apparatus but as an instrument of distributive justice. But Pound, according to Peter Nicholls, inhabited Fascist rhetoric yet distanced himself from its practice in Italy. The key to understanding this act may be a greater focus on Pound's economics rather than his fascist commitments or even anti-Semitism. Economics is the absolute ground from which everything else emerges as Pound states in Canto XCVIII. On this everything else rests. See Leon Surrette's *Pound in Purgatory: From Economic Radicalism to Anti-Semitism* (Urbana: Univ. of Illinois Press, 1999);

for Pound on banks and the bank wars see Roxana Preda's final chapters in her *Ezra Pound's (Post) Modern Poetics and Politics* (NY: Lang: 2001). Also see Peter Nicholls' critique of Pound's fascism in *Modernism/Modernity* (10: January 2003) 212–24.

6. Among the challenges is the way error undermines the textual authority of *The Cantos*. Pound's refusal to correct oversights of fact, reference or translation contradicts his understanding of fascism which privileges authority, discipline and order. At best, Pound treated errors in his text 'eclectically;' at best, 'the concept of "authorial intention" is [for Pound] lacking in neatness' Christine Froula writes with understatement. See Froula, *To Write Paradise, Style and Error in Pound's Cantos* (new Haven: Yale UP, 1984) 144 and Ch.3 'The Pound Error.'

7. Other important images, chronologically, include the youthful profile portrait of 1908–10 in London; the 1920 portrait of Pound by Wyndham Lewis; the spring 1923 photo standing with Ford, Joyce and Quinn; the 1932 painting of him energetically walking along the promenade at Rapallo by Rolando Monti; the 1938 oil by Wyndham Lewis showing him sloping back in an armchair, exhausted and brooding with half-shut eyes; the eager Pound photographed at his impromptu press conf. on board ship on his arrival in New York in 1939; the dapper Pound in front of the hotel in Rome where he stayed when making broadcasts; the mug shot taken on admission to St Elizabeths, 21 December 1945; his standing with his hand on the shoulder of William Carlos Williams just before his departure from America after his release; his fascist salute on his return to Italy, 9 July 1958. There are also photographs of Pound in old age in 1963 at Casa 131, Sant'Ambrogio and, poignantly, talking to Olga at the memorial service for Stravinsky in Venice. Mary Barnard in her autobiography remarks that his favorite photo of himself was taken in Rapallo in the late 1930's by James Angleton, one of the young editors of *Furioso* from Yale (Barnard, *Assault on Mount Helicon: A Literary Memoir* [Berkeley: Univ. of California Press, 1984, 160–1).

An interesting parallel is that the signature Hieratic Head of Pound, carved in 1914 and carried by Pound to Rapallo and later transported to the garden at Brunnenburg but now in the Raymond D. Nasher collection in the US, anticipated the 'cult of the Head' of Mussolini who promoted busts and statutes of himself with his jutting jaw and famous forehead during his reign (Calvino 38). The development of Mussolini's granite-like image in the 1930s – unsmiling, thin-lipped, shaven head – became an icon of Fascism at the same time it echoed the famous busts of Roman times.

8. See, for example, Robert Casillo, *The Genealogy of Demons.* (Evanston, Ill.: Northwestern Univ. Press, 1988) and Ronald Bush, 'Modernism, Fascism, and the Composition of Ezra Pound's *Pisan Cantos*,' *Modernism/Modernity* 2 (1995) 69–87.

9. The habits of those in Phase 12 include being 'driven from one self-conscious pose to another,' with the quality of the 'Forerunner' being 'fragmentary and violent. . . it is a phase of immense energy.' Additionally, one in this condition oscillates 'between the violent assertion of some commonplace pose, and a dogmatism which means nothing apart from the circumstance that created it' (Yeats, *A Vision* [New York: Macmillan – now Palgrave Macueillam, 1961] 127–8). Reconsidering, Yeats actually removed Pound from this circle to that

of Phase 23, 'The Receptive Man.' where one must 'kill all thought that would systematise the world, by doing a thing, not because he wants to... but because he can; that is to say, he sees all things from the point of view of his own technique, touches and tastes and investigates technically. He is, however, because of the nature of his energy, violent, anarchic' (164). Analogies to Pound are clear.

Works Cited

Ackroyd, Peter. *Ezra Pound*. London: Thames and Hudson, 1981.

Adamson, Walter L. *Avant-Garde Florence: From Modernism to Fascism*. Cambridge, MA: Harvard University Press, 1993.

Albright, Daniel. 'Early Cantos I-XLI,' *The Cambridge Companion to Ezra Pound*, ed. Ira B. Nadel. Cambridge: Cambridge University Press, 1999, 59–91.

Aldington, Richard '*Blast*,' *Egoist* 1 (15 July 1914) 273.

——. *Life for Life's Sake*. NY: Viking, 1941.

——. 'Presentation to Mr W.S. Blunt,' *Egoist* 1 (2 February 1914) 57.

——. *Richard Aldington: An Autobiography in Letters*, ed. Norman T. Gates. University Park, PA: Pennsylvania State Univ Press, 1991.

Alighieri, Dante. *The Divine Comedy*. tr. Allen Mandelbaum. London: Everyman, 1995.

Alldritt, Keith. *The Poet as Spy: The Life and Wild Times of Basil Bunting*. London: Aurum Press, 1998.

Bacigalupo, Massimo. *The Forméd Trace*. NY: Columbia University Press, 1980.

Barry, Iris. 'The Ezra Pound Period,' *The Bookman* (October 1931) [?] 159–71.

Beach, Sylvia. *Shakespeare and Company*. NY: Harcourt Brace & World, 1959.

Bosworth, R. J. W. *Mussolini*. London: Edward Arnold, 2002.

Bottome, Phyllis. *From the Life*. London: Faber and Faber, 1944.

Bricknell, Brad. *Literary Modernism and Musical Aesthetics*. Cambridge: Cambridge University Press, 2001.

Bridson, D.G. 'An Interview with Ezra Pound,' *New Directions* 17 (1961): 159–84.

Bunting, Basil. *Collected Poems*. New ed. Oxford: Oxford University Press, 1978.

Bukowski, Charles. *Beerspit Night and Cursing: The Correspondence of Charles Bukowski and Sheri Martinelli 1960–67*. ed. Steven Moore. Santa Rosa, CA: Black Sparrow Press, 2001.

Bush, Ronald. *The Genesis of Ezra Pound's Cantos*. 1976. Princeton: Princeton University Press, 1989.

——. '"Quiet, not Scornful"?' The Composition of *The Pisan Cantos, A Poem Containing History, The Cantos of Ezra Pound*, ed. Lawrence Rainey. Ann Arbor: University of Michigan Press, 1996. 169–211.

Calvino, Italo. 'Il Duce's Portraits,' *New Yorker* 6 January 2003: 34–39.

Coetzee, J.M. *Youth*. London: Secker and Warburg, 2002.

Cornell, Julian. *The Trial of Ezra Pound*. NY: John Day, 1966.

Creeley, Robert. 'Why Pound?' *Agenda* 17 (1979/80): 198–9.

Crosby, Caresse. *The Passionate Years*. NY: Dial, 1953.

Cunard, Nancy. *These Were the Hours*, ed. Hugh Ford. Carbondale: Southern Illinois University Press, 1969.

Dante Alighieri, *The Divine Comedy*. tr. Allen Mandelbaum. London: Everyman,1995.

de Rachewiltz, Mary. 'Fragments of An Atmosphere,' *Agenda* 17 (1979/80): 159–70.

Dasenbrock, Reed Way. *Imitating the Italians*. Baltimore: John Hopkins University Press, 1991.

204 *Works Cited*

Doolittle, Hilda. [H.D.] *Selected Poems*. NY: Grove Press, 1957.
Doordan, Dennis P. 'Political Things: Design in Fascist Italy,' *Designing Modernity*, ed. Wendy Kaplan. London: Thames and Hudson, 1995, 225–55.
Eliot, T. S. *The Letters of T.S. Eliot*, ed. Valerie Eliot, Vol. I.. NY: Harcourt Brace Jovanovich, 1988.
Emerson, Ralph Waldo. 'Experience,' Essays Second Series, *Essays and Lectures*. NY: Library of America, 1983.
——.*Journals and Miscellaneous Notebooks*, Vol 8. ed. William H. Gilman and J.E. Parson. Cambridge, MA: Harvard University Press, 1970.
Espey, John. *Ezra Pound's Mauberley*. 1955; Berkeley: University of California Press, 1974.
Fenollosa, Ernest. *The Chinese Written Character as a Medium of Poetry*. ed. Ezra Pound. San Francisco, CA: City Lights Books, 1983.
Fisher, Margaret. *Ezra Pound's Radio Operas: The BBC Experiments, 1931–1933*. Cambridge, MA: MIT Press, 2002.
Flory, Wendy Stallard. *The American Ezra Pound*. New Haven, CN: Yale University Press, 1989.
——.'Pound and antisemitism,' *The Cambridge Companion to Ezra Pound*, ed. Ira B. Nadel. Cambridge: Cambridge University Press, 1999, 284–300
Ford, Ford Madox. *It Was the Nightingale*. London: Heineman, 1934.
——.*Return to Yesterday*. London: Gollancz, 1931.
Foster, Roy. *W.B. Yeats, A Life I*. New York: Oxford University Press, 1997.
Fowler, H.W. *A Dictionary of Modern Usage*. London: Oxford University Press, 1957.
Froula, Christine. *To Write Paradise, Style and Error in Pound's Cantos*. New Haven, CN: Yale University Press, 1984.
Gallup, Donald. *Ezra Pound: A Bibliography*. Charlottesville, VA: University Press of Virginia Press, 1983.
Goldring, Douglas. *South Lodge*. London: Constable, 1943.
Goune, Iseult. *Letters to W.B. Yeats and Ezra Pound from Iseult Gonne*, ed. A. Norman Jeffares Anna MacBride White and Christina Bridgwater. London: Palgrave Macmillan, 2004.
Gregg, Frances. *The Mystic Leeway*. Ed. Ben Jones. Ottawa: Carleton University Press, 1995.
Guest, Barbara. *Herself Defined: The Poet H.D. and HerWorld*. Garden City, NY: Doubleday, 1984.
Hall, Donald. 'Fragments of Ezra Pound,' *Remembering Poets*. NY: Harper & Row, 1978. 111–99.
Hutchins, Patricia. *Ezra Pound's Kensington*. Chicago: Henry Regnery Company, 1965.
Jeffares, A. Norman. *W.B. Yeats: Man and Poet*. London: Routledge & Kegan Paul, 1949.
Josephson, Matthew. 'An Open Letter to Ezra Pound and other 'Exiles,' *transition* 13 (1928): 101–02.
Kamm, Henry. 'Pound in Silence, Returns to Paris,' *New York Times* 30 October 1965: 38.
Kenner, Hugh. *The Poetry of Ezra Pound*. London: Faber, 1951. *PEP*.
——.*The Pound Era*. Berkeley: University of California Press, 1971. *PE*.
Laughlin, James. 'A Collage for E.P.,' *Paris Review* 89 (1983): 154.
——.*Pound as Wuz, Essays and Lectures on Ezra Pound*. Saint Paul, MN: Greystone Press, 1987.

Longenbach, James. *Stone Cottage, Pound, Yeats and Modernism*. NY: Oxford University Press, 1988.
MacLeish, Archibald. *Riders on the Earth*. Boston: Houghton Mifflin, 1978.
McDonald, Gail. *Learning to Be Modern: Pound, Eliot and the American University*. Oxford: Clarendon Press, 1993.
Maddox, Brenda. *George's Ghosts: A New Life of W.B. Yeats*. London: Picador, 1999.
Martin, Wallace. *The New Age Under Orage*. Manchester: Manchester University Press, 1967.
Materer, Timothy, 'Make It Sell! Ezra Pound Advertises Modernism,' *Marketing Modernism*, ed. Kevin Dettmar and Stephen Watt. Ann Arbor: University of Michigan Press, 1996, 17–36.
Moody, A. David. 'Dante as the Young Pound's Virgil: Introduction to Some Early Drafts and Fragments,' *Agenda* 34 (1995/96) 65–88. Includes transcription of 'ORBI CANTUM PRIMUM . . . CANO' (ca. 1907).
Moore, Marianne. *Selected Letters of Marianne Moore*, ed. Bonnie Costello. London: Penguin, 1998. *SLMM*
Nadel, Ira B. 'E.P., 1964,' *Harvard Library Bulletin* N.S. 13 (2002): 59–68.
Norman, Charles. *Ezra Pound*. London: Macmillan – now Palgrave Macmillan, 1960.
O'Keeffe, Paul. *Some Sort of Genius: A Life of Wyndham Lewis*. London: Cape, 2000.
Olson, Charles. *Charles Olson and Ezra Pound*. ed. Catherine Seelye. NY: Grossman, 1972.
Packard, Reynolds. *Rome Was My Beat*. Secaucus, NJ: L. Stuart, 1975.
Patmore, Brigit. *My Friends When Young*. London: Heinemann, 1968.
Pea, Enrico. 'Thank You, Ezra Pound,' tr. D. Anderson. *Paideuma* 8 (1979): 443.
Perloff, Marjorie. *The Dance of the Intellect: Studies in the Poetry of the Pound Tradition*. Cambridge: Cambridge University Press, 1985.
——. *The Poetics of Indeterminacy: Rimbaud to Cage*. Princeton: Princeton University Press, 1981.
Pound, Ezra. *The Cantos*. NY: New Directions, 1995. 13th printing includes Cantos 72 and 73, the Italian Cantos. Ref. are to Canto and page number.
——. 'Chinese Poetry,' *To-Day* III (April–May 1918) 54–7, 93–5.
——. 'On Criticism in General,' *Criterion* I .2 (January 1923) 143–56.
——. 'Status Rerum,' *Poetry* 1 (January 1913) 125.
Qian, Zhaoming. *The Modernist Response to Chinese Art*. Charlottesville, VA: University. of Virginia Press, 2003.
Rainey, Lawrence. *Ezra Pound and the Monument of Culture, Text, History and The Malatesta Cantos*. Chicago: University. of Chicago Press, 1991.
Rapallo, Past and Present. Turin: Reynaud Illustrated Guide Books, 1925.
Reck, Michael. *Ezra Pound: A Close-Up*. NY: McGraw-Hill, 1967.
Redman, Timothy. *Ezra Pound and Italian Fascism*. Cambridge: Cambridge University. Press, 1991.
Robinson, Janice S. *H.D. The Life and Work of an American Poet*. Boston: Houghton Mifflin Company, 1982.
Rhys, Ernest. *Everyman Remembers*. London: J.M. Dent, 1931.
Santayana, George. *The Philosophy of George Santayana*. 2 vols. 2nd ed. La Salle, Illinois: Open Court, 1951.
——. *Realms of Being*. NY: Cooper Square Publishers, 1972.
Sitwell, Osbert. *Laughter in the Next Room*. London: Macmillan – now Palgrave Macmillan, 1949.

Stanley, Sandra Kumamoto. *Louis Zukofsky and the Transformation of a Modern American Poetics*. Berkeley: University. of California Press, 1994.

Stern, Richard. *Stitch*. NY: Harper & Row, 1965.

Stoicheff, Peter. *The Hall of Mirrors: Drafts & Fragments and The End of Ezra Pound's Cantos*. Ann Arbor: University. of Michigan Press, 1995.

Symons, Arthur. *The Symbolist Movement in Literature*, 2nd. ed. London, 1908.

Thomson, Virgil. *Virgil Thomson*. NY: Knopf, 1966.

Tietjens, Eunice. 'The End of Ezra Pound,' *Poetry* LX (1942): 38–40.

Tytell, John. *Ezra Pound: The Solitary Volcano*. NY: Doubleday, 1987.

Williams, William Carlos. *The Autobiography of William Carlos Williams*. NY: New Directions, 1967.

——.'III,' *The Cantos of Ezra Pound, Some Testimonials*. NY: Farrar & Rinehart, 1933. 5–7.

Wilhelm, J.J. *Ezra Pound in London and Paris 1908–1925*. University Park, PA: Pennsylvania State Univ. Press, 1990. Wilhelm 1.

——.*Ezra Pound, The Tragic Years 1925–1972*. University Park, PA: Pennyslvania State Univ. Press, 1994. Wilhelm 2.

Witemeyer, Hugh. *The Poetry of Ezra Pound: Forms and Renewal, 1908–1920*. Berkeley: Univ, of California Press, 1969.

Yeats, William Butler. *Essays and Introductions*. NY: Macmillan – now Palgrave Macmillan 1961. *E &I*.

——.*Letters of William Butler Yeats*. ed. Alan Wade. London: Rupert Hart-Davis, 1954.

——.*The Variorum Edition of the Poems of W.B. Yeats*, eds Peter Allt and Russell K. Alspach. NY: Macmillan – now Palgrave Macmillan, 1957.

Zukofsky, Louis. 'Ezra Pound,' *Prepositions: The Collected Critical Essays of Louis Zukofsky*, Expanded Edition. Berkeley: University. of California Press, 1981, 67–83.

Index